1982 Supplement

ADMINISTRATIVE LAW AND REGULATORY POLICY

1982 Supplement

ADMINISTRATIVE LAW AND REGULATORY POLICY

Stephen G. Breyer
Judge, United States Court of Appeals for the First Circuit

Richard B. Stewart
Professor of Law, Harvard Law School

Little, Brown and Company   *Boston and Toronto*

Library of Congress Catalog Card No. 78–71808

ISBN 0-316-10802-2

Third Printing

FG

Published simultaneously in Canada
by Little, Brown & Company (Canada) Limited

PRINTED IN THE UNITED STATES OF AMERICA

Contents

Chapter One.   Introduction   **1**

B.   The Focus of This Book: Administrative Law and
     Regulation   1

**Chapter Two.   The Uneasy Constitutional Position of
                 the Administrative Agency**   **3**

D.   The Nondelegation Doctrine   3
         Note on President Reagan's Executive Order 12991,
             Requiring Cost-Benefit Analysis in Regulatory
             Decision Making   3
E.   The Relation of the Executive to the Adminstrative
     Agencies   6

**Chapter Three.   The Problem of Administrative
                   Discretion**   **11**

B.   Criticisms of the Regulatory Process   11
         Senate Committee on the Judiciary, Report on S. 1080,
             the Regulatory Reform Act, 97th Cong., 1st Sess.   13
C.   Alternative Remedies for Regulatory Failure   16
         1A.   Encouraging Substantive Reform   16
         Breyer, Regulation and Its Reform   16

**Chapter Four.   The Scope of Judicial Review—
                  Questions of Fact and Law**   **21**

A.   Review of Questions of Fact   21
C.   Review of Questions of Law   22
D.   Direct Judicial Control of Administrative Discretion   24
         *Industrial Union Department, AFL-CIO v. American Petroleum
             Institute*   24

American Textile Mfrs. Institute v. Donovan 38
Note on Contemporary Hard Look Review 46

Chapter Five. Judicial Requirements of Clarity and Consistency **51**

A. Requiring Agencies to Narrow Their Discretion Through Adoption of Specific Rules 51
B. Requiring Agencies to Explain Their Decisions and the Requirement of Consistency in Adjudication 52
    Central Florida Enterprises, Inc. v. FCC 55
C. Rule Making versus Adjudication as Means of Developing Agency Policy 60
D. Consistency in Applying Regulations: "An Agency Must Follow Its Own Rules" 65
    United States v. Caceres 65
E. Estoppel and Res Judicata 70
    Schweiker v. Hansen 70

Chapter Six. Hearing Requirements in Economic Regulation and Taxation **75**

B. The Procedural Requirements of the APA and the Interplay Between Rule Making and Adjudication 75
    Note on Lower Court Reactions to *Vermont Yankee* 77
C. The Scope of the Right to Decision on the Record 79
    Seacoast Anti-Pollution League v. Costle 79
    Note on *Sierra Club v. Costle* and the Problem of White House and Congressional Off-the-Record Communications in Notice and Comment Rule Making 81
D. The Interaction Between Procedural Requirements and Regulatory Policies 86

Chapter Seven. Due Process Hearing Rights and the Positive State **91**

B. The Evolution of the New Due Process: The Definition of Interests Entitled to Procedural Protection 91
    Greenholtz v. Inmates of Nebraska Penal & Correctional Complex 91
    Vitek v. Jones 95
C. Determining What Process Is Due 100
    O'Bannon v. Town Court Nursing Center 102
D. Due Process in Particular Contexts 106

Chapter Eight. Organizing and Managing a Bureaucratic Agency: The FTC and Its Reform   **111**

B.   Problems Arising from the Combination of Conflicting Functions Within an Agency   111

     Hercules, Inc. v. EPA   111

     Association of National Advertisers, Inc. v. FTC   118

D.   Revitalizing the FTC: The Problem of False Advertising   124

     Central Hudson Gas & Electric Corp. v. Public Service

       Commn. of New York   128

Chapter Nine. The Availability and Timing of Judicial Review   **113**

A.   Jurisdiction and the Forms of Action   113

     Halperin v. Kissinger   139

B.   Reviewability   144

C.   Standing to Secure Judicial Review   146

     Notes and Questions on Recent Developments in the

       Law of Standing   146

D.   The Timing of Judicial Review   149

     FTC v. Standard Oil Co. of California   149

E.   Primary Jurisdiction   152

Chapter Ten. "Public Interest" Administrative Law: Representation and Disclosure   **153**

A.   Judicial Development of an Interest Representation Model of Administrative Law   153

B.   Public Disclosure of Agency Information and Decision Making   158

     Taxation With Representation Fund v. Internal Revenue

       Service   160

     Crysler Corp. v. Brown   164

Table of Cases

American Textile Mfrs., Institute v Donovan   38

Association of National Advertisers, Inc. v. FTC   118

Central Florida Enterprises, Inc. v. FCC   55

Central Hudson Gas & Electric Corp. v. Public Service Commn.
of New York   128

Chrysler Corp. v. Brown   164

Consumer Energy Council of America v. FERC   7

FTC v. Standard Oil Co. of California   149

Greenholtz v. Inmates of Nebraska Penal & Correctional
Complex   91

Halperin v. Kissinger   139

Hercules, Inc. v. EPA   111

Industrial Union Department, AFL-CIO v. American Petroleum
Institute   24

O'Bannon v. Town Court Nursing Center   102

Schweiker v. Hansen   70

Seacoast Anti-Pollution League v. Costle   79

Taxation With Representation Fund v. Internal Revenue
Service   160

United States v. Caceres   65

Vitek v. Jones   95

Preface

Our casebook, Administrative Law and Regulatory Policy, has three related aims. First, it provides material for the teaching of a traditional administrative law course, focusing for organizational purposes primarily upon procedure. Second, it integrates into its procedural structure substantive material deliberately chosen to allow the teacher to give a coherent, organized account of "regulation." Third, it also allows the teacher to focus upon the current "regulatory reform" debate.

This supplement carries forward these three themes. We have updated the material through the end of 1981, with an occasional look into 1982. Although the supplement does not purport to be comprehensive, we have tried to refer to both major procedural and major substantive developments. We have made a special effort to include material and discussion relevant to topical proposals for regulatory reform, including, for example, the legislative veto, the Bumpers amendment, cost-benefit proposals, and the procedural changes contained in S. 1080, which recently passed the Senate. The supplement, taken together with the teacher's manual, should also help the teacher use the text's substantive regulatory material to make general points of current relevance (as in the case of Chapter 8's discussion of 1970s FTC organization). For those who wish to supplement further the substantive material, we note that Breyer's Regulation and Its Reform (Harvard 1982), keyed to this book's organization, is now available.

Stephen Breyer
Richard Stewart

Cambridge, Massachusetts
June 1982

Chapter One

Introduction

B. THE FOCUS OF THIS BOOK: ADMINISTRATIVE LAW AND REGULATION

Page 9. At the end of line 30, add new callout 6a and accompanying footnote:

6a. For a good discussion of the functioning of an agency in the context of environmental regulation, we recommend B. Ackerman & E. Hassler, Clean Coal/Dirty Air (1981).

Page 19. At the end of the last line, add new callout 18a and accompanying footnote:

18a. One of the authors has just published a book developing in detail this framework of regulatory problems, tools, and solutions. It explains why and how the particular examples listed here can be generalized to cover most of the field of regulation. It is keyed to the substantive discussions contained in this casebook and elaborates upon them. It can be used as a supplementary text by those who wish to explore regulation systematically and in greater detail. S. Breyer, Regulation and Its Reform (1982).

Chapter Two

The Uneasy Constitutional Position of the Administrative Agency

D. THE NONDELEGATION DOCTRINE

Page 85. Add the following after line 16:

The nondelegation doctrine has recently reappeared in Supreme Court cases reviewing the Occupational Safety and Health Act of 1970, 29 U.S.C. §§651-678. Section 3(8) of the act defines an occupational safety and health standard as "a standard which requires conditions . . . reasonably necessary or appropriate to provide safe or healthful . . . places of employment." Section 6(b)(5) tells the secretary of labor that he or she "shall set the standard which most adequately assures, to the extent feasible, on the basis of the best available evidence that no employee will suffer material impairment of health."

Justice Rehnquist, in a concurring opinion in Industrial Union Department AFL-CIO v. American Petroleum Institute, 448 U.S. 607 (1980), and in a dissenting opinion (joined by Chief Justice Burger) in American Textile Manufacturers' Institute v. Donovan, 452 U.S. 490 (1981), argued that these statutory provisions represent an unconstitutional delegation of legislative power. A plurality of four justices in *Industrial Union* acknowledged the continuing power of the nondelegation doctrine by narrowly construing the secretary of labor's regulatory authority under the statute in order to avoid potential constitutional problems. Excerpts from the opinions in the two cases and further discussion of them are contained in chapter 4, at pp. 24-48 infra.

Page 95. Add the following Note after line 28:

Note on President Reagan's Executive Order 12991, Requiring Cost-Benefit Analysis in Regulatory Decision Making

Building on similar efforts by Presidents Nixon, Ford, and Carter, President Reagan has instituted a comprehensive program of internal executive branch review of regulations to ensure that they are justified and do not impose undue burdens on the economy

Executive Order 12991, 46 Fed. Reg. 13193, governs regulations issued by federal agencies, excluding "independent" agencies[60a], and regulations governed by the formal rule-making requirements of the APA or relating to military and foreign affairs functions or to agency organization, management, or personnel.

Section 2 of the order requires agencies in promulgating new regulations, reviewing existing regulations, or developing legislative proposals concerning regulation, to adhere to the following requirements "to the extent permitted by law":

(a) Administrative decisions shall be based on adequate information concerning the need for and consequences of proposed government action;
(b) Regulatory action shall not be undertaken unless the potential benefits to society from the regulation outweigh the potential costs to society;
(c) Regulatory objectives shall be chosen to maximize the net benefits to society;
(d) Among alternative approaches to any given regulatory objective, the alternative involving the least net cost to society shall be chosen. . . .

Section 3 of the order imposes special decision making procedures for "major" rules, defined as those that will have an annual effect on the economy of $100 million or more or will result in "major" price or cost increases or "significant" adverse effects on competition, employment, investment, productivity, innovation, or U.S. competition in world markets. Prior to issuing a notice of proposed rule making of or adoption of a final major rule, an agency must prepare, "and to the extent permitted by law consider," a Regulatory Impact Analysis containing the following information:

(1) A description of the potential benefits of the rule, including any beneficial effects that cannot be quantified in monetary terms, and the identification of those likely to receive the benefits;
(2) A description of the potential costs of the rule, including any adverse effects that cannot be quantified in monetary terms, and the identification of those likely to bear the costs;
(3) A determination of the potential net benefits of the rule, including an evaluation of effects that cannot be quantified in monetary terms;
(4) A description of alternative approaches that could substantially achieve the same regulatory goal at lower cost, together with an analysis of its potential benefit and costs and a brief explanation of the legal reasons why such alternatives, if proposed, could not be adopted; and
(5) Unless covered by the description required under paragraph (4) of this subsection, an explanation of any legal reasons why the rule cannot be based on the requirements set forth in Section 2 of this Order.

60a. Section 1(d) of the order excludes agencies specified in 44 U.S.C. §3502, which refers, without further elaboration, to "independent federal regulatory agencies."

Analyses must be transmitted by the director of the OMB, who is (subject to the President's Task Force on Regulatory Relief, headed by the vice-president) to "review any issues raised under this Order or ensure that they are presented to the President." Agencies must withhold final action until they have received and responded to the OMB's views on the rule. Procedures for review of existing rules and publication of regulatory agendas, and procedural exceptions for emergency rules or those subject to statutory deadlines, are incorporated in the order.

Section 9 of the order, entitled "judicial review," provides that "this Order is intended only to improve the internal management of the Federal government, and is not intended to create any right or benefit, substantive or procedural, enforceable at law by a party against the United States, its agencies, its officers or any person."

The initial operation of the review program is described in DeMuth, A Strong Beginning, Reg., Jan.-Feb. 1982, at 15. Ironically, some officials in the Reagan administration have complained that the procedures required by the order have allowed industry and other interest groups to block or delay administrative efforts at deregulation that are in consumers' interests.

NOTES AND QUESTIONS

1. Because the order's Section 2 requirements and its Section 3 requirement that agencies "consider" Regulatory Impact Analysis apply only "to the extent permitted by law," the order does not purport to require agencies to violate any statutory mandates or constraints. Consider, however, whether the procedural requirement that agencies automatically prepare such an analysis, which is subject to clearance by the OMB, isn't calculated to influence agency decisions in ways inconsistent with the letter or spirit of applicable statutes.

2. The order may also be subject to legal challenge where statutes (as they frequently do) explicitly vest decisional authority in a department head or agency official, as opposed to the president. For example, the Occupational Health and Safety Act provides that occupational health regulations shall be issued by the secretary of labor. In such a case, it may be argued, the order violates the statute by allowing the president or the director of the OMB to exercise or direct decision-making discretion and responsibility that Congress has lodged in another official. The counter-arguments are that the president's Article II responsibility to ensure faithful execution of the laws authorizes him to control the decision of department heads or other subordinate officials; that such directing power is implicit in the power to discharge such officials; that any congressional efforts to limit by statute the president's supervisory and directing powers would be unconstitutional; and that, given this constitu-

tional problem, congressional statutes vesting responsibility in subordinate officials should not be read as precluding the authority exercised
through Executive Order 12291.

For discussion of these and related issues, see Bruff, Presidential Power
and Administrative Rulemaking, 88 Yale L.J. 451 (1979); Note, Delegation and Regulatory Reform; Letting the President Change the Rules, 89
Yale L.J. 561 (1980).

3. Could the president validly apply Executive Order 12291 to the
Federal Trade Commission?

4. The order also raises important procedural questions, including the
extent to which the president and his advisees may confer off the record
with agency decision-makers after the public comment period has closed,
and the extent to which the exclusion of judicial review in Section 9 is
valid. We explore these questions in later chapters.

E. THE RELATION OF THE EXECUTIVE TO THE ADMINISTRATIVE AGENCIES

Page 98. Add the following after line 10:

The Ninth Circuit, in Chadha v. Immigration Service, 634 F.2d 408
(1980) (referred to in Casebook at 97, n.71), held unconstitutional a
statutory provision giving one house of Congress the right to "veto" the
attorney general's decision (taken pursuant to statute) to allow an otherwise deportable alien to remain in this country. The court concluded:
"Congress holds all legislative powers. We do not think that body would
confess itself unable to formulate deportation rules or policies applicable
to individual cases that are sufficiently clear for compliance by the Executive and for ascertainment by the Judiciary. We cannot accept that definite, uniform, and sensible criteria governing the conferral of government burdens and benefits on individuals should be replaced by a species
of nonlegislation, wherein the Executive branch becomes a sort of referee
in making an initial determination which has no independent force or
validity, even after review and approval by the Judiciary, save and except
for the exercise of final control by the unfettered discretion of Congress
as to each case. The defects of this procedure are aggravated by the
unicameral aspect of the statutory mechanism and the deficiencies of that
procedure preclude justifying congressional action as a separate and
independent way of adjudicating the status of aliens outside the executive
and judicial processes. In such a world, the Executive's duty of faithful
execution of the laws becomes meaningless, as the law to be executed in
a given case remains tentative until after action by the Executive has
ceased. The role of judicial review in determining the procedural or
substantive fairness of administrative action becomes equally nugatory

because ex parte influence on administrative decisionmakers, once condemned, now is made the norm. Such flexibility is but the structural twin of lawless rule. [634 F.2d at 434-435.]" The Supreme Court currently has the merits of this decision under review. Because there are jurisdictional and mootness questions involved, it is difficult to predict whether the Court will decide the basic constitutional question. See 102 S. Ct. 87 (1981) (consideration of jurisdiction postponed until hearing on merits).

In the meantime, the District of Columbia Circuit has held unconstitutional a provision of the National Gas Policy Act that instructed the Federal Energy Regulatory Commission to issue incremental pricing rules for natural gas ("phase II rules"). The provision stated that a phase II rule would take effect only if neither house of Congress adopted within thirty days a resolution disapproving the rule. Consumer Energy Council of America v. FERC, No. 80-2312 (D.C. Cir. Jan. 29, 1982). The Court reasoned that this one-house veto violated the Constitution's presentation clause, Art. I, sec. 7, as well as the separation of powers "implicit in Articles I, II, and III because it authorizes the legislature to share powers properly exercised by the other two branches."

CONSUMER ENERGY COUNCIL OF AMERICA v. FERC

No. 80-2312 (D.C. Cir. Jan. 29, 1982)

WILKEY, J. . . . Article I, Section 7 . . . [requires that bills, orders, resolutions and votes that require the concurrence of both houses also be] presented to the President of the United States. In each case the President may give either his approval, in which case the action of Congress becomes law, or his disapproval, in which case the action may not become law unless it is repassed by two-thirds of both the House and the Senate. These provisions [along with Article I, section 1] set up the fundamental prerequisites to the enactment of federal laws: bicameral passage of the legislation, and presentation for approval or disapproval by the President. . . .

There is little doubt as to Article I, Section 1's purpose in vesting all legislative powers "in a Congress" consisting of "a Senate and House of Representatives." Perhaps the greatest fear of the Framers was that in a representative democracy the Legislature would be capable of using its plenary lawmaking power to swallow up the other departments of the Government. . . .

A corollary fear was that national majorities would be able to exercise unconstrained power, thereby destroying the power of state governments. The answer to both concerns proved to be bicameralism. Requiring the concurrence of two branches in enacting laws would help prevent a single majority from undertaking to control the Federal Government.

And the Great Compromise, dividing the Congress into one branch directly representing the people and one branch representing the states, was devised as a means of preserving state power. The overriding objective of bicameralism, then, is to constrain the exercise of the federal legislative power by making sure that the Legislature can act only where representatives of two different constituencies are in agreement. . . . [T]he Framers were determined that the legislative power should be difficult to employ. The requirements of presentation to the President and bicameral concurrence ultimately serve the same fundamental purpose: to restrict the operation of the legislative power to those policies which meet the approval of three constituencies, or a supermajority of two. If the legislative veto represents an exercise of the legislative power, then, it must be exercised only in compliance with these constitutional requirements.

Congressional amici[72a] argue that Article I, Section 7 does not apply because FERC's Phase II rule was never an effective law, but merely a proposal to be accepted or rejected by Congress through the one-house disapproval mechanism. . . . The contention that the Phase II rule was a mere legislative proposal [however,] . . . is easily refuted by comparing the status of the rule to that of a bill introduced in Congress. If neither house of Congress acts to approve a bill, the bill dies; but when neither house acts to disapprove an agency rule, the rule becomes law. . . .

It has [also] been suggested that the nonobjection of either house is merely a condition precedent to the effectiveness of the rule, such that the rule never gains legal effect until the condition is satisfied. . . . [But] merely styling something as a condition on a grant of power does not make that condition constitutional. Otherwise Congress could, for example, provide that all rights and duties established by legislation are conditioned on the vote of either house of Congress to eliminate them, thus enabling instant repeal of all statutes by simple resolution. . . .

It suffices here that in practical effect the House's veto changed national incremental pricing policy. . . .

[The veto made "a social policy judgment," an "assessment that is peculiarly legislative in nature" because it is a "predictive assessment, using public participation and collective decisionmaking, with democratic accountability as the final test of judgment."] Congress attempted to do by one house what the Constitution requires be done only by both houses and the President. Section 202(c) is therefore unconstitutional. . . .

Congressional amici [further] argue that the House's veto of the Phase II rule by definition did not interfere with the Executive's administration of the statute because FERC is not part of the Executive Branch. The Commission is an independent regulatory agency "within the Depart-

---

72a. [Since all parties to the suit agreed that the veto was unconstitutional, the arguments in its favor were presented by the two houses of Congress, in amicus briefs.—Ed].

ment [of Energy]" for purposes of its budget, but functionally independent because its members "shall hold office for a term of four years and may be removed by the President only for inefficiency, neglect of duty, or malfeasance in office." Since the Supreme Court has upheld the constitutionality of such agency independence, Congressional amici argue that it is clear that the President can have no claim to participation in the making of FERC's rules: "FERC performs only those functions as assigned to it by Congress; it derives no independent authority from the Constitution, and separation of powers principles do not apply to it."

The contention that the separation of powers doctrine does not apply to independent agencies is manifestly groundless. . . . It is true that the President, as representative of the Executive, does not have a claim to control the decisionmaking of independent agencies. But it is an enormous, and unwarranted, jump from this to the conclusion that Congress may itself interfere with an independent agency's decisions without regard to separation of powers. Although FERC is substantially independent of the Executive, it nonetheless performs executive functions. The constitutionality of agency independence has not turned on a determination that certain agency functions are properly legislative rather than executive in nature. . . .

[T]he constitutionality of the one-house veto does not depend on whether it is used against an executive agency or an independent agency. There has been a general breakdown in any distinction between the functions of the two types of agency, and in practice the interference by Congress is identical in either case. Indeed, it is ironic that Congressional amici attempt to place great significance on the Commission's independence and on the need for having a politically accountable check on the agency's decision. The fundamental justification for making agencies independent is that since they exercise adjudicatory powers requiring impartial expertise, political interference is undesirable. By then turning around and asserting that this independence is a justification for the one-house veto, Congress attempts simultaneously to decrease the power of the Executive and increase its own power. . . .

Congressional veto proponents contend, however, that the one-house veto is simply one of many techniques Congress may use in carrying out its responsibility to oversee the administration of the laws. The error in this argument is that the one-house veto provides Congress with a fundamentally different kind of authority over administrative rulemaking than it otherwise would have. When Congress conducts investigations or hearings, or enacts a "report and wait" requirement, or threatens to reduce appropriations, or imposes reporting requirements, or engages in other modes of oversight, its ability to influence the agency derives almost entirely from its ability to pass a statute requiring a different agency action or reducing the agency's appropriations. These oversight methods enable Congress to inquire "into *past* executive branch action in order to influence *future* executive branch performance." Congress' supervisory power thus comes directly from its legislative power.

The one house veto, on the other hand, effectively enables Congress "to participate prospectively in the approval or disapproval of . . . law 'enacted' by the executive branch pursuant to a delegation of authority by Congress." In effect, Congress is able to expand its role from one of oversight, with an eye to legislative revision, to one of shared administration. . . . Not only does this expand the congressional power, but it may also expand the total national power. Because of the veto, the rulemaking agency is given greater power than Congress might otherwise delegate; and Congress normally will let rules take effect unless so clearly undesirable that a veto is deemed warranted. . . .

The fundamental problem of the one-house veto, then, is that it represents an attempt by Congress to retain direct control over delegated administrative power. Congress may provide detailed rules of conduct to be administered without discretion by administrative officers, or it may provide broad policy guidance and leave the details to be filled in by administrative officers exercising substantial discretion. It may not, however, insert one of its houses as an effective administrative decisionmaker. . . .

Page 99. Add the following at the end of the page:

The Senate has recently passed a major regulatory reform bill, S. 1080. As amended on the floor of the Senate, that bill now includes a legislative veto provision that allows the two houses of Congress, acting jointly, to veto any substantive rule-making decision of an administrative agency. (There are a few exceptions.) The provision states in part that "any final rule [of an agency] . . . shall be considered a recommendation of the agency to the Congress and shall have no force and effect as a rule unless [after the passage of a specified time Congress has not 'vetoed' it]." S. 1080, §801 et seq., as passed by the Senate, 128 Cong. Rec. S. 2720 (daily ed. March 24, 1982).

Chapter Three

The Problem of Administrative Discretion

B. CRITICISMS OF THE REGULATORY PROCESS

Page 135. Add the following after line 5:

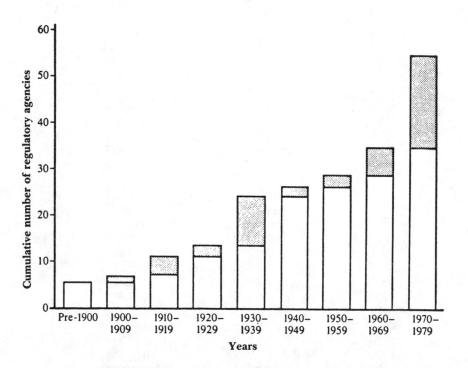

Growth of federal regulatory agencies. The shaded areas represent the new agencies created during the decade. (Source: M. Weidenbaum, "The Trend of Government Regulation of Business," paper prepared for the Hoover Institute Conference on Regulation, Stanford University, July 9, 1979)

CUMULATIVE GROWTH OF FEDERAL REGULATIONS PAGES IN THE FEDERAL REGISTER.

Year	Number of pages	Cumulative pages
1936	2,599	2,599
1937	3,445	6,044
1938	3,160	9,204
1939	5,007	14,211
1940	5,307	19,518
1941	6,877	26,395
1942	11,134	37,529
1943	17,553	55,082
1944	15,194	70,276
1945	15,508	85,784
1946	14,736	100,520
1947	8,902	109,422
1948	9,608	119,030
1949	7,952	126,982
1950	9,562	136,544
1951	13,175	149,719
1952	11,896	161,615
1953	8,912	170,527
1954	9,910	180,437
1955	10,196	190,633
1956	10,528	201,161
1957	11,156	212,317
1958	10,579	222,896
1959	11,113	234,009
1960	14,479	248,488
1961	12,789	261,277
1962	13,226	274,503
1963	14,842	289,345
1964	19,304	308,649
1965	17,206	325,855
1966	16,850	342,705
1967	21,088	363,793
1968	20,072	383,865
1969	20,466	404,331
1970	20,036	424,367
1971	25,447	449,814
1972	28,924	478,738
1973	35,572	514,310
1974	45,422	559,732
1975	60,221	619,953
1976	57,072	677,025
1977	65,603	742,628
Projected 1981		Over 1 million

Source: W. Buhler, Calculating the Full Costs of Government Regulation, Office of the Librarian, Federal Register, 1978.

97th Cong., 1st Sess. 17-50 passim (1981)

THE EFFECTIVENESS OF REGULATION

[This document, prepared as a justification for the Regulatory Reform Bill currently in Congress, provides an overview of the various criticisms and doubts about regulation that underlie some of the current calls for reform. It is highly impressionistic, noting the wide range of studies and the numerous anecdotes that cast doubt on the effectiveness of regulation, and also noting other contrary studies that seek to rebut those doubts. It begins by distinguishing between "economic regulation"—as for example of airlines, trucking, or natural gas—and "social regulation"—as for example of the environment, health, and safety. As to the former, the debate is typically framed in terms of regulation or deregulation. As to the latter, the debate typically focuses on how to make regulation more effective or less burdensome. The report collects studies that it believes are relevant to this latter issue, showing social regulation's benefits and its costs. It finds the studies overall to be inconclusive—a fact that the report believes suggests that regulation is not working well. The flavor of the report can be conveyed to some extent in a short summary of, and by a few brief excerpts from, the discussion of benefits and costs of social regulation.]

THE BENEFITS OF REGULATION

[Information about benefits, while sparse, is sometimes available. There are numerous studies showing significant benefits to health from increased control of air and water pollution. In summarizing those studies,] a report prepared by the Center for Policy Alternatives at the Massachusetts Institute of Technology . . . concluded that "substantial benefits have been realized from federal environmental, health and safety regulations." . . . [In the area of auto safety, for example,] a 1976 study by the General Accounting Office concluded that the safety devices required for passenger cars in the 1966 to 1968 model years resulted in from 15 to 25 percent fewer deaths and injuries, in the 1969 to 1970 model years in [from] 25 to 30 percent fewer deaths and injuries, but in the 1971 to 1973 model years in no benefits. . . . A 1977 CRS study reviewing the data of the Bureau of Labor Statistics and the National Safety Council, noted a decrease in occupational fatality and injury rates between 1974 and 1975. . . .

[On the other hand, other independent scholars, such as Paul MacAvoy of Yale and Robert Crandall of Brookings, have written that so far there is "very little evidence" of improved human health or safety due to regulatory programs. Professors Zeckhauser and Nichols, for example, reviewed accident/lost work day rates in 1972-1975 (after OSHA), noting little change from 1960-1970 (before OSHA). They concluded:]

"Both politically and practically [OSHA] has been a failure. It has generated fierce antagonism in the business community and is viewed by many as the quintessential government intrusion. And it has had virtually no noticeable impact on work-related injuries and illnesses. . . ."

A volume just published by the Brookings Institution makes a corresponding judgment: "While plausible explanations can be offered for why OSHA inspections should be found to increase the observed accident rate, the fact remains that analysis fails to uncover convincing evidence that OSHA has succeeded in lowering the accident rate.

These studies provide a devastating critique of OSHA's efforts to improve occupational safety, indicating that OSHA had little or no effect on accident rates, even in targeted industries where its resources were focused. L. Lave, The Strategy of Social Regulation 102 (1981). . . ."

Other studies make a more limited critique of the relative effectiveness of certain regulations. Bruce Ackerman and William Hassler, in their new study of efforts to control pollution from coal burning under the 1977 Clean Air Act Amendments, relate their conclusion that: "Congress's well-intentioned effort to improve the administrative process has driven EPA to an extraordinary decision that will cost the public tens of billions of dollars to achieve environmental goals that could be reached more cheaply, more quickly, and more surely by other means. Indeed, the agency action is so inept that some of the nation's most populous areas will end up with a *worse* environment than would have resulted if the new policy had never been put into effect. B. Ackerman & W. Hassler, Clean Coal/Dirty Air 2 (1981) (emphasis in original). . . ."

[In the report's view, the very uncertainty about benefits has led to public hostility to regulation in part because there is greater certainty that regulation has imposed severe costs on industry.]

[THE COSTS OF REGULATION]

[The direct costs of federal regulation—expenditures by federal agencies—can be measured fairly easily. Expenditures on regulation increased from $866 million ($539 million for "social," $327 million for "economic") in 1970 to $6.937 billion in 1981 ($5.8 billion for "social," $1.0 billion for "economic"). Adjusted for inflation, this latter figure comes to $3.2 billion in 1970 dollars, representing a real average annual rate of increase of 6 percent.

The more important costs, however, include the costs of *complying* with regulations. In a well-known study, Professor Murray Weidenbaum, now chairman of the Council of Economic Advisors, concluded:]

ESTIMATED COST OF FEDERAL REGULATION OF BUSINESS
[Fiscal years, in billions of dollars]

	1977	1978	1979	Estimated 1980
Administrative costs	$4.1	$4.9	$5.5	$6.0
Compliance costs	82.0	98.0	110.0	120.0
Total	86.1	102.9	115.5	126.0

From: M. Weidenbaum, "Cost of Regulation and Benefits of Reform" 11 (1980) (Center for the Study of American Business Publ. No. 35).

The Office of Management and Budget has at various times ventured its own estimates of regulatory costs. In 1975, OMB estimated the total cost of regulation as between $113.3 to $135.4 billion. These figures were subsequently criticized by the General Accounting Office. 6 Study on Federal Regulation, supra at 63-66. More recently, OMB has predicted that total regulatory costs could reach $500 billion per year by the end of the 1980's unless unnecessary regulations are eliminated. . . .

Over the last decade, regulation has served to aggravate price increases already proceeding at a severe rate. "The industries most subject to health and safety and environmental quality regulation—automobile manufacturing; paper; chemicals; stone, clay, and glass; primary metals; non-fuel mining; and construction—have generally experienced larger price increases in the 1970's than other, less-regulated industries." . . . Between 1969 and 1973 prices in the most heavily regulated industries rose by more than 30 percent, while prices in unregulated manufacturing increased by 14 percent. [In Professor MacAvoy's view, these price increases were due to regulation and were passed on to consumers.] . . .

For example, in 1978, various features mandated by federal regulation increased the price of the average passenger car by $666.   . In that same year it was estimated that requirements imposed by regulation added between $1,500 and $2,500 to the cost of a typical new house. . .

A Congressional Research Service study estimated that the costs of implementing section 504 of the Rehabilitation Act to the New York Metropolitan Transit Authority and the New York Station Island Rapid Transit System to be between $201 and $314 million per year.   .

New York City Mayor Edward Koch estimates federal and state mandates over the next four years will cost that city $6.25 billion in expense-budget dollars; . . and 1.66 billion in lost revenues. While generally supportive of regulation's policy objectives, Mayor Koch warned of the "lack of comprehension by those who write them as to the cumulative impact on single city, and even the nation." . . .

[Moreover,] . . . due to regulation it now takes $54 million and ten years to bring a new drug to market. . . . [Regulations may well be] responsible for about one third of the increase in [drug] costs between 1960 and 1975. . . . In the eight years from 1979 to 1987   . environmental regulations could cost the copper industry up to 28,000 full time jobs, that is, 32.9 percent of [its] . . . work force. . .   [In the electric power industry,] regulatory costs [may] amount to 44.88 percent of total production costs. [For example, in 1960 it cost $15,000 to build a mile of transmission line; in 1977 it cost over $95,000, with regulatory costs accounting for more than half the difference.] . . . [Such regulatory costs mean higher interest rates, making it particulary difficult for small firms to invest.] It has been estimated that environmental protection and job safety regulations cost the economy about one fourth of the potential average annual increase in productivity. . .

We believe that, based on available information, one can conclude that the compliance costs of regulation are excessive. Such a conclusion can be based on the sheer magnitude of those costs without reference to the achievements of regulation. The data on these costs is extensive, coming from a variety of different sources, including industry, government, and private researchers. It is impossible to conclude that all these estimates are completely wrong, distorted by self interest or bias, or otherwise useless for policy guidance. . . .

[In many instances, the benefits of regulation do not justify the costs imposed. At a minimum the severity of costs and uncertainty about benefits explain the "impulse for reform."]

C. ALTERNATIVE REMEDIES FOR REGULATORY FAILURE

Page 138. Add the following after line 29:

1A. Encouraging Substantive Reform

BREYER, REGULATION AND ITS REFORM (1982)

Several generic proposals would encourage substantive reform, and, in particular, substantive change toward less restrictive methods of regulation. These proposals are of two sorts: (1) those that encourage the agencies to adopt more competitive or less restrictive proposals by imposing an "impact statement" requirement; and (2) those that encourage Congress and the president to examine regulatory programs individually and in detail.

A. IMPACT STATEMENTS

The success in leading agencies of the Environmental Impact Statements to take account of the environment has led regulatory reformers to propose other impact statement requirements, designed to influence the substantive direction of agency policy. The most significant proposals would encourage agencies to adopt less costly or less restrictive methods of regulation. President Ford, by executive order, required the agencies to write an "inflationary impact statement." The agency would determine how much its proposed action would raise costs and whether there were alternative, less costly ways of dealing with the problem. President Carter withdrew this order, substituting an order requiring a "regulatory impact statement." Before the agency takes any major action, it must write a statement setting out the action's objectives and alternative ways of achieving them. It must then justify its action as better than any alternative. President Reagan has also required agencies to consider less restrictive alternatives and to use cost-benefit analyses.

This approach, which President Reagan has embodied in an Executive

Order, also forms part of S. 1080, the regulatory reform bill that passed the Senate in March 1982. That bill would have agencies issue a "regulatory analysis" of any major rule. The analysis would state the economic and noneconomic costs and benefits and would explore the possibility of less restrictive ways of achieving the regulation's objectives, explaining why they were not satisfactory. . . .

In addition to their ability to focus the agencies upon factors currently of interest to Congress, the strength of many of these impact statements is that they provide a justification for the Office of Management and Budget, the Council of Economic Advisors, and the Department of Justice (Antitrust Division) to intervene in agency proceedings and to present their views. These agencies are institutionally disposed to stress the need for competition, the importance of incentives, the need to take account of costs, and the difficulties of classical regulation. Their presence in the proceeding can force the agency to take more serious account of these considerations. . . .

Intervention based upon the impact statement can also force the White House staff to pay attention to issues and decisions that might otherwise pass unnoticed. Involvement by the Council of Economic Advisors in some major regulatory proceedings, for example, has led the White House to develop a firm position, which, in turn, has strongly influenced the agency's decision toward less restrictive regulation. Finally, if the impact statement is reviewable in court, action that is unreasonable in terms of the statement can be set aside. Thus, the Justice Department might urge the courts to set aside ICC action that impeded entry into the trucking business on the grounds that the ICC had not written (indeed, could not write) . . . [an] impact statement showing that a restrictive entry policy was needed to carry out the purposes of trucking regulation.

There are several major weaknesses of the impact statement approach. (1) It is difficult to find a single factor, or even a small number of factors, that *all* agencies would do better to focus upon. The ICC, for example, might do better to focus on the need for competition, but that is not so serious a problem for OSHA. (2) The final decision remains with the agency. (3) It is not difficult to write a plausible justification for almost any decision along the lines required by the statement. [C]lassical regulation, even when far too restrictive and undesirable, is never without plausible justification. In every instance one can find claims, evidence, and argument that will support regulation. Weighing of arguments and careful judgment is needed before concluding that a particular regulatory program or action is undesirable. Thus, it may not be difficult for agencies to reach a decision and then to write whatever impact statement is needed to justify it. [I]n many agencies it is common practice first to reach a decision and then to have a special opinion-writing section compose a statement in justification.

B. ENCOURAGING STEP-BY-STEP REFORM

There are also proposals that would encourage step-by-step, detailed examination of individual agencies. Detailed congressional oversight, for example, helped bring about airline and trucking deregulation. Executive branch study, when combined with congressional support, has also recently brought about major change in the railroad and banking industries. But how can Congress and the executive be encouraged to continue to conduct this type of oversight and reform? The major proposal advocated as a way to do so is "sunset" legislation.

Sunset legislation is designed to force Congress to consider regulatory reform on an agency-by-agency basis. It provides that an agency, together with its rules and regulations, will simply cease to exist as of a certain date unless Congress specifically enacts legislation that extends the agency's life. The threat of extinction should lead Congress to reconsider the need for a regulatory program before it disappears. Typically, sunset legislation also provides a comprehensive set of criteria, which Congress, after investigation, is to use in determining whether the agency's life should be prolonged. Several states, including Colorado and Florida, have adopted sunset laws. Congress has occasionally inserted sunset provisions into laws creating new regulatory agencies, such as the Federal Energy Administration, which was to have expired on June 30, 1976.

There are two major problems with the sunset approach. First, there is no guarantee that Congress will address itself seriously to the reform question and undertake the detailed work required. It may well simply reenact the old program automatically, as it did with the Federal Energy Administration. Or pressed by the demand for quick action, it may simply attack administrative waste without examining the fundamental objectives of the program. Second, the approach may condemn to extinction those agencies that are the subject of serious political controversy. It is far more difficult to pass legislation through Congress than to stop legislation from being passed. To give an obvious example, a few senators can filibuster and prevent a bill's enactment. Even without a filibuster, a determined minority can take advantage of time pressures, the committee system, and floor rules to delay or halt unfavorable legislation. The proponents of sunset laws seek to use this very fact to force serious reexamination of agencies. Yet the obverse side of the coin is that a minority within Congress could destroy the Federal Trade Commission, OSHA, or virtually any other agency. These defects suggest that the sunset approach needs modifications. . . .

One such modification would have the president appoint a special committee, whose members would include the chairman of the Council of Economic Advisors, the attorney general, and perhaps, members of Congress, to review regulatory programs individually and in detail on a ten-year schedule. The president would be required to send reform recommendations to Congress, where they would be automatically discharged from committee and voted upon on the floor after one year. This discharge provision is designed as a trigger to force those with political authority to take agency reform seriously, because they know they will have to vote on it publicly. The committee's makeup is designed to include persons who represent "procompetitive" institutions and thus are likely to favor a "least restrictive alternative" approach to regulation. Of course, one cannot predict whether the committee's meetings would be attended by only low-level staff, whether the recommendations would be significant, or whether reform could pass Congress.

Page 164. At the end of the page, add the following new footnote:

38a. The Regulatory Reform Act of 1982. On March 24, 1982, the Senate passed S. 1080, the Regulatory Reform Act, which it had under consideration for several years. The bill grew out of a study of regulation made in the mid-1970s by the Senate Committee on Governmental Affairs. It represents an amalgam of proposals by that committee, the Senate Committee on the Judiciary, and two different administrations. For its text, see 128 Cong. Rec. S. 2713 et seq. (daily ed. March 24, 1982).

The bill combines several different approaches to regulatory reform, which are discussed elsewhere in this text and supplement. We summarize its main features here.

(1) Procedures governing informal "notice and comment rule making (APA §553) are modified to make the process more formal. The agencies must publish more detailed notices, they must make greater efforts to encourage public participation, and they must create a rule-making file containing virtually all the data relied upon in creating the rule. This file "shall constitute the rulemaking record for purposes of review." (Moreover, it shall contain any written comments sent by the White House as well as an explanation of any changes in a proposed rule made as a result of White House intervention—a requirement likely to make it more difficult for a president to control his own agencies.) See supplement to chapter 5, infra.

(2) Elaborate analyses are required for "major rules"—defined as those likely to have a major impact on the economy. This proposal is patterned after President Reagan's Executive Order. See supplement to chapter 2, supra. Before promulgating a major rule, the agency must prepare a preliminary regulatory analysis containing a description of benefits, costs, reasonably less intrusive and more flexible alternatives, sources of funding, and sources of scientific data. It must also explain why the benefits of the proposed rule are likely to justify its costs and to prove more cost-effective than the alternatives, unless doing so is "expressly or by necessary implication inconsistent with the provisions of the [agency's] enabling statute." A final regulatory analysis will also explain

how the rule is cost-justified. These regulatory analyses will not be subject to judicial review except that they "shall constitute part of the whole rulemaking record of agency action for the purpose of judicial review of the rule."

(3) All existing major rules of agencies shall be reviewed on a schedule under criteria roughly similar to those contained in the regulatory analysis provisions.

(4) Every six months, each agency shall publish an agenda of proposed rules upon which it is working. It shall also establish deadlines. The president will make an annual regulatory activities report to Congress.

(5) The Bumpers Amendment attached to S. 1080 requires the courts, on review, to scrutinize agency activity more carefully. They are to pay somewhat less heed to what the agency says on questions of law. See supplement to chapter 4, infra.

(6) Certain changes are made in venue and other similar procedural requirements.

(7) A two-house legislative veto is enacted, applicable to nearly all agency rule making. See supplement to chapter 2, supra.

Chapter Four

The Scope of Judicial Review—Questions of Fact and Law

A. REVIEW OF QUESTIONS OF FACT

Page 193. Add the following after line 23:

(d) A recent set of cases in the First Circuit illustrates the close relation of "burden of proof" to the more general question of how a court should review agency fact finding. The National Labor Relations Act §8(a)(3) makes it an unfair labor practice for an employer "by discrimination in regard to . . . tenure of employment . . . to encourage or discourage membership in any labor organization." 29 U.S.C. §158(a)(3).

While this statute obviously forbids discharging an employee because, say, he or she is a union organizer, the NLRB has found it difficult to apply to mixed-motive cases—cases in which an employer seems to impose discipline both for a legitimate reason *and* as retaliation for union activities. To allow employers to discharge freely in such cases might well undermine the statute's purpose. But, since employers are often hostile to union organizing, to forbid discharge no matter how good or important the legitimate cause would effectively grant union organizers total job security—also contrary to the statute's purpose. Because the factual pattern of the cases before the courts led them to believe that the board was moving too far in this latter direction, they reversed its efforts to apply an "in-part" test—a test that would have forbidden the discharge as long as an anti-union motive played *some* role in the decision.[35a] The First Circuit, for example, insisted that the "bad" motive not only be present but that it constitute a necessary condition for the discharge. NLRB v. Eastern Smelting & Refining Corp., 598 F.2d 666, 671 (1st Cir. 1979). Eventually the board and the First Circuit agreed on a set of ground rules for such cases: In a "dual motive" case "the initial inquiry is whether the Board has made

---

35a. See Youngstown Osteopathic Hospital Assn., 21 N.L.R.B. 574 (1976).

a prima facie showing that a 'significant improper motivation' underlay the Company's action." In making this prima facie case, the board must establish the "requisite knowledge by the Company of union activity." The "bad reason may [then] be shown by independent evidence or by the circumstances of the discharge itself." NLRB v. Eastern Smelting & Refining Corp., 598 F.2d at 670. See NLRB v. Cable Vision, 666 F.2d 1, 8 (1st Cir. 1981). Thereafter, the burden shifts to the company to "prove that it had a good reason, sufficient in itself, to produce" the discharge. Statler Industries, Inc. v. NLRB, 644 F.2d 902, 905 (1st Cir. 1981)·

The court went on to state that the board "may not reject the employer's proof [of good and sufficient motive], absent a reasonable basis," NLRB v. Eastern Smelting & Refining Corp., 598 F.2d at 671 n.12, and that the employer need only bring the evidentiary scales back into "equipoise." NLRB v. Cable Vision, 660 F.2d at 13. But the board made it clear that it intended to force the employer to *overcome* the board's prima facie case of violation. *Wright Line*, 251 NLRB No. 150. The First Circuit then struck down the board's *Wright Line* test insofar as that test required the employer to *overcome* the prima facie case. The Court held that the statutes require the board to prove a violation by a "preponderance" of the evidence. The board could not, therefore, ask the employer to prove itself innocent. Rather, the board could impose upon the employer only a "burden of *production*"; NLRB v. Wright Line, 662 F.2d 899 (1st Cir. 1981).

Underneath this technical language and complex set of decisions is an important practical point. It is quite possible that the courts feared that the agency was using its fact-finding power—the power to find anti-union discrimination as a fact—to provide job security to union organizers, contrary to the NLRA's language and intent. The board's *Wright Line* test would have aggravated this tendency because of the practical difficulty of an employer proving that its hostility to the union played *no* significant part in a discharge decision. Thus, the court's insistence in *Wright Line* on the burden-of-production/burden-of-proof distinction may have been an effort to bring the board's fact finding under control. By forcing the board to certify that, after hearing both sides, the board still believes that the evidence—by a preponderance—shows a violation, the court forces the agency to focus on what Congress told it to do and prevents it from using its fact-finding power for other purposes. See NLRB v· Transportation Management Corp., No. 81-1537 (1st Cir. 1982) (Breyer, J., concurring).

C. REVIEW OF QUESTIONS OF LAW

Page 258. Add the following after line 5:

You might consider the following conceptual framework for dealing with "questions of law" issues. Begin with Justice Frankfurter, writing for the Court in Social Security Board v. Nierotko, 327 U.S. 358 (1946). In that case, the Court stressed the importance of Congressional intent. The Court was asked to review an administrative determination of a legal question—"whether 'back pay' is to be treated as wages" within the terms of the statute. The Court wrote:

"But it is urged by petitioner that the administrative construction on the question of whether 'back pay' is to be treated as wages should lead us to follow the agencies' determination. There is a suggestion that the administrative decision should be treated as conclusive, and reliance for that argument is placed upon Labor Board v. Hearst Publications, 322 U.S. 111, 130, and Gray v. Powell, 314 U.S. 402, 411. . . . The Social Security Board and the Treasury were compelled to decide, administratively, whether or not to treat 'back pay' as wages; and their expert judgment is entitled, as we have said, to great weight. [Citing *Skidmore.*] The very fact that judicial review has been accorded, however, makes evident that such decisions are only conclusive as to properly supported findings of fact. Both *Hearst Publications,* p. 131, and Gray v. Powell, p. 411, advert to the limitations of administrative interpretations. Administrative determinations must have a basis in law and must be within the granted authority. Administration, when it interprets a statute so as to make it apply to particular circumstances, acts as a delegate to the legislative power. Congress might have declared that 'back pay' awards under the Labor Act should or should not be treated as wages. Congress might have delegated to the Social Security Board to determine what compensation paid by employers to employees should be treated as wages. Except as such interpretive power may be included in the agencies' administrative functions, Congress did neither. An agency may not finally decide the limits of its statutory power. That is a judicial function. Congress used a well understood word—"wages"—to indicate the receipts which were to govern taxes and benefits under the Social Security Act. There may be borderline payments to employees on which courts would follow administrative determinations as to whether such payments were or were not wages under the act

"We conclude, however, that the Board's interpretation of this statute to exclude back pay goes beyond the boundaries of administrative routine and the statutory limits."

What should a court do, however, when Congress is silent as to the extent it intends a reviewing court to respect an agency's judgment on a matter of law? Such is often the case. What factors ought the court to consider in determining probable Congressional intent? See L Jaffe, Judicial Review, Questions of Law, 69 Harv. L. Rev. 239 (1955). For the authors' views, see Constance v. Secretary of HHS, No. 81-1322 (1st Cir. March 5, 1982). See generally Ford Motor Credit Co. v. Milhollin, 444 U.S. 555, 556 (1979).

The extent to which courts should "respect" or "defer to" agency views about questions of law is at the heart of the current regulatory reform debate surrounding the Bumpers Amendment. It will be discussed later in the supplement to this chapter

D. DIRECT JUDICIAL CONTROL OF ADMINISTRATIVE DISCRETION

Page 288. Add the following cases after line 10:

INDUSTRIAL UNION DEPARTMENT, AFL-CIO v. AMERICAN PETROLEUM INSTITUTE

448 U.S. 607 (1980)

MR. JUSTICE STEVENS announced the judgment of the Court and delivered an opinion, in which THE CHIEF JUSTICE and MR. JUSTICE STEWART joined and in Parts I, II, III-A, III-B, III-C, and III-E of which MR. JUSTICE POWELL joined.

[Industry challenged the adoption by the secretary of labor of a regulatory standard limiting occupational exposure to benzene Under the Occupational Health and Safety Act, the Occupational Health and Safety Administration (OSHA), within the Department of Labor, is responsible for developing such standards.]

The Act delegates broad authority to the Secretary to promulgate different kinds of standards. The basic definition of an "occupational safety and health standard" is found in §3(8), [of the Occupational Safety and Health Act,] which provides·

> The term "occupational safety and health standard" means a standard which requires conditions, or the adoption or use of one or more practices, means, methods, operations, or processes, reasonably necessary or appropriate to provide safe or healthful employment and places of employment. 84 Stat. 1591, 29 U.S.C. §652(8).

Where toxic materials or harmful physical agents are concerned, a standard must also comply with §6(b)(5), which provides.

> The Secretary, in promulgating standards dealing with toxic materials or harmful physical agents under this subsection, shall set the standard which most adequately assures, to the extent feasible, on the basis of the best available evidence, that no employee will suffer material impairment of health or functional capacity even if such employee has regular exposure to the hazard dealt with by such standard for the period of his working life. 84 Stat. 1594, 29 U.S.C. §655(b)(5).

Wherever the toxic material to be regulated is a carcinogen, the Secretary has taken the position that no safe exposure level can be determined and that §6(b)(5) requires him to set an exposure limit at the lowest technologically feasible level that will not impair the viability of the industries regulated. In this case, after having determined that there is a causal connection between benzene and leukemia (a cancer of the white blood cells), the Secretary set an exposure limit on airborne concentrations of benzene of one part benzene per million parts of air (1 ppm), regulated dermal and eye contact with solutions containing benzene, and imposed complex monitoring and medical testing requirements on employers whose workplaces contain 0.5 ppm or more of benzene.

On pre-enforcement review pursuant to 29 U.S.C. §655(f), the United States Court of Appeals for the Fifth Circuit held the regulation invalid. American Petroleum Institute v. OSHA, 581 F.2d 493 (1978).

Reading the two provisions together, the Fifth Circuit held that the Secretary was under a duty to determine whether the benefits expected from the new standard bore a reasonable relationship to the costs that it imposed. . . . The court noted that OSHA had made an estimate of the costs of compliance, but that the record lacked substantial evidence of any discernible benefits.

We agree with the Fifth Circuit's holding that §3(8) requires the Secretary to find, as a threshold matter, that the toxic substance in question poses a significant health risk in the workplace and that a new, lower standard is therefore "reasonably necessary or appropriate to provide safe or healthful employment and places of employment." Unless and until such a finding is made, it is not necessary to address the further question whether the Court of Appeals correctly held that there must be a reasonable correlation between costs and benefits, or whether, as the federal parties argue, the Secretary is then required by §6(b)(5) to promulgate a standard that goes as far as technologically and economically possible to eliminate the risk. . . .

I

Benzene is a familiar and important commodity. It is a colorless, aromatic liquid that evaporates rapidly under ordinary atmospheric conditions. Approximately 11 billion pounds of benzene were produced in the United States in 1976. Ninety-four percent of that total was produced by the petroleum and petrochemical industries, with the remainder produced by the steel industry as a byproduct of coking operations. Benzene is used in manufacturing a variety of products including motor fuels (which may contain as much as 2% benzene), solvents, detergents, pesticides, and other organic chemicals. . . .

The entire population of the United States is exposed to small quantities of benzene, ranging from a few parts per billion to 0.5 ppm, in the ambient air. . . . [O]ne million workers are subject to additional low-level exposures as a consequence of their employment. The majority of these employees work in gasoline service stations, benzene production (petroleum refineries and coking operations), chemical processing, benzene transportation, rubber manufacturing, and laboratory operations.

Benzene is a toxic substance. . . . Exposure to high concentrations produces an almost immediate effect on the central nervous system. Inhalation of concentrations of 20,000 ppm can be fatal within minutes; exposures in the range of 250 to 500 ppm can cause vertigo, nausea, and other symptoms of mild poisoning. . . . Persistent exposures at levels above 25-40 ppm may lead to blood deficiencies and diseases of the blood-forming organs, including aplastic anemia, which is generally fatal.

[As authorized by the act, the secretary in 1971 adopted as the federal standard the American National Standards Institute "consensus standard" for occupational exposure to benzene of 10 ppm averaged over an eight-hour period. The National Institute for Occupational Safety and Health (NIOSH), OSHA's research arm, concluded, on the basis of epidemiological studies correlating exposure levels of 150-600 ppm over extended periods and increased cancer incidence by exposed workers, that benzene caused leukemia. Although the studies failed to establish dose-response relations that would predict cancer incidence at lower exposure levels, NIOSH recommended that the exposure limit be set as low as possible.]

[OSHA proposed a "permanent" standard of 1 ppm. It] did not ask for comments as to whether or not benzene presented a significant health risk at exposures of 10 ppm or less. Rather, it asked for comments as to whether 1 ppm was the minimum feasible exposure limit. As OSHA's Deputy Director of Health Standards, Grover Wrenn, testified at the hearing, this formulation of the issue to be considered by the Agency was consistent with OSHA's general policy with respect to carcinogens. Whenever a carcinogen is involved, OSHA will presume that no safe level of exposure exists in the absence of clear proof establishing such a level and will accordingly set the exposure limit at the lowest level feasible. . . .

The permanent standard is expressly inapplicable to the storage, transportation, distribution, sale, or use of gasoline or other fuels subsequent to discharge from bulk terminals. This exception is particularly significant in light of the fact that over 795,000 gas station employees, who are exposed to an average of 102,700 gallons of gasoline (containing up to 2% benzene) annually, are thus excluded from the protection of the standard.

As presently formulated, the benzene standard is an expensive way of providing some additional protection for a relatively small number of employees. According to OSHA's figures, the standard will require capital investments in engineering controls of approximately $266 million, first-year operating costs (for monitoring, medical testing, employee training, and respirators) of $187 million to $205 million and recurring annual costs of approximately $34 million. 43 Fed. Reg. 5934 (1978). The figures outlined in OSHA's explanation of the costs of compliance to various industries indicate that only 35,000 employees would gain any benefit from the regulation in terms of a reduction in their exposure to benzene. Over two-thirds of these workers (24,450) are employed in the rubber-manufacturing industry. Compliance costs in that industry are estimated to be rather low with no capital costs and initial operating expenses estimated at only $34 million ($1,390 per employee); recurring annual costs would also be rather low, totaling less than $1 million. By contrast, the segment of the petroleum refining industry that produces benzene would be required to incur $24 million in capital costs and $600,000 in first-year operating expenses to provide additional protection for 300 workers ($82,000 per employee), while the petrochemical industry would be required to incur $20.9 million in capital costs and $1 million in initial operating expenses for the benefit of 552 employees ($39,675 per employee).

Although OSHA did not quantify the benefits to each category of worker in terms of decreased exposure to benzene, it appears from the economic impact study done at OSHA's direction that those benefits may be relatively small. Thus, although the current exposure limit is 10 ppm, the actual exposures outlined in that study are often considerably lower. For example, for the period 1970-1975 the petrochemical industry reported that, out of a total of 496 employees exposed to benzene, only 53 were exposed to levels between 1 and 5 ppm and only 7 (all at the same plant) were exposed to between 5 and 10 ppm. . . .

II

Any discussion of the 1 ppm exposure limit must, of course, begin with the Agency's rationale for imposing that limit. The written explanation of the standard fills 184 pages of the printed appendix. Much of it is devoted to a discussion of the voluminous evidence of the adverse effects of exposure to benzene at levels of concentration well above 10 ppm. This discussion demonstrates that there is ample justification for regulating occupational exposure to benzene and that the prior limit of 10 ppm, with a ceiling of 25 ppm (or a peak of 50 ppm) was reasonable. It does not, however, provide direct support for the Agency's conclusion that the limit should be reduced from 10 ppm to 1 ppm.

The evidence in the administrative record of adverse effects of benzene exposure at 10 ppm is sketchy at best. OSHA noted that there was "no dispute" that certain nonmalignant blood disorders, evidenced by a reduction in the level of red or white cells or platelets in the blood, could result from exposures of 25-40 ppm. It then stated that several studies had indicated that relatively slight changes in normal blood values could result from exposures below 25 ppm and perhaps below 10 ppm. OSHA did not attempt to make any estimate based on these studies of how significant the risk of nonmalignant disease would be at exposures of 10 ppm or less. Rather, it stated that because of the lack of data concerning the linkage between low-level exposures and blood abnormalities, it was impossible to construct a dose-response curve at this time. . . .

With respect to leukemia, evidence of an increased risk (i.e., a risk greater than that borne by the general population) due to benzene exposures at or below 10 ppm was even sketchier. . . . [T]here was only one study that provided any evidence of such an increased risk. That study, conducted by the Dow Chemical Co., uncovered three leukemia deaths, versus 0.2 expected deaths, out of a population of 594 workers; it appeared that the three workers had never been exposed to more than 2 to 9 ppm of benzene. The authors of the study, however, concluded that it could not be viewed as proof of a relationship between low-level benzene exposure and leukemia because all three workers had probably been occupationally exposed to a number of other potentially carcinogenic chemicals at other points in their careers and because no leukemia deaths had been uncovered among workers who had been exposed to much higher levels of benzene. . . .

[OSHA concluded] that some benefits were likely to result from reducing the exposure limit from 10 ppm to 1 ppm. This conclusion was based, again, not on evidence, but rather on the assumption that the risk of leukemia will decrease as exposure levels decrease. Although the Agency had found it impossible to construct a dose-response curve that would predict with any accuracy the number of leukemias that could be expected to result from exposures at 10 ppm, at 1 ppm, or at any intermediate level, it nevertheless "determined that the benefits of the proposed standard are likely to be appreciable."

It is noteworthy that at no point in its lengthy explanation did the Agency quote or even cite §3(8) of the Act. It made no finding that any of the provisions of the new standard were "reasonably necessary or appropriate to provide safe or healthful employment and *places* of employment."

III

. . . In the Government's view, §3(8)'s definition of the term "standard" has no legal significance or at best merely requires that a standard not be totally irrational. It takes the position that §6(b)(5) is controlling and that it requires OSHA to promulgate a standard that either gives an absolute assurance of safety for each and every worker or reduces exposures to the lowest level feasible. The Government interprets "feasible" as meaning technologically achievable at a cost that would not impair the viability of the industries subject to the regulation.

The respondent industry representatives, on the other hand, argue that the Court of Appeals was correct in holding that the "reasonably necessary and appropriate" language of §3(8), along with the feasibility requirement of §6(b)(5), requires the Agency to quantify both the costs and the benefits of a proposed rule and to conclude that they are roughly commensurate.

In our view, it is not necessary to decide whether either the Government or industry is entirely correct. For we think it is clear that §3(8) does apply to all permanent standards promulgated under the Act and that it requires the Secretary, before issuing any standard, to determine that it is reasonably necessary and appropriate to remedy a significant risk of material health impairment. . . .

Because the Secretary did not make the required threshold finding in these cases, we have no occasion to determine whether costs must be weighed against benefits in an appropriate case.

A

. . . [W]e think it is clear that the statute was not designed to require employers to provide absolutely risk-free workplaces whenever it is technologically feasible to do so, so long as the cost is not great enough to destroy an entire industry. Rather, both the language and structure of the Act, as well as its legislative history, indicate that it was intended to require the elimination, as far as feasible, of significant risks of harm.

B

Therefore, before he can promulgate *any* permanent health or safety standard, the Secretary is required to make a threshold finding that a place of employment is unsafe—in the sense that significant risks are present and can be eliminated or lessened by a change in practices. . . .

In the absence of a clear mandate in the Act, it is unreasonable to assume that Congress intended to give the Secretary the unprecedented power over American industry that would result from the Government's view of §§3(8) and 6(b)(5), coupled with OSHA's cancer policy. Expert testimony that a substance is probably a human carcinogen—either because it has caused cancer in animals or because individuals have contracted cancer following extremely high exposures—would justify the conclusion that the substance poses some risk of serious harm no matter how minute the exposure and no matter how many experts testified that they regarded the risk as insignificant. That conclusion would in turn justify pervasive regulation limited only by the constraint of feasibility. In light of the fact that there are literally thousands of substances used in the workplace that have been identified as carcinogens or suspect carcinogens, the Government's theory would give OSHA power to impose enormous costs that might produce little, if any, discernible benefit.[85a]

If the Government were correct in arguing that neither §3(8) nor §6(b)(5) requires that the risk from a toxic substance be quantified sufficiently to enable the Secretary to characterize it as significant in an understandable way, the statute would make such a "sweeping delegation of legislative power" that it might be unconstitutional under the Court's reasoning in A. L. A. Schechter Poultry Corp. v. United States, 295 U.S. 495, 539 and Panama Refining Co. v. Ryan, 293 U.S. 388. A construction of the statute that avoids this kind of open-ended grant should certainly be favored.

C

The legislative history also supports the conclusion that Congress was concerned, not with absolute safety, but with the elimination of significant harm. . . .

D

. . . As we read the statute, the burden was on the Agency to show, on the basis of substantial evidence, that it is at least more likely than not that long-term exposure to 10 ppm of benzene presents a significant risk of material health impairment. Ordinarily, it is the proponent of a rule or order who has the burden of proof in administrative proceedings. . . .

In this case OSHA did not even attempt to carry its burden of proof. The closest it came to making a finding that benzene presented a significant risk of harm in the workplace was its statement that the benefits to be derived from lowering the permissible exposure level from 10 to 1 ppm were "likely" to be "appreciable." The Court of Appeals held that this finding was not supported by substantial evidence. Of greater importance, even if it were supported by substantial evidence, such a finding

85a. OSHA's proposed generic cancer policy, 42 Fed. Reg. 54149 (1977), indicates that this possibility is not merely hypothetical. Under its proposal, whenever there is a certain quantum of proof—either from animal experiments, or, less frequently, from epidemiological studies—that a substance causes cancer at any exposure level, an emergency temporary standard would be promulgated immediately, requiring employers to provide monitoring and medical examinations and to reduce exposures to the lowest feasible level. A proposed rule would then be issued along the same lines, with objecting employers effectively foreclosed from presenting evidence that there is little or no risk associated with current exposure levels. . . .

The scope of the proposed regulation is indicated by the fact that NIOSH has published a list of 2,415 potential occupational carcinogens. . . . OSHA has tentatively concluded that 269 of these substances have been proved to be carcinogens and therefore should be subject to full regulation. . . .

would not be sufficient to satisfy the Agency's obligations under the Act. . . .

Contrary to the Government's contentions, imposing a burden on the Agency of demonstrating a significant risk of harm will not strip it of its ability to regulate carcinogens, nor will it require the Agency to wait for deaths to occur before taking any action. First, the requirement that a "significant" risk be identified is not a mathematical straitjacket. It is the Agency's responsibility to determine, in the first instance, what it considers to be a "significant" risk. Some risks are plainly acceptable and others are plainly unacceptable. If, for example, the odds are one in a billion that a person will die from cancer by taking a drink of chlorinated water, the risk clearly could not be considered significant. On the other hand, if the odds are one in a thousand that regular inhalation of gasoline vapors that are 2% benzene will be fatal, a reasonable person might well consider the risk significant and take appropriate steps to decrease or eliminate it. Although the Agency has no duty to calculate the exact probability of harm, it does have an obligation to find that a significant risk is present before it can characterize a place of employment as "unsafe."

Second, OSHA is not required to support its finding that a significant risk exists with anything approaching scientific certainty. Although the Agency's findings must be supported by substantial evidence, 29 U.S.C. §655(f), §6(b)(5) specifically allows the Secretary to regulate on the basis of the "best available evidence." As several Courts of Appeals have held, this provision requires a reviewing court to give OSHA some leeway where its findings must be made on the frontiers of scientific knowledge. . . .

It should also be noted that, in setting a permissible exposure level in reliance on less-than-perfect methods, OSHA would have the benefit of a backstop in the form of monitoring and medical testing. Thus, if OSHA determined that the permissible exposure limit should be set at 5 ppm, it could still require monitoring and medical testing for employees exposed to lower levels. By doing so, it could keep a constant check on the validity of the assumptions made in developing the permissible exposure limit, giving it a sound evidentiary basis for decreasing the limit if it was initially set too high. · .

E

Because our review of these cases has involved a more detailed examination of the record than is customary, it must be emphasized that we have neither made any factual determinations of our own, nor have we rejected any factual findings made by the Secretary. . . .

In this case the record makes it perfectly clear that the Secretary relied squarely on a special policy for carcinogens that imposed the burden on industry of proving the existence of a safe level of exposure, thereby avoiding the Secretary's threshold responsibility of establishing the need for more stringent standards. In so interpreting his statutory authority, the Secretary exceeded his power.

[Part IV, dealing with OSHA's regulation of dermal contact, is omitted.]

The judgment of the Court of Appeals remanding the petition for review to the Secretary for further proceedings is affirmed.

It is so ordered.

MR. CHIEF JUSTICE BURGER, concurring.

. . . The judicial function does not extend to substantive revision of regulatory policy. That function lies elsewhere—in Congressional and Executive oversight or amendatory legislation—although to be sure the boundaries are often ill-defined and indistinct.

Nevertheless, when discharging his duties under the statute, the Secretary is well admonished to remember that a heavy responsibility burdens his authority. Inherent in this statutory scheme is authority to refrain from regulation of insignificant or de minimis risks. . . .

MR. JUSTICE POWELL, concurring in part and in the judgment. . . .

[Justice Powell found that OSHA had not relied solely on its assumption that no safe threshold exposure for a carcinogen exists, but had also claimed that the specific facts of record, including evidence of adverse health effects of levels of benzene exposure substantially higher than 10 ppm, established that the 1 ppm standard adopted was reasonably necessary to deal with a significant health risk. The Justice concluded that the record failed to establish "substantial evidence" for such a finding.]

. . . But even if one assumes that OSHA properly met this burden, see . . . (Marshall, J., dissenting), I conclude that the statute also requires the agency to determine that the economic effects of its standard bear a reasonable relationship to the expected benefits. An occupational health standard is neither "reasonably necessary" nor "feasible," as required by statute, if it calls for expenditures wholly disproportionate to the expected health and safety benefits. . . . It is simply unreasonable to believe that Congress intended OSHA to pursue the desirable goal of risk-free workplaces to the extent that the economic viability of particular industries—or significant segments thereof—is threatened. . . .

. . . [Such a policy] would impair the ability of American industries to compete effectively with foreign businesses and to provide employment for American workers.[85b]

85b. Congress has assigned OSHA an extremely difficult and complex task, and the guidance afforded OSHA is considerably less than clear. The agency's primary responsibility, reflected in its title, is to minimize health and safety risks in the workplace. Yet the economic health of our highly industrialized society requires a high rate of employment and an adequate response to increasingly vigorous foreign competition. There can be little doubt that Congress intended OSHA to balance reasonably the societal interest in health and safety with the often conflicting goal of maintaining a strong national economy.

. . . Perhaps more significantly, however, OSHA's interpretation of §6(b)(5) would force it to regulate in a manner inconsistent with the important health and safety purposes of the legislation we construe today. Thousands of toxic substances present risks that fairly could be characterized as "significant." . . . Even if OSHA succeeded in selecting the gravest risks for earliest regulation, a standard-setting process that ignored economic considerations would result in a serious misallocation of resources and a lower effective level of safety than could be achieved under standards set with reference to the comparative benefits available at a lower cost. I would not attribute such an irrational intention to Congress.

In this case, OSHA did find that the "substantial costs" of the benzene regulations are justified. See supra, at 665-666. But the record before us contains neither adequate documentation of this conclusion, nor any evidence that OSHA weighed the relevant considerations. . . .

MR. JUSTICE REHNQUIST, concurring in the judgment.

In considering the alternative interpretations . . . [of the statute] my colleagues manifest a good deal of uncertainty, and ultimately divide over whether the Secretary produced sufficient evidence that the proposed standard for benzene will result in any appreciable benefits at all. This uncertainty, I would suggest, is eminently justified, since I believe that this litigation presents the Court with what has to be one of the most difficult issues that could confront a decisionmaker: whether the statistical possibility of future deaths should ever be disregarded in light of the economic costs of preventing those deaths. I would also suggest that the widely varying positions advanced in the briefs of the parties and in the opinions of Mr. Justice Stevens, the Chief Justice, Mr. Justice Powell, and Mr. Justice Marshall demonstrate, perhaps better than any other fact, that Congress, the governmental body best suited and most obligated to make the choice confronting us in this litigation, has improperly delegated that choice to the Secretary of Labor and, derivatively, to this Court.

I

In his Second Treatise of Civil Government, published in 1690, John Locke wrote that "[t]he power of the legislative, being derived from the people by a positive voluntary grant and institution, can be no other than what that positive grant conveyed, which being only to make laws, and not to make legislators, the legislative can have no power to transfer their authority of making laws and place it in other hands." Two hundred years later, this Court expressly recognized the existence of and the necessity for limits on Congress' ability to delegate its authority to representatives of the Executive Branch: "That Congress cannot delegate legislative power to the President is a principle universally recognized as vital to the integrity and maintenance of the system of government ordained by the Constitution." Field v. Clark, 143 U.S. 649, 692 (1892).

The rule against delegation of legislative power is not, however, so cardinal a principle as to allow for no exception. The Framers of the Constitution were practical statesmen. . . .

[The Justice discussed the history of the doctrine that Congress may not delegate "legislative" powers to administrative agencies without adequate standards to guide its exercise.] . . .

Viewing the legislation at issue here in light of these principles, I believe that it fails to pass muster. Read literally, the relevant portion of §6(b)(5) is completely precatory, admonishing the Secretary to adopt the most protective standard if he can, but excusing him from that duty if he cannot. In the case of a hazardous substance for which a "safe" level is either unknown or impractical, the language of §6(b)(5) gives the Secretary absolutely no indication where on the continuum of relative safety he should draw his line. Especially in light of the importance of the interests at stake, I have no doubt that the provision at issue, standing alone, would violate the doctrine against uncanalized delegations of legislative power. For me the remaining question, then, is whether additional standards are ascertainable from the legislative history or statutory context of §6(b)(5) or, if not, whether such a standardless delegation was justifiable in light of the "inherent necessities" of the situation.

II

One of the primary sources looked to by this Court in adding gloss to an otherwise broad grant of legislative authority is the legislative history of the statute in question.

[The Justice reviewed the legislative history of §6(b)(5), which originally required OSHA to prevent injury to workers' health, without regard to feasibility. The words "to the extent feasible" were added during the Senate floor debates.]

. . . I believe that the legislative history demonstrates that the feasibility requirement, as employed in §6(b)(5), is a legislative mirage, appearing to some Members but not to others, and assuming any form desired by the beholder. . . .

In sum, the legislative history contains nothing to indicate that the language "to the extent feasible" does anything other than render what had been a clear, if somewhat unrealistic, standard largely, if not entirely, precatory. There is certainly nothing to indicate that these words, as used in §6(b)(5), are limited to technological and economic feasibility. . . .

III

. . . [I]n some cases this Court has abided by a rule of necessity, upholding broad delegations of authority where it would be "unreasonable and impracticable to compel Congress to prescribe detailed rules" regarding a particular policy or situation. . . .

. . . But no need for such an evasive standard as "feasibility" is apparent in the present cases. In drafting §6(b)(5), Congress was faced with a clear, if difficult, choice between balancing statistical lives and industrial resources or authorizing the Secretary to elevate human life above all concerns save massive dislocation in an affected industry. That Congress recognized the difficulty of this choice is clear from the [floor debate] remark of Senator Saxbe, who stated that "[w]hen we come to saying that an employer must guarantee that such an employee is protected from any possible harm, I think it will be one of the most difficult areas we are going to have to ascertain." . . .

. . . That Congress chose, intentionally or unintentionally, to pass this difficult choice on to the Secretary is evident from the spectral quality of the standard it selected and is capsulized in Senator Saxbe's unfulfilled promise that "the terms that we are passing back and forth are going to have to be identified."

IV

As formulated and enforced by this Court, the nondelegation doctrine serves three important functions. First, and most abstractly, it ensures to the extent consistent with orderly governmental administration that important choices of social policy are made by Congress, the branch of our Government most responsive to the popular will. . . . Second, the doctrine guarantees that, to the extent Congress finds it necessary to delegate authority, it provides the recipient of that authority with an "intelligible principle" to guide the exercise of the delegated discretion. . . . Third, and derivative of the second, the doctrine ensures that courts charged with reviewing the exercise of delegated legislative discretion will be able to test that exercise against ascertainable standards.

I believe the legislation at issue here fails on all three counts. . . . I would suggest that the standard of "feasibility" renders meaningful judicial review impossible.

We ought not to shy away from our judicial duty to invalidate unconstitutional delegations of legislative authority solely out of concern that we should thereby reinvigorate discredited constitutional doctrines of the pre-New Deal era. If the nondelegation doctrine has fallen into the same desuetude as have substantive due process and restrictive interpretations of the Commerce Clause, it is, as one writer has phrased it, "a case of death by association." J. Ely, Democracy and Distrust, A Theory of Judicial Review 133 (1980). Indeed, a number of observers have suggested that this Court should once more take up its burden of ensuring that Congress does not unnecessarily delegate important choices of social policy to politically unresponsive administrators.[85c] Other observers, as might be imagined, have disagreed.[85d]

If we are ever to reshoulder the burden of ensuring that Congress itself make the critical policy decisions, these are surely the cases in which to do it. It is difficult to imagine a more obvious example of Congress simply avoiding a choice which was both fundamental for purposes of the statute and yet politically so divisive that the necessary decision or compromise was difficult, if not impossible, to hammer out in the legislative forge. . . . When fundamental policy decisions underlying important legislation about to be enacted are to be made, the buck stops with Congress and the President insofar as he exercises his constitutional role in the legislative process. . . . Accordingly, for the reasons stated above, I concur in the judgment of the Court affirming the judgment of the Court of Appeals.

MR. JUSTICE MARSHALL, with whom MR. JUSTICE BRENNAN, MR. JUSTICE WHITE, and MR. JUSTICE BLACKMUN join, dissenting.

In cases of statutory construction, this Court's authority is limited. If the statutory language and legislative intent are plain, the judicial inquiry is at an end. Under our jurisprudence, it is presumed that ill-considered or unwise legislation will be corrected through the democratic process; a court is not permitted to distort a statute's meaning in order to make it conform with the Justices' own views of sound social policy. See TVA v. Hill, 437 U.S. 153 (1978).

Today's decision flagrantly disregards these restrictions on judicial authority. The plurality ignores the plain meaning of the Occupational Safety and Health Act of 1970 in order to bring the authority of the Secretary of Labor in line with the plurality's own views of proper regulatory policy. The unfortunate consequence is that the Federal Government's efforts to protect American workers from cancer and other crippling diseases may be substantially impaired. . . .

The plurality's conclusion . . . is based on its interpretation of 29 U.S.C. §652(8), which defines an occupational safety and health standard as one "which requires conditions . . . reasonably necessary or appropriate to provide safe or healthful employment. . . ." According to the plurality, a standard is not "reasonably necessary or appropriate" unless the Secre-

85c. See J. Ely, Democracy and Distrust, A Theory of Judicial Review 131-134 (1980); J. Freedman, Crisis and Legitimacy, The Administrative Process and American Government 78-94 (1978); T. Lowi, The End of Liberalism: Ideology, Policy, and the Crisis of Public Authority 129-146, 297-299 (1969); Wright, Beyond Discretionary Justice, 81 Yale L.J. 575, 582-587 (1972); Waist-Deep in Regulation, Washington Post, Nov. 3, 1979, p. A10, col. 1. Cf. W. Douglas, Go East, Young Man 217 (1974).

85d. See K. Davis, Discretionary Justice: A Preliminary Inquiry 49-51 (1969); Stewart, The Reformation of American Administrative Law, 88 Harv. L. Rev. 1669, 1693-1697 (1975). Cf. Jaffe, The Illusion of the Ideal Administration, 86 Harv. L. Rev. 1183, 1190, n.37 (1973).

tary is able to show that it is "at least more likely than not," ante, at 653, that the risk he seeks to regulate is a "significant" one. Ibid. Nothing in the statute's language or legislative history, however, indicates that the "reasonably necessary or appropriate" language should be given this meaning. . . .

. . . Contrary to the plurality's suggestion, the Secretary did not rely blindly on some Draconian carcinogen "policy." . . . If he had, it would have been sufficient for him to have observed that benzene is a carcinogen, a proposition that respondents do not dispute. Instead, the Secretary gathered over 50 volumes of exhibits and testimony and offered a detailed and evenhanded discussion of the relationship between exposure to benzene at all recorded exposure levels and chromosomal damage, aplastic anemia, and leukemia. In that discussion he evaluated, and took seriously, respondents' evidence of a safe exposure level. . . .

[The Justice reviewed the record in detail.]

In this case the Secretary found that exposure to benzene at levels above 1 ppm posed a definite albeit unquantifiable risk of chromosomal damage, nonmalignant blood disorders, and leukemia. The existing evidence was sufficient to justify the conclusion that such a risk was presented, but it did not permit even rough quantification of that risk. Discounting for the various scientific uncertainties, the Secretary gave "careful consideration to the question of whether th[e] substantial costs" of the standard "are justified in light of the hazards of exposure to benzene," and concluded that "these costs are necessary in order to effectuate the statutory purpose . . . and to adequately protect employees from the hazards of exposure to benzene." 43 Fed. Reg. 5941 (1978).

In these circumstances it seems clear that the Secretary found a risk that is "significant" in the sense that the word is normally used. . . .

The Court might . . . allow the Secretary to attempt to make a very rough quantification of the risk imposed by a carcinogenic substance, and give considerable deference to his finding that the risk was significant. If so, the Court would permit the Secretary to promulgate precisely the same regulation involved in this case if he had not relied on a carcinogen "policy," but undertaken a review of the evidence and the expert testimony and concluded, on the basis of conservative assumptions, that the risk addressed is a significant one. Any other interpretation of the plurality's approach would allow a court to displace the agency's judgment with its own subjective conception of "significance," a duty to be performed without statutory guidance. . . .

Because the approach taken by the plurality is so plainly irreconcilable with the Court's proper institutional role, I am certain that it will not stand the test of time. In all likelihood, today's decision will come to be regarded as an extreme reaction to a regulatory scheme that, as the Members of the plurality perceived it, imposed an unduly harsh burden on regulated industries. But as the Constitution "does not enact Mr.

Herbert Spencer's Social Statics," Lochner v. New York, 198 U.S. 45, 75 (1905) (Holmes, J., dissenting), so the responsibility to scrutinize federal administrative action does not authorize this Court to strike its own balance between the costs and benefits of occupational safety standards. I am confident that the approach taken by the plurality today, like that in *Lochner* itself, will eventually be abandoned, and that the representative branches of government will once again be allowed to determine the level of safety and health protection to be accorded to the American worker.

AMERICAN TEXTILE MANUFACTURERS' INSTITUTE v. DONOVAN

101 S. Ct. 2478 (1981)

MR. JUSTICE BRENNAN delivered the opinion of the Court.
[Textile manufacturers sought judicial review of an OSHA regulation limiting occupational exposure to cotton dust, contending that the OSH Act requires OSHA to weigh costs and benefits in framing standards. The court of appeals upheld the regulation, agreeing with OSHA's contention that the act requires it to mandate the use of all economic and technologically feasible means to eliminate or reduce significant risks of material health impairment.]

I

Byssinosis, known in its more severe manifestations as "brown lung" disease, is a serious and potentially disabling respiratory disease primarily caused by the inhalation of cotton dust.

. . In its most serious form, byssinosis is a chronic and irreversible obstructive pulmonary disease, clinically similar to chronic bronchitis or emphysema, and can be severely disabling. At worst, as is true of other respiratory diseases including bronchitis, emphysema, and asthma, byssinosis can create an additional strain on cardiovascular functions and can contribute to death from heart failure.[85e]

85e. Descriptions of the disease by individual mill workers, presented in hearings on the Cotton Dust Standard before an administrative law judge, are more vivid: "When they started speeding the looms up the dust got finer and more and more people started leaving the mill with breathing problems. My mother had to leave the mill in the early fifties. Before she left, her breathing got so short she just couldn't hold out to work. My stepfather left the mill on account of breaching [sic] problems. He had coughing spells til he couldn't breath, like a child's whooping cough. Both my sisters who work in the mill have breathing problems. My husband had to give up his job when he was only fifty-four years old because of the breathing problems." Ct. of App. J.A. 3791. "I am only fifty-seven years old and I am retired and I can't even get to go to church because of my breathing. I get short of breath just walking around the house or dressing [or] sometimes just watching T.V. I cough all the time." Id., at 3793.

. . . Estimates indicate that at least 35,000 employed and retired cotton mill workers, or 1 in 12 such workers, suffers from the most disabling form of byssinosis.

[In 1970, OSHA adopted a standard setting a permissible exposure limit (PEL) of 1000 micrograms per cubic meter (1000 $\mu g/m^3$) averaged over an eight-hour workday. In 1976 it proposed to lower the standard to 200 $\mu g/m^3$. In 1978 it adopted new standards.]

The Cotton Dust Standard promulgated by OSHA establishes mandatory PELs over an 8-hour period of 200 $\mu g/m^3$ for yarn manufacturing, 750 $\mu g/m^3$ for slashing and weaving operations, and 500 $\mu g/m^3$ for all other processes in the cotton industry. . . . These levels represent a relaxation of the proposed PEL of 200 $\mu g/m^3$ for all segments of the cotton industry.

[OSHA estimated costs of complying with the standard at $543 million.] . . .

In enacting the Cotton Dust Standard, OSHA interpreted the Act to require adoption of the most stringent standard to protect against material health impairment, bounded only by technological and economic feasibility. . . . OSHA therefore rejected the industry's alternative proposal for a PEL of 500 $\mu g/m^3$ in yarn manufacturing, a proposal which would produce a 25% prevalence of at least Grade ½ byssinosis. The agency expressly found the Standard to be both technologically and economically feasible based on the evidence in the record as a whole. Although recognizing that permitted levels of exposure to cotton dust would still cause some byssinosis, OSHA nevertheless rejected the union proposal for a 100 $\mu g/m^3$ PEL because it was not within the "technological capabilities of the industry."

II

The principal question presented in this case is whether the Occupational Safety and Health Act requires the Secretary, in promulgating a standard pursuant to §6(b)(5) of the Act, 29 U.S.C. §655(b)(5), to determine that the costs of the standard bear a reasonable relationship to its benefits. Relying on §§6(b)(5) and 3(8) of the Act, . . . petitioners urge not only that OSHA must show that a standard addresses a significant risk of material health impairment, see Industrial Union Department v. American Petroleum Institute, . . . 448 U.S., at 639 . . . (plurality opinion), but also that OSHA must demonstrate that the reduction in risk of material health impairment is significant in light of the costs of attaining that reduction. . . . Respondents on the other hand contend that the Act requires OSHA to promulgate standards that eliminate or reduce such risks "to the extent such protection is technologically and economically feasible." . . . To resolve this debate, we must turn to the language, structure, and legislative history of the Occupational Safety and Health Act.

A

. . . Section 6(b)(5) of the Act, 29 U.S.C. §655(b)(5) (emphasis added), provides:

> The Secretary, in promulgating standards dealing with toxic materials or harmful physical agents under this subsection, shall set the standard which most adequately assures, *to the extent feasible*, on the basis of the best available evidence, that no employee will suffer material impairment of health or functional capacity even if such employee has regular exposure to the hazard dealt with by such standard for the period of his working life.

. . . The plain meaning of the word "feasible" supports respondents' interpretation of the statute. According to Webster's Third New International Dictionary of the English Language, "feasible" means "capable of being done, executed, or effected." Id., at 831 (1976). . . . Congress itself defined the basic relationship between costs and benefits, by placing the "benefit" of worker health above all other considerations save those making attainment of this "benefit" unachievable. Any standard based on a balancing of costs and benefits by the Secretary that strikes a different balance than that struck by Congress would be inconsistent with the command set forth in §6(b)(5). Thus, cost-benefit analysis by OSHA is not required by the statute because feasibility analysis is. . . .

B

. . . Section 3(8) of the Act, 29 U.S.C. §652(8) (emphasis added), provides:

> The term "occupational safety and health standard" means a standard which requires conditions, or the adoption or use of one or more practices, means, methods, operations, or processes, *reasonably necessary or appropriate* to provide safe or healthful employment and places of employment.

Taken alone, the phrase "reasonably necessary or appropriate" might be construed to contemplate some balancing of the costs and benefits of a standard. Petitioners urge that, so construed, §3(8) engrafts a cost-benefit analysis requirement on the issuance of §6(b)(5) standards, even if §6(b)(5) itself does not authorize such analysis.

. . . Agreement with petitioners' argument that §3(8) imposes an additional and overriding requirement of cost-benefit analysis on the issuance of §6(b)(5) standards would eviscerate the "to the extent feasible" requirement. Standards would inevitably be set at the level indicated by cost-benefit analysis, and not at the level specified by §6(b)(5). . . . We cannot believe that Congress intended the general terms of §3(8) to countermand the specific feasibility requirement of §6(b)(5). Adoption of petitioners' interpretation would effectively write §6(b)(5) out of the Act. . . .

C

The legislative history of the Act, while concededly not crystal clear, provides general support for respondents' interpretation of the Act. . . .

[The Court then considered the technological and economic feasibility of the control requirements imposed by the OSHA regulation. Section 6(f) requires that OSHA determinations in promulgating occupational health and safety regulations be supported by "substantial evidence." The Court found "substantial evidence" for OSHA's determination that controls would cost the textile industry $543 million, and that the industry could absorb this cost without significant loss of sales or shut-down of capacity. Justice Stewart dissented on the ground that the study relied upon by OSHA for its cost estimates had assumed a less stringent level of controls than that eventually adopted by OSHA, and therefore couldn't represent "substantial evidence." OSHA claimed that this discrepancy, which would produce an underestimation of actual control costs, was offset by other erroneous assumptions in the study that produced an overestimate. Justice Stewart found no evidence for OSHA's conclusion that these errors would cancel out. The Court found that the study represented the best cost evidence available, and that OSHA had acted reasonably in acting on the basis of the study.

Justice Rehnquist, joined by Chief Justice Berger dissented on the ground that the OSHA provisions in question are an unconstitutional delegation of legislative power. This opinion repeats, in summary form, the basic points made in Justice Rehnquist's *Benzene* (Industrial Union Department, AFL-CIO v. American Petroleum Institute) dissent. Justice Powell did not participate in the decision.]

NOTES AND QUESTIONS

1. The *Benzene* plurality opinion appears to rest ultimately on use of a clear statement technique similar to that employed in *Overton Park* and *Mow Sun Wang*. The opinion asserts: "In the absence of a clear mandate in the Act, it is unreasonable to assume that Congress [gave OSHA the] unprecedented power over American industry" that OSHA's view of its statutory authority and responsibility would entail. Is this an appropriate use of the clear statement technique? Why didn't the Court employ the same technique in *Cotton Dust* to require cost-benefit analysis?

2. Are *Cotton Dust* (American Textile Mfrs. Inst. v. Donovan) and the *Benzene* plurality consistent? The *Benzene* plurality limits OSHA to the regulation of "significant" risks. But how can the significance of a risk be determined in isolation from the cost of eliminating that risk? Wouldn't we judge a quite minor risk "significant" for regulatory purposes if it would be very cheaply and easily eliminated? If so, shouldn't the *extent* to which we seek to control a major risk also reflect a consideration of costs?

3. Are you persuaded, as *Cotton Dust* appears to hold, that Congress required OSHA to mandate industry use of all technologically and economically feasible controls whenever it finds a "significant" occupational health risk? Shouldn't OSHA have discretion to set priorities and to require less than all feasible controls in particular circumstances? See Note, The Supreme Court, 1980 Term, 95 Harv. L. Rev. 93, 319-329 (1981).

Why should courts presume or perhaps pretend that Congress has decided issues that it did not squarely address and arguably never considered or anticipated? For discussion, see Note, Intent, Clear Statements, and the Common Law: Statutory Interpretation in the Supreme Court, 95 Harv. L. Rev. 892 (1982). Perhaps courts do so in order to narrow statutory delegation of authority that would otherwise be unconstitutional. The *Benzene* plurality expressed fear that unless OSHA's regulatory authority were narrowly construed, it might represent an unconstitutional delegation of legislative power. *Cotton Dust* may reflect a similar concern.

4. If the OSH Act is an unconstitutional delegation of legislative authority, shouldn't the courts simply invalidate it in order to force Congress to reconsider the matter, rather than rewriting the act in accordance with judicial notions of sound policy?

On the other hand, is it the courts' appropriate role to force Congress explicitly to resolve all significant legal and policy issues in an administrative program? Is this a feasible or wise enterprise? Consider the problems presented in *Benzene* and *Cotton Dust.* Congress, when it created OSHA, presumably had quite fuzzy information about likely risks and compliance costs in various industries, the future state of the economy, the development of risk assessment and cost-benefit methodologies, and other relevant factors. If Justice Rehnquist's approach were followed, what options would be open to Congress if it wished to pass legislation? Assuming that it wanted to avoid widespread plant shutdowns, would it be required either (a) to mandate installations of all technologically and economically feasible controls whenever a nonzero health risk was established, or (b) to require OSHA to impose controls up to the point that a legislatively specified cost-benefit threshold, such as $1,000,000 per life saved, was reached? Consider also that, given the division of views in Congress on controversial regulatory questions, adoption of Justice Rehnquist's approach might disable Congress from passing regulatory legislation at all.[85f]

85f. Moreover, there is developing criticism of excessive specificity in regulatory statutes. See, e.g., B. Ackerman & W. Hassler, Clean Coal/Dirty Air (1981). Ackerman and Hassler argue that Congress's efforts to specify in detail the means of implementing air pollution policies have often been scientifically and technically naive, unduly influenced by parochial or partisan concerns, and have become rapidly obsolescent. They argue that Congress should define the "bottom line" objectives of clean air policy and leave implementation choices to the EPA.

5. Detailed statutes may become rapidly obsolescent in the face of changing technologies and social and economic conditions. See generally G. Calabiesi, A Common Law for the Age of Statutes (1982).

But interpreting statutes to allow agencies substantial discretion to change their policies may not be the answer to the problem of obsolescence. As *Scenic Hudson* indicates, mission-oriented agencies may, if left to their own devices, cling to their established ways, ignoring new societal concerns and priorities. The *Benzene* plurality may be understood as an attempted cure for obsolescent agency policies. The policy of a healthy environment at almost any cost may have been understandable in the early 1970s, when OSHA was established; the economy was booming and environmental concerns were the top priority. That policy may be less appropriate today, when economic concerns are uppermost.

Is the solution to problems of statutory and agency obsolescence a combination of (1) statutes that allow for substantial administrative discretion and (2) a system of presidential control over agency decisions to ensure that they adjust to changing national priorities? Consider in this respect President Reagan's Executive Order 12991, requiring, "to the extent permitted by law," cost-benefit analysis in connection with agency promulgation of "major rules," described at p. 3, supra. Does *Cotton Dust* preclude the application of the cost-benefit requirements of the order to the promulgation of occupational health standards? Should it?

An alternative solution to the obsolescence problem might be a combination of broad delegations and the legislative veto. See p. 6, supra.

6. Now reconsider the role of the courts. Should it be limited to defining the appropriate law-making role of *other institutions*— Congress, the agencies, and the president? Or should the courts have some law-making role as well? Can these two tasks be neatly separated?

In the context of broadcast regulation, the Supreme Court has recently overturned several decisions of the D.C. Circuit that had used clear statement principles to require more stringent regulation by the FCC. See FCC v. WNCN, 101 S. Ct. 1266 (1981), *rev'g* 610 F.2d 838 (D.C. Cir. 1979), which had held that the "public interest" standard of the Communications Act requires the FCC to review past or anticipated changes in a radio station's entertainment programming (e.g., classical to rock) on transfer or renewal of license, rejecting the FCC's reliance on competition to provide program diversity; FCC v. National Citizens Committee for Broadcasting, 436 U.S. 775 (1978), *rev'g in part* 555 F.2d 938 (D.C. Cir. 1977), which had held that a principle of "diversity" implicit in the act obliges the FCC to require divestiture by newspapers of broadcast stations in the same community (the FCC had prohibited such cross-ownership only prospectively).

The Court struck a direct blow for deregulation in FCC v. Midwest Video Corp., 440 U.S. 689 (1979), holding that the Communications Act did not empower the FCC to require that all cable television systems provide a minimum capacity of twenty channels and access to third parties. The Court (6 3) distinguished United States v. Southwestern Cable Co., 392 U.S. 157 (1968), and United States v. Midwest Video Corp, 406 U.S. 649 (1972), which had sustained FCC restrictions on cable television because of its impact on over-the-air broadcasting (which the FCC is charged with regulating). Here the FCC had exceeded its jurisdiction by going further and imposing common-carrier obligations on cable systems.[85g]

See generally Note, Intent, Clear Statements, and the Common Law: Statutory Interpretation in the Supreme Court, 95 Harv. L. Rev. 892 (1982).

Page 289. Add the following after line 15:

There are, however, continuing indications in the cases of a somewhat greater willingness by courts than in the past to set aside agency action as arbitrary and capricious.[87a]

Page 291. Add the following after line 2:

In 1975 Senator Bumpers introduced a bill to amend the Administrative Procedure Act to require specifically that courts review all questions of law "de novo." S. 2408, 94th Cong., 1st Sess. (1975). After debate and criticism the bill was modified and reintroduced in 1979 and 1980. As of March 1982, when S. 1080 passed the Senate, its key provisions would do the following.

(1) They would add the word "independently" to §706(a) of the APA (so that it would read "the reviewing court shall *independently* decide all relevant questions of law").

85g. The Communications Act authorizes the FCC to issue and review broadcast licenses and regulate broadcasters' conduct in "the public interest, convenience and necessity." The legislative history provides no more definite standards for the commission's award of licenses that may be worth hundreds of million of dollars or its regulation of broadcast practices touching sensitive issues of the speech. Justice Rehnquist joined the Court in each of the three FCC cases described above. Is such action consistent with his *Benzene* and *Cotton Dust* dissents?

87a. See Health Systems of Oklahoma, Inc., v. Norman, 589 F.2d 486 (10th Cir. 1978) (agency refusal to accept and consider application filed fifty-five minutes late held arbitrary and capricious); Hurley v. United States, 575 F.2d 792 (10th Cir. 1978) (no rational basis for personnel decision adverse to government employee); Robert E. Derecktor of Rhode Island, Inc. v. Goldschmidt, 506 F. Supp. 1059 (D.R.I. 1980) (disqualification of bids arbitrary and capricious); Community Nutrition Institute v. Berglund, 493 F. Supp. 488 (D.D.C. 1980) (Agriculture Department school lunch program regulations permitting sale of fortified snack foods during lunch irrational and arbitrary).

See also Lockhart, Irrational but Not Arbitrary: Should Reviewing Courts Draw So Fine a Line?, 1979 Utah L. Rev. 649.

(2) They would add a sentence concerning §706(a)(2)(C), which now instructs a court to set aside agency action "in excess of statutory jurisdiction, authority or limitations, or short of statutory right." The new sentence states that "the court shall require that action by the agency is within the scope of the agency jurisdiction or authority on the basis of the language of the statute or, in the event of ambiguity, other evidence of ascertainable legislative intent."

(3) They would add another new sentence stating, "In making determinations on other questions of law, the court shall not accord any presumption in favor of or against agency action, but, in reaching its independent judgment concerning an agency's interpretation of a statutory provision, the court shall give the agency interpretation such weight as it warrants, taking into account the discretionary authority provided to the agency by law." See S. 1080, 128 Cong. Rec. S. 2713 (daily ed. March 24, 1982). The House version of the regulatory reform legislation would not make the third change; it does not contain any "no presumption" language. H.R. 746, 97th Cong., 2d Sess. (as reported Feb. 25, 1982).

The supporters of the Bumpers Amendment want to send the courts a "signal." They know that courts now defer to agencies on many legal matters, the exact degree of deference depending upon a host of factors, including the nature of the legal decisions at issue. The object of Senator Bumpers's proposal is to encourage more active court review and less deference.

The basic aim of the proposal is to assure agency fidelity to congressional statutes. Agency decisions will have to be more carefully supported in the record, and agency employees will have to be more careful. Judges will be encouraged to learn more about the technical bases for agency decisions—to learn statistics, if necessary, and to understand scientific language and reasoning. Fewer irrational agency decisions will take effect. In other words, Bumpers's proposal represents one line of response to the problem of regulation. If that problem is seen to be agencies that are out of control, Bumpers's response is to give the courts more power to hold them in check.

Critics of the proposal argue its drawbacks: if its intent is to signal the courts to defer less to the agencies, how much less deference ought there to be? Are judges to rehear the merits of, say, the "separations manual" for allocating the joint costs of telephone service? Do courts have the time or the resources to examine such decisions de novo? From a political perspective, one cannot be certain which groups will be favored. The business community, for example, might like to see OSHA take greater care, but it may feel that greater scrutiny of the Nuclear Regulatory Commission means only longer delays in issuing licenses. From the perspective of regulatory policy, the effect of the proposal is also indeterminate. As the example of natural gas regulation makes clear, it is sometimes the courts, not the agencies, that seek to expand the scope of regulation. By slowing down agency proceedings and examining more closely the relation of the agency decision to the authorizing statute, will stricter review mean less experimentation? Will it make agencies hesitate to look for new but less restrictive ways to carry out their mandate?

Moreover, to what extent are courts likely to bring about better substantive policies by giving agency decisions a closer look? Appellate judges base their decisions on a record. This record typically reflects a trial, a hearing, or some other procedure under which lawyers present evidence and make arguments. This system is fair (at least if the contesting parties have roughly equivalent resources), for the parties have a roughly equivalent chance to present their own side of the story and to contest that of their opponents. It may be reasonably accurate in cases of typically adjudicative matters, such as who did what to whom when. But are these typical courtroom procedures accurate in hotly contested, uncertain matters of *legislative* policy? Is carnauba wax really dangerous? What about saccharine? A record on these subjects made at length by paid advocates reflects what they choose to put in it. Such a record, once made, is not readily changed; the judge who reviews the record cannot use the telephone to clarify obscurity or to discover, by calling different experts, the present state of scientific knowledge. When, from society's point of view, what really counts is that a matter be decided *fairly*, court-type procedure and judicial review may help. If society, however, is vitally interested in the *accuracy* of the result and if *legislative* facts are at issue, can more extensive court review help?

For a history of the controversy surrounding this amendment and the approach to reform that it embodies see O'Reilly, Deference Makes a Difference: A Study of Impacts of the Bumpers Judicial Review Amendments, 49 U. Cinn. L. Rev. 739 (1980). The Judicial Conference of the United States has taken a position somewhat hostile to the amendment. See 127 Cong. Rec. H. 4824 (daily ed. July 23, 1981) and subsequent testimony before the Administrative Law Subcommittee of the House Committee on the Judiciary, Sept. 10, 1981.

Page 299. Add the following Note after line 8:

Note on Contemporary Hard-Look Review

The "hard look" or "adequate consideration" approach to review is frequently employed in federal court review of federal regulatory and other administration decisions. Most courts of appeals and many district courts have employed the basic technique exemplified in *Scenic Hudson*. They demand that the agency's opinion address all legally relevant considerations, discuss alternatives to the decision and explain the decision made; that the decision meet contrary views, data, and analysis; and that the reasons and analysis in the decision find support in the record.[96a] The ultimate effort is to determine whether the agency has taken a hard look at relevant data, analysis, considerations, and alternatives. One commentator has argued that this approach to review is premised on a decision-making ideal of global rationality rather than incremental muddling-through. See Diver, Policymaking Paradigms in Administrative Law, 95 Harv. L. Rev. 393 (1981).

The courts set aside agency decisions that fail to satisfy these requirements, although the agency is typically left free upon remand to reach the same result if adequately justified on the basis of further proceedings. A large number of these decisions involve agency regulations, reflecting the fact that agencies (for reasons discussed in chapters 5 and 6) have turned increasingly to rule making in order to formulate and implement policy.

Hard-look review has reached its fullest flowering in the decisions of the District of Columbia Circuit Court of Appeals, which has borne the brunt of reviewing responsibility for technically complex regulation, particularly in the environmental field. For example, National Lime Association v. EPA, 627 F.2d 416 (D.C. Cir. 1980), set aside Environmental Protection Agency regulations for control of air pollution from lime plants after an elaborate review of available control techniques, the adequacy and representativeness of the EPA's testing data, and the EPA's failure to deal adequately with industry criticisms of its position. In Sierra Club v. Costle, 657 F.2d 298 (D.C. Cir. 1981), the court ultimately sustained the EPA's regulations for control of emissions from coal-fired power plants after an even more elaborate review of technological and economic issues. The opinion occupies 133 pages in the Federal Reports and includes an appendix containing twenty-four tables and technical charts.

The Supreme Court's decision in Vermont Yankee Nuclear Power Corp. v. Natural Resources Defense Counsel, 435 U.S. 519 (1978), Case-

---

96a. See, e.g., Digital Equip. Corp. v. Diamon, 653 F.2d 701 (1st Cir. 1981) (failure of Patent and Trademark Office to examine relevant factors and adequately justify decision); McCulloch Gas Processing Corp v. Department of Energy, 650 F.2d 1216 (Temp. Emer. Ct. App. 1981) (failure of Department of Energy to consider relevant factors; inadequate explanation; inadequate record); Central Power & Light Co. v. United States, 634 F.2d 137 (5th Cir. 1980), cert. denied, 102 S. Ct. 128 (1981) (failure of the ICC to respond to substantial criticisms from regulated firms; inadequate explanation of decision; failure to deal with obvious problems in agency position); Argo-Collier Truck Lines v. United States, 611 F.2d 149 (6th Cir. 1979) (ICC failure to articulate basis for findings or address objections); City Federal Savings and Loan Ass'n v. Federal Home Loan Bank Board, 600 F.2d 681 (7th Cir. 1979) (failure to address protesting parties' serious objections to board's action); National Treasury Employees' Union v. Campbell, 589 F.2d 669 (D.C. Cir. 1978) (Civil Service Commission must explain grounds for decision and relate it to supporting data); United States v. Nova Scotia Food Prods., 568 F.2d 240 (2d Cir 1977) (FDA failure to disclose supporting data disabled regulated firms from commenting on data, potentially preventing FDA from considering relevant factors: FDA opinion failed to deal with vital questions)

book at p. 516, denied federal courts general law-making powers to impose new procedural requirements on federal agencies. It has been argued that hard-look review is inconsistent with *Vermont Yankee* because, as a practical matter, such review often requires the agency to generate extensive records, write lengthy opinions, respond to outside criticism, or take other essentially procedural steps that are not required by the Administrative Procedure Act of the relevant organic statute. See Public Systems v. Federal Energy Regulatory Commission, 606 F.2d 973, 983, 986 (D.C. Cir. 1979) (Robb, J., dissenting). But the plurality opinion in *Benzene* and, to a lesser extent, the Court's *Cotton Dust* opinion indicate that the Supreme Court continues to engage in a form of hard-look review.

For discussion, see Rodgers, A Hard Look at *Vermont Yankee:* Environmental Law Under Close Scrutiny, 67 Geo. L.J. 699 (1979); Stewart & Sunstein, Public Programs and Private Rights, 95 Harv. L. Rev. 1293 (1982).

Page 306. Add the following after line 24:

The difficulties faced by courts in reviewing engineering and economic issues remain serious. Nonetheless, judges brave voluminous records and dauntingly difficult technical issues in order to enforce hard-look review, relying on the arguments of counsel, their law clerks, and their own study and pluck. Notable examples include National Lime Association v. EPA and Sierra Club v. Costle, discussed supra. In concluding her voluminous opinion in Sierra Club v. Costle, 657 F.2d at 410, Judge Wald summed up the contemporary enterprise of judging in this way: "Since the issues in this proceeding were joined in 1973 . . . we have had several lawsuits, almost four years of substantive and procedural maneuvering before the EPA, and now this extended court challenge. In the interim, Congress has amended the Clean Air Act once and may be ready to do so again. The standard we uphold has already been in effect for almost two years, and could be revised within another two years.

"We reach our decision after interminable record searching (and considerable soul searching). We have read the record with as hard a look as mortal judges can probably give its thousands of pages.[102a] We have adopted a simple and straight-forward standard of review, probed the

102a. "Cf. Rodgers, Judicial Review of Risk Assessments: The Role of Decision Theory in Unscrambling the *Benzene* Decision, 11 Envt'l L. 301, 302, 309 (1981) ('[T]he suspicion has arisen, certainly among practitioners who can say such things, that the grand synthesizing principle that tells us whether the court will dig deeply or bow cursorily depends exclusively on whether the judge agrees with the result of the administrative decision. . . . Few practitioners believe that judges read, much less studiously follow, the monstrous records thrust before them. Nor do these records deserve reading, contrived and formless as they are')."

agency's rationale, studied its references (and those of appellants), endeavored to understand them where they were intelligible (parts were simply impenetrable), and on close questions given the agency the benefit of the doubt out of deference for the terrible complexity of its job. We are not engineers, computer modelers, economists or statisticians, although many of the documents in this record require such expertise—and more.

"Cases like this highlight the critical responsibilities Congress has entrusted to the courts in proceedings of such length, complexity and disorder. Conflicting interests play fiercely for enormous stakes, advocates are prolific and agile, obfuscation runs high, common sense correspondingly low, the public interest is often obscured.

"We cannot redo the agency's job; Congress has told us, at least in proceedings under this Act, that it will not brook reversal for small procedural errors; *Vermont Yankee* reinforces the admonition. So in the end we can only make our best effort to understand, to see if the result makes sense, and to assure that nothing unlawful or irrational has taken place. In this case, we have taken a long while to come to a short conclusion: the rule is reasonable.

"Affirmed."

Chapter Five

Judicial Requirements of Clarity and Consistency

A. REQUIRING AGENCIES TO NARROW THEIR DISCRETION THROUGH ADOPTION OF SPECIFIC RULES

Page 321. Add the following after line 13:

In recent years, the *Holmes* requirement that administrators adopt standards for dispensing scarce welfare benefits has been enforced by the federal courts in a variety of contexts. Carey v. Quern, 588 F.2d 230 (7th Cir. 1978), for example, involved a municipal general relief program under which unemployed relief recipients could receive a clothing allowance "as needed." The court held that due process was violated by the program administrators' failure to adopt guidelines for determining when as-needed allowances should be given. Ressler v. Landrieu, 502 F. Supp. 324 (D. Alaska 1980), required the US Department of Housing and Urban Development to adopt specific standards to limit the discretion of owners of rent-subsidized housing to deny tenancy to otherwise qualified applicants on the ground that they might be abusive or disruptive tenants. HUD was also required to develop hearing procedures to ensure that owners adhered to such standards in making tenancy decisions. See also Holbrook v. Pitt, 643 F.2d 1261 (7th Cir. 1981) (absence of standards for retroactive benefit payments to tenants in federally subsidized housing violates due process).

Historic Green Springs, Inc. v. Bergland, 497 F. Supp. 839 (E.D. Va. 1980), overturned the federal government's designation of 14,000 acres of land as a national historic landmark. The designation, which had the effect of limiting federally assisted commercial development within the area, was held to violate due process because no ascertainable standards for designation had been developed.

Page 332. Add the following to footnote 15:

See Tribe, Perspectives on *Bakke;* Equal Protection, Procedural Fairness, or Structural Justice, 92 Harv. L. Rev. 864 (1978) (discussing "structural" benefits of individualized decisions).

B. REQUIRING AGENCIES TO EXPLAIN THEIR DECISIONS AND THE REQUIREMENT OF CONSISTENCY IN ADJUDICATION

Page 358. Add the following after line 31:

Several recent decisions have invalidated the application of newly adopted general guidelines or regulations to conduct occurring before their adoption, where the application would have serious adverse financial consequences. For example, Daughters of Miriam Center for the Aged v. Mathews, 590 F.2d 1250 (3d Cir. 1978), invalidated an item change in policy regarding use of accelerated depreciation by nursing homes in determining the amount of Medicare reimbursement. In 1967, HEW adopted regulations allowing nursing homes a choice between straight line and accelerated depreciation. HEW belatedly realized that the regulation would create a loophole by allowing homes to recoup the bulk of their investment from Medicare by using accelerated depreciation in the early years of operation, and then make high profits by leaving the Medicare program and serving commercial patients during later years. In 1970 HEW modified the regulations to eliminate accelerated depreciation for new homes or new assets, and to provide for recapture by HEW of any post-1970 excess of accelerated (over straight-line) depreciation if a home left the Medicare program, or if its percentage of Medicare patients dropped by a specified percentage. In 1972, HEW's Provider Reimbursement Manual, which interprets and elaborates upon Medicare regulations, was modified to provide for recapture of excess pre-1970 depreciation enjoyed by homes that leave the program or experience a drop in Medicare patients. HEW applied this new guideline to recapture excess pre-1970 depreciation from the Daughters of Miriam Center, which had experienced a substantial decline in the percentage of its patients on Medicare as a result of new HEW regulations tightening Medicare eligibility requirements. The court set aside HEW's action, sharply distinguishing "retroactive" administrative impositions from those accomplished by statute: " . . . It is now well accepted that 'courts do not substitute their social and economic beliefs for the judgment of legislative bodies, who are elected to pass laws,' and that ' "[f]or protection against abuses by legislatures the people must resort to the polls, not to the courts" ' The constitutional legitimacy that inheres in Congress by virtue of its accountability to the electorate is absent, however, from the administrative process, and consequently, serious questions are continually being raised—and with increased frequency—regarding the legitimacy of the administrative apparatus within the framework of American government. Near the center of the growing concern over legitimacy lies the apprehension that the critical choices of our society will more and more be made by administrative personnel who ofttime are not, as a practical matter, accountable to anyone and whose decisions are immune from challenge. . . ."

The court also emphasized that in modifying the manual in 1972, HEW had dispensed with notice and comment rule making on the ground that the ruling was "interpretive," and that the ruling accordingly could not control the court's interpretation of the applicable statute and regulations.

The court concluded that pre-1970 application of the recapture policy might be justified in the case of a home that voluntarily left the Medicare program, but that it could not be justified in the case of a home, like Miriam Center, that continued in the program and suffered an involuntary drop in its Medicare patient percentage because of changed HEW eligibility regulations. The court also considered that: " . . . In a retroactivity challenge, such as the present one, a critical question is how the challenger's conduct, or the conduct of others in its class, would have differed if the rule in issue had applied from the start. In the Center's case, that question may be answered with a degree of certainty. Had the Center been apprised in 1967, when it first joined the Medicare program, that upon choosing to depreciate its capital assets on an accelerated basis it also assumed the risk that should its utilization by Medicare patients substantially decrease in the future it would be vulnerable to recapture of the excess depreciation already taken, the Center undoubtedly would have opted for the straight-line method. . . .

. . . When the 'rules of the game' were suddenly modified, HEW claimed that the Center owed the Medicare program over $148,000. This severe impact upon the Center's finances, overturning its settled expectations, outweighs the negligible public interest in applying the new provision retroactively to it." See also Natural Gas Pipeline Co. of America v. FERC, 590 F.2d 664 (7th Cir. 1979), and Standard Oil Co. v. Department of Energy, 596 F.2d 1029 (Temp. Emer. Ct. App., 1978), invalidating changes in energy price regulations that were applied to conduct occurring before the changes.

Page 393. Add the following after line 5:

The possibilities of an "auction" system, or even "deregulation of television," have become greater as a result of several developments: (1) There is a growing realization that in many communities there is no "scarcity" of spectrum space. AM, FM, and TV channels are available for the asking. See Brenner, Communications Regulation in the Eighties: The Vanishing Drawbridge, 33 Ad. L. Rev. 255 (1981). (2) There is a growing possibility of competition from many small local low-power TV stations, TV communicated via satellite, and in particular from cable TV, which has recently been deregulated. See Bensen & Crandall, The Deregulation of Cable Television, 44 J.L. & Contemp. Prob. 77 (1981); Symposium, 69 Calif. L. Rev. 442 (1981). (3) The FCC has deregulated much of radio, removing rules related to (a) nonentertainment programming, (b) commercials, (c) "community ascertainment," and (d) program logging. 46 Fed. Reg. 13888 (Feb. 24, 1981). Indeed, if former Commissioner Robinson has been converted to an "auction" approach, others may have been converted as well. See Robinson, The Federal Communications Commission: An Essay on Regulatory Watchdogs, 64 U. Va. L. Rev. 169 (1978); Seraso, Communications Law, N.Y.U. Ann. Survey of Am. Law, Issue 2, at 305 (1980).

The Supreme Court appears to be firmly allied with the deregulation effort. See FCC v. WNCN Listener & Guild, 101 S. Ct. 1266 (1981) (FCC not required to consider entertainment format changes in connection with renewal or transfer of radio licenses, but may rely on competition to achieve diversity); FCC v. Midwest Video Corp., 440 U.S. 689 (1979) (FCC lacks authority to require cable television companies to provide minimum number of channels and provide access to third parties). FCC v. National Citizens Committee for Broadcasting, 436 U.S. 775 (1978) (FCC not required to order divestiture of all newpaper owned local broadcast stations).

Page 394. Add the following after line 23:

In FCC v. National Citizens Committee for Broadcasting, 436 U.S. 775 (1978), the Court reviewed FCC rules forbidding future acquisition of common ownership of a broadcast station and a daily newspaper located in the same community and requiring "divestiture" of one or the other in sixteen "egregious" cases. In upholding the FCC (and reversing a circuit court decision requiring still more divestiture) Justice Marshall, writing for the Court, stated the following about renewal expectations: "In the past, the Commission has consistently acted on the theory that preserving continuity of meritorious service furthers the public interest, both in its direct consequence of bringing proved broadcast service to the public, and in its indirect consequence of rewarding—and avoiding losses to—licensees who have invested the money and effort necessary to produce quality performance. Thus, although a broadcast license must be renewed every three years, and the licensee must satisfy the Commission that renewal will serve the public interest, both the Commission and the courts have recognized that a licensee who has given meritorious service has a 'legitimate renewal expectanc[y]' that is 'implicit in the

structure of the Act' and should not be destroyed absent good cause.
. . . Accordingly, while diversification of ownership is a relevant factor in
the context of license renewal as well as initial licensing, the Commission
has long considered the past performance of the incumbent as the most
important factor in deciding whether to grant license renewal and
thereby to allow the existing owner to continue in operation. Even where
an incumbent is challenged by a competing applicant who offers greater
potential in terms of diversification, the Commission's general practice
has been to go with the 'proved product' and grant renewal if the incumbent has rendered meritorious service. . . ."

This language has been taken as authority for the FCC to give an
incumbent an advantage for "meritorious service." See Central Florida
Enterprises Inc. v. FCC, 598 F.2d 37, 44 (D.C. Cir. 1978).

Page 395. Add the following at the end of footnote 47c:

The FCC order discontinuing these proceedings, 69 F.C.C. 2d 419
(1977), was affirmed, National Black Media Coalition v. FCC, 559 F.2d
578 (D.C. Cir. 1978).

Page 395. Add the following after line 26:

The District of Columbia Circuit Court of Appeals reversed the commission's decision to renew Cowles's television license and remanded the
case for new proceedings:

CENTRAL FLORIDA ENTERPRISES, INC. v. FCC
598 F.2d 37 (D.C. Cir. 1978).

WILKEY, J. [The two main contenders for Cowles's license on renewal
were Cowles and Central. The commission voted for Cowles, 4-3. In
reviewing the proceedings the Court noted that the commission had
decided the following: (1) Cowles would receive a small demerit because
its main studio was not in the community served. (2) Cowles's parent,
CCI, had engaged in serious fraud, but Cowles was held to be "insulated"
from the findings of the fraud because Cowles itself was not involved. (3)
Central earned a clear preference on the "standard comparative" issue
of diversification because Cowles's parent (CCI) owned other broadcast
and newspaper interests (but these were located far away from Cowles's
station in Daytona Beach, Florida). (4) The "need for industry stability"
and Cowles's "local autonomy" in management diminished the significance of Central's preference. (5) In considering the standard comparative issue—best practicable service—Central deserved a plus for
minority group (black) participation, and its management/ownership

integration was meritorious. But this merit was not sufficient to outweigh Cowles's good prior-service record. (6) Cowles's past service, which the ALJ characterized as "thoroughly acceptable," in fact was "superior." This means that it was "sound, favorable and substantially above a level of mediocre service which might just minimally warrant renewal."]

. . . [W]e hold that the Commission acted unreasonably and without substantial record support in this matter and we remand for further proceedings.

The Commission's rationale in this case is thoroughly unsatisfying. The Commission purported to be conducting a full hearing whose content is governed by the 1965 Policy Statement. It found favorably to Central on each of diversification, integration and minority participation, and adversely to Cowles on the studio move question. Then simply on the basis of a wholly noncomparative assessment of Cowles' past performance as "substantial," the Commission confirmed Cowles' "renewal expectancy." Even were we to agree (and we do not agree) with the Commission's trivialization of each of Central's advantages, we still would be unable to sustain its action here. The Commission nowhere even vaguely described how it aggregated its findings into the decisive balance; rather, we are told that the conclusion is based on "administrative 'feel.'" Such intuitional forms of decision-making, completely opaque to judicial review, fall somewhere on the distant side of arbitrary.

The Commission's treatment of the standard comparative issues— diversification of media ownership and best practicable service—is the most worrisome aspect of this case. The Commission plainly disfavors use of the 1965 criteria in comparative renewal proceedings. This in turn is largely because the Commission dislikes the idea of comparative renewal proceedings altogether—or at least those that accord no presumptive weight to incumbency *per se.* As long as the renewal hearings were carried on in a completely ad hoc manner, it was little noticed that they were not really comparative. But the restatement of the comparative criteria in 1965 imposed an orderliness on the inquiry which made it obvious when applicants were not in fact on an equal footing. This would never have been a problem if the Commission had been able to distinguish in its rules between hearings comparing only new applicants and comparative renewal hearings. This it was unable to do and the 1965 Policy Statement has since governed comparative renewal proceedings more or less by default.

Since the 1965 Statement admits little room for a presumption of renewal, the Commission has reconstructed the criteria in a manner creating a de facto presumption. Whether justified in precedent or logic, the process has been straightforward and comports at least formally with the requirement of a "full hearing": (1) the criteria of diversification and integration were converted from structural questions (challengers usually prevailed on the simple numbers) to functional questions regarding the consequences of other media ownership and autonomous management (but challengers could rarely show injury to the public service); (2) a finding of "substantial," if not above average, past performance by the incumbent would be given decisive weight; and (3) other comparative or designated issues favoring the challenger would be noted, but would not be dispositive "even in conjunction with other factors," unless pertaining to grievous misconduct by the incumbent.

This usual procedure, we believe, although the Commission nowhere tells us, is essentially what occurred here. The development of Commission policy on comparative renewal hearings has now departed sufficiently from the established law, statutory and judicial precedent, that the Commission's handling of the facts of this case make embarrassingly clear that the FCC has practically erected a presumption of renewal that is inconsistent with the full hearing requirement of §309(e). . . .

[The Court then questioned the reasonableness of the commission's findings on each of the "designated issues": Why was Cowles given only a "slight" demerit when it moved its main studio to Daytona Beach, contrary to FCC regulations? Why was Cowles "insulated" from its parent CCI's involvement in mail fraud, since at least two persons were principal officers of both Cowles and the other CCI subsidiaries that were directly involved?

More importantly, why was Central not given a "clear preference" on "diversification," since Cowles's parent owned other media outlets? The fact that CCI gave Cowles's managers "autonomy" might be sufficient "to withstand the competition of a 'nothing' competitor," but Central is a more substantial challenger. If a challenger, in the face of a "management autonomy" claim, must prove that concentration of media ownership *actually* had an adverse effect on programming, he will never win. "Given the likely difficulties of proof in such matters, widespread reliance on the autonomy excuse would effectively repeal the diversification criterion." Thus it was unreasonable for the commission to find the diversification preference for Central of "little decisional significance." It must reconsider.

Finally, why were Central's preferences as to integration of ownership and management and minority participation insufficient to outweigh Cowles's past record? The commission never directly compared the factors predicting how Cowles will do (namely, its past record) with the criteria predicting how Central will do. Of course, since Central has no past record, in its case these predictors are "integration" and "minority participation." Central prevailed on these latter two criteria, which supposedly (according to the FCC's policies) predict how it will perform. Although the commission said that Cowles, too, did well on "management/ownership" integration because of its "management autonomy" policy, such a finding makes nonsense of the "integration" criterion. Of course, the commission characterized Cowles's past performance as "superior," but it went on to say that this word meant "substantial," or, at least not clearly better than the performance of other stations in the area. How can such average past performance—even if "average" here means "good" or "solid"—overcome, as a predictor of future performance, two preferences on each of the structural criteria that the FCC has said predict future performance? In any event, the commission has not explained why "good past performance" is likely to predict better future performance than is success on the two FCC "structural" criteria.]

On remand, the Commission will have occasion to reconsider its characterization of Cowles' past performance and to articulate clearly the manner in which its findings are integrated into the comparative analysis.

On Petition for Rehearing

Per curiam. The FCC and intervenors in this matter . . . complain . . . that our opinion disregards the "legitimate renewal expectancies implicit in the structure of the [Communications] Act." . . .

We set aside the [Cowles] renewal. Our principal reason for doing so was that the Commission's manner of "balancing" its findings was wholly unintelligible, based, it was said, on "administrative 'feel.' " Admittedly, licensing in the public interest entails a good many discretionary choices, but even if some of them rest inescapably on agency intuition (not a comfortable idea), we may at least insist that they do not contradict whatever rules for choosing do exist. We think it plain that the Commission violated the rules. . . . The dispositive question is, of course, the relevance of the incumbent's past performance. We thought it relevant "only insofar as it predicts whether future performance will be better or worse than that of competing applicants." . . . The Commission nowhere articulated how Cowles' unexceptional, if solid, past performance supported a finding that its future service would be better than Central's. In fact, as we have noted, *Central prevailed on each of the questions* [integration and minority participation] *supposedly predicting which applicant would better perform*—the same criteria the Commission uses for this purpose in non-renewal comparative hearings. . . .

However [the commission now wants to use the past record for a different, nonpredictive purpose. It wishes to give some extra advantage to incumbency pure and simple. Thus, it now argues that] ". . . renewal expectancies . . . are provided in order to promote security of tenure and to induce efforts and investments, furthering the public interest, that may not be devoted by a licensee without reasonable security." Pursuant to these expectancies a "substantial" or "meritorious" past record is a relevant factor to be weighed in the incumbent's favor. In this sense, a "meritorious" past record deserves appropriate weight in the overall "public interest" determination, irrespective of the predictive value of past performance and, contrary to the panel's view . . ., irrespective of any finding concerning the challenger's likely future performance. . . . This we admit, appears at least a plausible construction of the "public interest."

The trouble is, apart from several unenlightening recitals that there are expectations implicit in the Act, *there were few intimations that this was the Commission's inchoate rationale. . . . The place for a new rationale in this case, if one is to be logically developed, is on remand.* Moreover, if through rule-making or adjudication the Commission decides to accord weight to such noncomparative values as industry stability, it will have to do so in a manner that is susceptible of judicial review. This would seem to require that the Commission describe with at least rough clarity how it takes into account past performance, and how that factor is balanced alongside its findings under the comparative criteria. Although mathematical precision is, of course, impossible, something more than the Commission's customary recitals, "completely opaque to judicial review," must be provided. The choice of procedures through which an intelligible analysis could be composed is, as we have said, for the Commission.

Since the FCC petition for rehearing displayed a certain agitated concern that our decision in this case would destroy legitimate renewal expectancies of licensees, with baleful commercial consequences and harm to the general public, we thought it relevant to inquire of the Commission as to just how strong those renewal expectancies have been in the past, based on the action actually taken by the Commission and reviewing court.

The history of comparative renewal proceedings since 1 January 1961 (the date from which the data was requested) discloses that incumbents rarely have lost, and then only because they were disqualified on some noncomparative ground. From 1961 to 1978 the Commission has conducted seventeen comparative television license renewal proceedings, seven of which are still pending. In only two cases did the incumbent lose its license, and in *neither* of those cases were the comparative criteria the grounds of decision. In one case the incumbent was disqualified because of its fraudulent conduct, and in the other the incumbent failed to pursue its renewal application, so the challenger won by default.

The story is not much different in radio licensing. No license has been denied on a comparative basis.[47d]

Plainly, incumbents can "expect" in a statistical sense that their license will be renewed. We doubt that any realistic appraisal of the remand in this single case, calling upon the Commission to perform its duty in

47d. From 1961 to 1978 there were thirty-one comparative radio renewal proceedings, twelve of which are still pending. No incumbent radio licensee has been displaced on the basis of the comparative criteria. Three licensees were disqualified for misconduct, five other renewal applications were dismissed, and the challengers' applications granted. . . .

accord with its own expressed standards, could reasonably create the nervous apprehension among licensees claimed by the Commission. The only legitimate fear which should move licensees is the fear of their own substandard performance, and that would be all to the public good.

How precisely does the court of appeals intend for the commission to make renewal decisions? What effect would you expect the opinion in *Central Florida* to have? See Note, 92 Harv. L. Rev. 1801 (1979). See also Gottfried v. FCC, 655 F.2d 297 (D.C. Cir. 1981) (commission must consider efforts to help the hard of hearing when it renews "public," but not "commercial," television licenses). For additional discussion and criticism of the renewal process, see Brinkman, The Policy Paralysis in WESH, 32 Fed. Com. L.J. 55 (1980).

Former Commissioner Glenn Robinson has described the comparative licensing process as an exercise in "regulatory futility." He now favors an "auction" system of allocation. As to his prior opposition to auctions, (quoting an English judge) he states, "the matter does not appear to me now as it appears to have appeared to me then." We recommend his article, The Federal Communications Commission: An Essay on Regulatory Watchdogs, 64 U. Va. L. Rev 169 (1978).

C. RULE MAKING VERSUS ADJUDICATION AS MEANS OF DEVELOPING AGENCY POLICY

Page 405. At the end of line 34, add new callout 59a and the accompanying footnote:

59a. For additional discussion of the considerations involved in the choice between rule making and adjudication see Mayton, The Legislative Resolution of the Rulemaking vs. Adjudication Problem in Agency Lawmaking, 1980 Duke L.J. 103 (1980); Pierce, The Choice Between Adjudicating and Rulemaking for Formulating and Implementing Energy Policy, 31 Hastings L.J. 1 (1979); Note, NLRB Rulemaking: Political Reality versus Procedural Fairness, 89 Yale L.J. 982 (1980).

Page 420. Add the following at the end of the page:

3. In some instances agencies have been attacked, generally without success, for employing rule-making procedures when the proceeding is assertedly adjudicatory in character. For example, Hercules Inc. v. EPA, 598 F.2d 91 (D.C. Cir. 1978), upheld the EPA's authority to adopt pollution control requirements through rule making, even though the resulting rules apply to only a single plant. FTC v. Brigadier Industries Corp., 613 F.2d 1110 (D.C. Cir. 1979), held that the issuance of subpoenas

during a rule-making proceeding did not transform it into an adjudication requiring that full adjudicatory procedures be employed.

The Ninth Circuit has extended *Wyman-Gordon* to limit agencies' ability to modify policy through adjudication rather than rule making.

Patel v. INS, 638 F.2d 1199 (9th Cir. 1980), involved a series of shifts in immigration policy concerning adjustment of the status of a deportable alien to that of an alien admitted for permanent residence. Ordinarily, aliens so admitted must obtain a certification from the Labor Department that their presence will not be detrimental to the US labor force, but there is an "investor exemption" from this requirement. In 1967, the INS adopted a regulation creating an investor exemption for aliens engaged in an agricultural and commercial enterprise in which they had invested a "substantial amount of capital." In 1973 the regulation was amended to require that the alien invest at least $10,000 in the enterprise and have at least one year's training or experience qualifying him or her to engage in such enterprise. At the time, the service initially proposed but ultimately failed to adopt in the regulations an additional "job-creation" requirement that the investment tend to expand employment opportunities in the United States. In 1976 the INS amended the regulations to include a requirement that the enterprise employ citizens or aliens lawfully admitted to permanent residence, other than the investing alien or his or her spouse and children.

In re Heitland, 14 I & N Dec. 563 (BIA 1974), *aff'd*, 551 F.2d 495 (2d Cir.), *cert. denied*, 434 U.S. 819 (1977), involved an INS decision in a case arising under the 1967 regulations. Overruling prior interpretations of the 1967 regulations, the INS held that in order to qualify as "substantial," the investment must create new job opportunities. The INS decision in *Heitland* stated in dicta that this requirement would also apply in cases arising under the 1973 regulation. The INS, in In re Ruangswang, I.D. 2546 (BIA 1976), applied the *Heitland* job-creation requirement to a case arising under the 1973 regulations, denying the alien in question eligibility for adjustment of status. The Ninth Circuit reversed, 591 F.2d 39 (9th Cir. 1978). It held that the INS could not, through adjudication, add a new requirement to the explicit and limited terms of the 1973 regulation, and that it would in any event be an abuse of discretion to apply the *Heitland* requirement to Ruangswang, who had completed her investment before *Heitland* was decided.

In *Patel*, the court faced a case arising under the 1973 regulations in which the alien had made his investment after *Heitland* but failed to meet the job-creation requirement. The court set aside the INS order of deportation, holding that *Wyman-Gordon* precluded enforcement of the job-creation requirement in *Patel*.

". . . *Heitland*, like *Excelsior*, created a broad requirement of prospective application. It stated that aliens attempting to qualify for the investor exemption under the 1973 regulation would be required to show, in addition to requirements set forth in the regulation, that their investment expands job opportunities in the United States. Only months before, the INS itself had recognized the desirability of establishing a job-creation standard by rulemaking when it proposed the 1973 regulation. . . . INS eventually failed to include the job-creation standard in its rule. Under the authority of *Wyman-Gordon,* we conclude that if the INS wished to add the job-creation criterion, it should have done so in a rulemaking procedure. See 2 Davis, Administrative Law Treatise §7:25 at 124 (1979).

We recognize, of course, that there are differences between *Heitland* and *Excelsior.* Unlike the NLRB in *Excelsior,* the Board in *Heitland* applied the job-creation criterion to the alien before it (although the criterion in *Heitland* was applied to the 'substantial amount of capital' requirement of the pre-1973 regulation, not to the 1973 regulation which was in effect for purposes of the instant case); and the Board in *Heitland* did not attempt a quasi-rulemaking procedure as did the NLRB in *Excelsior.* Nonetheless, *Heitland* did prospectively pronounce a broad, generally applicable requirement, without then applying that requirement to aliens seeking exemptions under the 1973 regulation. It was an abuse of discretion to thus circumvent the rulemaking procedures of the APA.''

The court distinguished *Bell Aerospace* on the ground that the classification of buyers for collective bargaining purposes involves many variables, which are best treated through case-by-case adjudication: ''. . . In contrast, the job-creation criterion of *Heitland* does not call for a case-by-case determination. It may be stated and applied as a general rule even though the result may vary from case to case. . . .

In addition to our conclusion that *Heitland* was an improper circumvention of rulemaking procedure, we also conclude that the Board abused its discretion by applying the job-creation criterion to Patel. Although Patel invested money and applied for the investor exemption well after *Heitland* was decided, we doubt that he could have clearly determined what he must do to qualify for the exemption. The INS had been sending aliens confusing signals. In promulgating the 1973 regulation, the INS had expressly eliminated language similar to the job-creation criterion of *Heitland.* When the Board decided in *Heitland* that the criterion applied to the out-of-date, pre-1973 regulation, it only obscurely stated in dictum that it would also be applied to the 1973 regulation. . . . It was not until 1976 that the regulation was amended to include clearly the job-creation criterion.

The hardship Patel has experienced as a result of his failure to comply with the job-creation criterion is great. . . .

. . . In view of the agency's confusion with respect to the job-creation criterion and the resulting hardship to Patel, we hold that the Board abused its discretion in applying that criterion in this case. Thus, we reverse the Board's denial of Patel's application for adjustment of status, and remand to the Board for exercise of discretion in relation to that application."

The Ninth Circuit has followed *Patel* in a variety of similar immigration cases. See Konishi v. INS, 661 F.2d 818 (9th Cir. 1981), and decision there cited. The Second Circuit has reached a contrary conclusion. In Mehta v. INS, 574 F.2d 701 (2d Cir. 1978), it concluded that the INS could continue to apply the job-creation requirement to cases arising under the 1973 regulations as it had to cases arising under the 1967 regulations. Invoking *Chenery*, it held that the INS was not required to adopt the job-creation requirement through rule making. It further held that, since Mehta had not made his investment until after the *Heitland* decision by the INS, it would not be unfair to apply the job creation requirement to him.

In Francis Ford, Inc. v. FTC, Nos. 79-7647, 79-7654 (9th Cir. Aug. 24, 1981), a panel of the Ninth Circuit applied the logic of *Patel* to a regulatory case.

The FTC entered a cease- and desist-order against an Oregon Ford dealer, concluding that its practice with respect to repossessed cars was an unfair trade practice. The dealer credited the debtor for the wholesale value of the car, but then deducted from this figure an allowance for dealer's overhead and lost profits as well as the direct expenses of refurbishing the car. On reselling the car at retail, the dealer pocketed the entire difference between the sale price and the adjusted wholesale price. The dealer's practice was apparently common in the industry.

In a comprehensive but uncompleted rule-making proceeding on credit practices, the FTC proposed to deal with the practice of charging debtors overhead and lost profits in calculating debtor's *deficiencies* in connection with the sale of repossessed cars.

Invoking *Patel*, the court held the FTC should also address the problem of accounting for surpluses through rule making. Because the FTC's decision in *Francis Ford* had "widespread application" to repossession practices (and the FTC undertook to publicize it as such), the court ruled that the FTC "has exceeded its authority by proceeding to create new law by adjudication rather than by rulemaking."

The panel opinion has been withdrawn pending disposition of the FTC's petition for rehearing. Is *Francis Ford* compelled by *Patel*? Is it consistent with *Chenery* and *Bell Aerospace*?

Appeal of FTC Line of Business Litigation, 595 F.2d 685 (D.C. Cir. 1978), *cert. denied*, 439 U.S. 958 (1979), held that the FTC imposition of a new program of reporting requirements on hundreds of companies was not rule making and that the FTC accordingly did not have to comply with APA rule-making procedures before implementing the program.

In order to obtain information on sales and industrial concentration in various product markets, the FTC served identical Line of Business (LB) reporting orders on 450 corporations and identical Corporate Patterns (CP) reporting orders on 1100 corporations. The commission acted pursuant to §6(b) of the Federal Trade Commission Act, empowering the FTC to require businesses to file informational reports concerning their "business, conduct [and] practices."

The court, drawing on the legislative history of the APA, concluded that the act distinguishes three forms of agency activity: rule making, adjudication, and investigation. It held that because the issuance of investigative orders is addressed by §555(c), the FTC was not required to follow the rule-making procedures of §553(c) before instituting the LB and CP reporting programs. The court was evidently concerned that a contrary ruling might unduly hamper an agency's ability to gather information. But should §555(c) be read as excluding compliance with other requirements of the APA? Why shouldn't the FTC have complied with notice and comment procedures in instituting new, broad-scale reporting requirements whose compliance costs are substantial and whose value is disputed?

Page 444. Add the following after line 2:

The net result of this regulatory approach, in the authors' view, was a very severe shortage of natural gas. Breyer & MacAvoy, The Natural Gas Shortage and the Regulation of Natural Gas Producers, 86 Harv. L. Rev. 941 (1973). The shortage first took the form of a running-down of gas resources, but by the early 1970s there was a severe shortage of gas for heating and other uses during the winter months.

As a result, in 1978 Congress enacted the Natural Gas Policy Act, 15 U.S.C. §§3301-3432. The act allowed the price of most "new" natural gas to rise, by a certain percentage each year, in accordance with a fixed schedule. It also provided for the eventual deregulation of much "new gas." Gas from new onshore wells deeper than 5000 feet, for example, would be deregulated in 1985, and all new onshore gas would escape regulation by 1987. New offshore gas was also deregulated. (Congress could by joint resolution delay deregulation for eighteen additional months.) In the meantime, the price increases would be "allocated" in a way designed to raise the price of gas used for *industrial*— not for residential—purposes.

The price increase "allocation" system thus created is enormously complicated, involving more than thirty possible classifications of natural gas with different and changing ceiling prices. To begin to understand intuitively the complexity, consider a pipeline that buys gas from different suppliers in the field. Some of these will have higher prices than others, depending on whether they are selling gas that is "old," "new," "offshore," "onshore," etc. The pipeline then averages, or "rolls in," all its supplies to determine the average cost. It cannot sell to all customers at prices reflecting this average, however, for it must pass through higher costs to industrial customers first, so that they bear most of the burden of the new, higher-cost "incremental" gas. If there is more such high-cost gas than is used by industrial customers, the extra cost is next added to the bills of other customers, according to a system of priorities. Now, considering the fact that each pipeline has a different mix of high-cost/-low-cost suppliers and a different mix of industrial/residential customers, it is apparent that this system can yield very different prices for gas that (economically speaking) costs the same to produce and to transport, depending on which pipeline sells it. This misallocation and the resulting pattern of incentives to firms to locate near a "low price" pipeline, as well as the administrative complexity, is a price being paid for the continued effort to control the "rents" that residential users would otherwise have to pay to companies that own older, cheaper gas supplies.

This whole system, however, is supposed to be temporary or transitional, allowing gas prices to rise to approach free market levels by the time new gas is totally deregulated in the mid or late 1980s. Some have expressed doubt about whether such deregulation will actually occur. See MacAvoy, The Natural Gas Policy Act of 1978, 19 Nat. Resources J. 811 (1979). Others have urged that deregulation be speeded up, sometimes accompanying this suggestion with a proposal to impose a windfall profits tax on the accompanying rents. See generally Breyer, Regulation and Its Reform, chs. 8, 13 (1982).

D. CONSISTENCY IN APPLYING REGULATIONS: "AN AGENCY MUST FOLLOW ITS OWN RULES"

Page 457. Add the following case after line 29:

UNITED STATES v. CACERES

440 U.S. 741 (1979)

[United States v. Caceres held that a defendant in a criminal prosecution may not exclude evidence obtained in violation of administrative regulations. Internal Revenue Service regulations required Justice Department approval before electronic surveillance of meetings between taxpayers and IRS agents was undertaken. The IRS conducted surveillance of a meeting in which the defendant attempted to bribe an agent. The surveillance was approved by relevant IRS officials, but because time was short, Justice Department approval was not obtained until after the monitoring of conversations that led to defendant's conviction. The surveillance did not violate any constitutional or statutory requirement. In sustaining the conviction, Justice Stevens's opinion for the Court stated as follows:]

[This is not] a case in which the Due Process Clause is implicated because an individual has reasonably relied on agency regulations promulgated for his guidance or benefit. ... Agency violations of their own regulations, whether or not also in violation of the Constitution, may well be inconsistent with the standards of agency action which the APA directs the courts to enforce.[90a] Indeed, some of our most important decisions holding agencies bound by their regulations have been in cases originally brought under the APA.

But this is not an APA case, and the remedy sought is not invalidation of the agency action. Rather, we are dealing with a criminal prosecution in which respondent seeks judicial enforcement of the agency regulations by means of the exclusionary rule. ... [W]e decline to adopt any rigid rule requiring federal courts to exclude any evidence obtained as a result of a violation of these rules. ... [W]e cannot ignore the possibility that a rigid application of an exclusionary rule to every regulatory violation could have a serious deterrent impact on the formulation of additional standards to govern prosecutorial and police procedures. Here, the Executive itself has provided for internal sanctions in cases of knowing violations of the electronic-surveillance regulations. To go beyond that, and require exclusion in every case, would take away from the Executive Department the primary responsibility for fashioning the appropriate remedy for the violation of its regulations. But since the content, and indeed the existence, of the regulations would remain within the Executive's sole authority, the result might well be fewer and less protective regulations. In the long run, it is far better to have rules like those contained in the IRS Manual, and to tolerate occasional erroneous administration of the kind displayed by this record, than either to have no rules except those mandated by statute, or to have them framed in a mere precatory form. ...

Reversed.

MR. JUSTICE MARSHALL, with whom MR. JUSTICE BRENNAN joins, dissenting. ...

90a. Vitarelli v. Seaton, [359 U.S. 535, 547 (1959), described in Casebook at 606] (Frankfurter, J., concurring in part and dissenting in part). ("This judicially-evolved rule of administrative law is now firmly established and, if I may add, rightly so. He that takes the procedural sword shall perish with that sword").

Even as a matter of administrative law, however, it seems clear that agencies are not required, at the risk of invalidation of their action, to follow all of their rules, even those properly classified as "internal." In American Farm Lines v. Black Ball Freight Service, 397 U.S. 532, 538, for example, ICC rules requiring certain information to be included in applications had not been followed. This Court rejected the argument that the agency action was therefore invalid, concluding that the Commission was "entitled to a measure of discretion in administering its own procedural rules in such a manner as it deems necessary to resolve quickly and correctly urgent transportation problems."

In a long line of cases beginning with Bridges v. Wixon, 326 U.S. 135, 152-153 (1945), this Court has held that "one under investigation . . . is legally entitled to insist upon the observance of rules" promulgated by an executive or legislative body for his protection. See . . . Morton v. Ruiz, 415 U.S. 199, 235 (1974); . . . Vitarelli v. Seaton, 359 U.S. 535 (1959); Service v. Dulles, 354 U.S. 363 (1957); United States ex rel. Accardi v. Shaughnessy, 347 U.S. 260 (1954). Underlying these decisions is a judgment, central to our concept of due process, that government officials no less than private citizens are bound by rules of law. Where individual interests are implicated, the Due Process Clause requires that an executive agency adhere to the standards by which it professes its action to be judged. . . .

This Court has consistently demanded governmental compliance with regulations designed to safeguard individual interests even when the rules were not mandated by the Constitution or federal statute. In United States ex rel. Accardi v. Shaughnessy, supra, the Court granted a writ of habeas corpus where the Attorney General had disregarded applicable procedures for the Board of Immigration Appeals' suspension of deportation orders. Although the Attorney General had final power to deport the petitioner and had not statutory or constitutional obligation to provide for intermediate action by the Board, this Court held that while suspension procedures were in effect, "the Attorney General denies himself the right to sidestep the Board or dictate its decision." 347 U.S., at 267. On similar reasoning, the Court in Service v. Dulles vacated a Foreign Service officer's national security discharge. While acknowledging that the Secretary of State was not obligated to adopt "rigorous substantive and procedureal safeguards," the Court nonetheless held that "having done so he could not, so long as the Regulations remained unchanged, proceed without regard to them." 354 U.S., at 388. Similarly, in Vitarelli v. Seaton we demanded adherence to Department of the Interior employee-discharge procedures that were "generous beyond the requirements that bind [the] agency." 359 U.S., at 547. . . . And most recently, in Morton v. Ruiz, we declined to permit the Bureau of Indian Affairs to depart from internal rules for establishing assistance-eligibility requirements although the procedures were "more rigorous than otherwise would be required." 415 U.S., at 235.90b. . .

90b. Although not always expressly predicated on the Due Process Clause, these decisions are explicable in no other terms. The complaints in only two of the cases, Vitarelli v. Seaton, 359 U.S. 535 (1959), and Service v. Dulles, 354 U.S. 363 (1957), invoked the Administrative Procedure Act. . . . In neither of these cases was the Act even mentioned in the Court's opinions. Rather, *Vitarelli* followed *Service*, see 359 U.S., at 539-540, which in turn had relied on United States ex rel. Accardi v. Shaughnessy, 347 U.S. 260 (1954). See 354 U. S., at 373, 386-387. Both *Accardi* and its predecessor, Bridges v. Wixon, 326 U. S. 135 (1945), were habeas corpus cases. . . .

To make subjective reliance controlling in due process analysis deflects inquiry from the relevant constitutional issue, the legitimacy of government conduct. . . .

Moreover, the Court's focus on subjective reliance is inconsistent with our prior decisions enforcing due process guarantees. In Bridges v. Wixon, 326 U.S. 135 (1945), we vacated a deportation order because the Immigration and Naturalization Service had failed to observe regulations requiring that witness statements be made under oath, even though the petitioner's statements were not involved and he had not invoked the regulations at his deportation hearing. . . .

Similarly, the petitioner in Vitarelli v. Seaton, 359 U.S. 535 (1959), was in no meaningful sense prejudiced by the Department of the Interior's departure from regulations governing employee discharges for national security reasons. After the petitioner filed suit, he received a revised notice of dismissal which complied with all applicable regulations. Despite the petitioner's inability to demonstrate that adherence to agency regulations would have affected the decision to discharge him, this Court ordered reinstatement.

Implicit in these decisions, and in the Due Process Clause itself, is the premise that regulations bind with equal force whether or not they are outcome determinative. As its very terms make manifest, the Due Process Clause is first and foremost a guarantor of *process.* It embodies a commitment to procedural regularity independent of result. . . .

Finally, the Court declines to order suppression because "a rigid application of an exclusionary rule to every regulatory violation could have a serious deterrent impact on the formulation of additional standards to govern prosecutorial and police procedures." No support is offered for that speculation. Under today's decision, regulations largely unenforced by the IRS will be unenforceable by the courts. I cannot share the Court's apparent conviction that much would be lost if the agency were to withdraw such rules in protest against judicial enforcement. Presumably Congress, which has been repeatedly dissuaded by the IRS from legislating in the area, would then step into the breach. In the event of congressional action, this Court could not so cavalierly tolerate unauthorized electronic surveillance. . . .

QUESTIONS

1. Why should the requirement that agencies follow their own regulations be enforced only in cases falling under the Administrative Proce-

---

[T]hese decisions have been uniformly, and I believe properly, interpreted as resting on due process foundation. [Citing lower court decisions.] See generally Berger, Do Regulations Really Bind Regulators, 62 Nw. U.L. Rev. 137 (1967).

dure Act? Recall that the APA was not in existence when *Arizona Grocery* was decided.

2. Does due process require that agencies follow their own regulations? If Justice Marshall's position were accepted, would federal courts be required to hear and resolve claims that state administrators had not followed state regulations? Would such "federalization" of state administrative law be desirable?

Shouldn't a litigant at least be required to show that he relied upon agency regulations and was prejudiced by their violation in order to obtain relief on due process grounds?

3. President Reagan's Executive Order 12991 requiring use of cost-benefit analysis, described at p. 13, supra, contains the following provision: "Section 9. *Judicial Review.* This Order is intended only to improve the internal management of the Federal government, and is not intended to create any right or benefit, substantive or procedural, enforceable at law by a party against the United States, its agencies, its officers or any person. The determinations made by agencies under Section 4 of this Order, and any Regulatory Impact Analyses for any rule, shall be made part of the whole record of agency action in connection with the rule."

Suppose that a federal agency adopts a regulation without following the cost-benefit analysis required by the order. A firm subject to the regulation brings suit to set it aside, alleging that the regulation would not have been adopted at all or would have been less rigorous if the cost-benefit analysis had been performed and considered. What result?

Does the *Arizona Grocery* principle require an agency to adhere to established practices, even though they have not been formally specified through regulations? National Conservation Political Action Committee v. Federal Election Commission, 626 F.2d 953 (D.C. Cir. 1980), invalidated a FEC advisory opinion favorable to the Democratic National Committee (DNC) because of a failure to provide public notice of the DNC's request for the opinion. Both the relevant statute and regulations provided that requests for advisory opinions would be made public, but neither required FEC publication of their receipt. FEC, however, had regularly published notice of advisory opinion requests in the Federal Register. The commission then announced that such notice would be published in its weekly newsletter. The DNC request was not noticed in either publication. The court concluded as follows: "Thus, appellants, who justifiably relied upon the Commission's practice of publishing requests, were effectively denied the opportunity to comment upon the DNC's request during the comment period provided for by the Act[91a]

91a. "Section 312(c) of the Act provides in pertinent part: 'The Commission shall, before rendering an advisory opinion with respect to such request, provide any interested party

and by the Commission's own regulations.91b Agencies are under an obligation to follow their own regulations, procedures, and precedents, or provide a rational explanation for their departures. . . . In addition, prior notice is required where a private party justifiably relies upon an agency's past practice and is substantially affected by a change in that practice. . . . Thus, Congress' mandate, the Commission's regulations, and considerations of fundamental fairness lead us to conclude that [the advisory opinion] was unlawfully issued and is without force and effect."

Page 457. Add the following to end of footnote 91:

Does the principle of *Arizona Grocery* preclude an agency from adopting a regulation, modifying the regulation, and then relying upon the modified regulation to impose financial loss on a person whose conduct conformed to the original regulation and occurred before the regulation was modified? See Daughters of Miriam Center for the Aged v. Mathews, 590 F.2d 1250 (3d Cir. 1978) discussed at p. 52, supra.

Does the principle of *Arizona Grocery* preclude an agency that has imposed certain requirements in a regulation from adopting, in the course of an adjudication, an additional requirement to impose a deprivation on a person who conformed to the regulation? See Patel v. INS, 638 F.2d 1199 (9th Cir. 1980), discussed at p. 61, supra.

E. ESTOPPEL AND RES JUDICATA

Page 459. Add the following after line 33:

SCHWEIKER v. HANSEN

450 U.S. 785 (1981)

Per curiam. On June 12, 1974, respondent met for about 15 minutes with Don Connelly, a field representative of the Social Security Administration (SSA), and orally inquired of him whether she was eligible for "mother's insurance benefits" under §202(g) of the Social Security Act (Act), 64 Stat. 485, as amended, 42 U.S.C. §402(g). Connelly erroneously told her that she was not, and she left the SSA office without having filed

---

with an opportunity to transmit written comments to the Commission with respect to such request.' 2 U.S.C. §437f(c) (1976)."

91b. "11 C.F.R. § 112.3 (1979) provides in pertinent part:

'(a) Interested persons are invited to submit written comments concerning advisory opinion requests.

(b) Written comments may be submitted within 10 calendar days of the date the request is made public at the Commission. The Commission may in its discretion shorten or extend the comment period on a particular request where there is reasonable cause for doing so.' "

a written application. By the Act's terms, such benefits are available only to one who, among other qualifications, "has filed application." 42 U.S.C. §402 (g)(1)(D). By a regulation promulgated pursuant to the Act, only written applications satisfy the "filed application" requirement. 20 CFR §404.601 (1974). The SSA's Claims Manual, an internal Adminstration handbook, instructs field representatives to advise applicants of the advantages of filing written applications and to recommend to applicants who are uncertain about their eligibility that they file written applications. Connelly, however, did not recommend to respondent that she file a written application; nor did he advise her of the advantages of doing so. [Respondent eventually filed a written application and began receiving benefits in 1975.] The question is whether Connelly's erroneous statement and neglect of the Claims Manual estop petitioner, the Secretary of Health and Human Services, from denying retroactive benefits to respondent for a period in which she was eligible for benefits but had not filed a written application. . . .

Respondent then brought this lawsuit in the District Court for the District of Vermont, which held that the written-application requirement was "unreasonably restrictive" as applied to the facts of this case. A divided panel of the Court of Appeals for the Second Circuit affirmed. It agreed with petitioner as an initial matter that the regulation requiring a written application is valid and that the Claims Manual has no legally binding effect. But it considered the written-application requirement a mere "procedural requirement" of lesser import than the fact that respondent in June 1974 had been "substantively eligible" for the benefits. In such circumstances, the majority held, "misinformation provided by a Government official combined with a showing of misconduct (even if it does not rise to the level of a violation of a legally binding rule) should be sufficient to require estoppel." . . .

Judge Friendly dissented. He argued that the majority's conclusion is irreconcilable with decisions of this Court, e.g., Federal Crop Insurance Corp. v. Merrill, 332 U.S. 380. . . .

We agree with the dissent. . . .

Connelly erred in telling respondent that she was ineligible for the benefit she sought. . . . But at worst, Connelly's conduct did not cause respondent to take action, cf. Federal Crop Insurance Corp. v. Merrill, supra, or fail to take action, cf. Montana v. Kennedy, supra, that respondent could not correct at any time.

Similarly, there is no doubt that Connelly failed to follow the Claims Manual in neglecting to recommend that respondent file a written application and in neglecting to advise her of the advantages of a written application. But the Claims Manual is not a regulation. It has no legal force, and it does not bind the SSA. Rather, it is a 13-volume handbook for internal use by thousands of SSA employees, including the hundreds of employees who receive untold numbers of oral inquiries like respondent's each year. If Connelly's minor breach of such a manual suffices to estop petitioner, then the Government is put "at risk that every alleged failure by an agent to follow instructions to the last detail in one of a thousand cases will deprive it of the benefit of the written application requirement which experience has taught to be essential to the honest and effective administration of the Social Security Laws." 619 F.2d. at 956 (Friendly, J., dissenting). See United States v. Caceres, 440 U.S. 741, 755-756 (1979). . . .

[MR. JUSTICE MARSHALL, joined by MR. JUSTICE BRENNAN, dissented.]

See also Jackson v. United States, 573 F.2d 1189 (Ct. Claims 1978) (soldier injured in combat maneuvers may not recover damages on theory that government recruiter's representation that he would not be assigned to such maneuvers; *Merrill* invoked).

QUESTION

What is the difference between cases holding the government "estopped," and those, see Casebook at pp. 355-358, holding that agencies may not, through adjudication, engage in certain "retroactive" changes of law or policy?

Page 459. Add to end of footnote 95:

See also Note, Equitable Estoppel of Government, 79 Colum. L. Rev. 551 (1979).

Page 462. Add the following after paragraph (e):

(f) In proceedings to certify a collective bargaining unit, the NLRB ruled that certain employees were within the bargaining unit. In subsequent unfair labor practice proceedings involving the same unit, the board invoked res judicata in refusing to reconsider the appropriateness of classifying them as members of the unit. Held, the board must reconsider the question; the evidentiary record in the first proceeding was defective (in part due to the employer's counsel), while that in the second proceeding was more complete. Burns Electronic Security Services, Inc. v. NLRB, 624 F.2d 403 (2d Cir. 1980). But see Mosher Steel Co. v. NLRB, 568 F.2d 436 (5th Cir 1978) (board may not, at instance of union, reopen, in second related proceeding, finding of employee misconduct in first proceeding in which union had full opportunity to litigate issue).

Page 462. Add the following after Question 2:

3. In Parklane Hosiery Co., Inc. v. Shore, 439 U.S. 322 (1979), the Court held that the Seventh Amendment right to jury trial was not vi-

olated when (1) the SEC sued a corporation and its controlling shareholders, directors, and officers in federal district court for violation of the securities laws, and obtained an injunction following a nonjury trial; and (2) other shareholders of the corporation, who did not participate in the SEC proceeding, brought suit against the same defendants for damages, and successfully invoked the SEC's judgment "offensively" as collateral estoppel on the question of violation.

Suppose that the first proceeding had been an administrative proceeding before the SEC rather than a court suit. Would the Seventh Amendment ruling have been the same? Cf. Bowen v. U.S., 570 F.2d 1311 (7th Cir. 1978). See Note, the Collateral Estoppel Effect of Administrative Agency Actions in Federal Civil Litigation, 46 Geo. Wash. L. Rev. 65 (1977).

Chapter Six

Hearing Requirements in Economic Regulation and Taxation

B. THE PROCEDURAL REQUIREMENTS OF THE APA AND THE INTERPLAY BETWEEN RULE MAKING AND ADJUDICATION

Page 491. Add the following after paragraph 5:

6. The courts have often failed to follow the restrictive approach adopted by *Florida East Coast* in the context of *rule making* in determining whether *adjudicatory* proceedings are subject to formal trial-type procedures under the APA. Linguistically, the test is the same for the two types of procedures; §§553(c) and 556-7 apply to cases where "rules are required by statute to be determined on the record after opportunity for an agency hearing," while §§554 and 556-7 apply to cases of "adjudication required by statute to be determined on the record after opportunity for an agency hearing." But, in cases of adjudication, courts are readier to find that an organic statute triggers formal hearing procedures even though it does not contain the words "hearing" and "on the record." For example, Seacoast Anti-Pollution League v. Costle, 572 F.2d 872 (1st Cir.), *cert. denied*, 439 U.S. 824 (1978), held that APA formal adjudication procedures must be followed in an EPA proceeding on issuance of a thermal discharge permit for a nuclear power plant even though the governing statute provided only for decision "after opportunity for public hearing," and did not require decision "on the record." The court stated that "we are willing to presume that, unless a statute otherwise specifies, an adjudicatory hearing subject to judicial review must be on the record."[37a] It asserted that an opposite presumption should apply in rule making.

37a. See also cases cited at Casebook, p. 525 n.88. But cf. United States Lines v. FMC, 584 F.2d 519 (D.C. Cir. 1978), holding that a "quasi adjudicatory" proceeding to amend a joint shipping service agreement that carries with it antitrust immunity was not subject to §§554 and 556-7 trial-type procedures where the statute provided for decision "after notice and hearing."

Why are courts readier to imply trial-type procedural formalities in adjudication than in rule making? Undoubtedly tradition and black-letter constitutional law, which ordinarily require a trial-type hearing in tax or regulatory adjudication but not in rule making, exert a powerful influence. Courts may also believe that trial-type procedures pose a lesser threat to efficient administration in adjudication than in rule making, which often involves more parties and a wider range of issues.[37b]

Although trial-type hearing requirements are more readily implied in adjudication than rule making, courts as well as agencies are displaying concern that automatic insistence on trial-type formalities in regulatory adjudication can seriously impede effective administration. The Environmental Protection Agency, for example, has sought to limit adjudicatory hearings by requiring those seeking an evidentiary trial to make a threshold showing of disputed facts warranting such a procedure. Costle v. Pacific Legal Foundation, 445 U.S. 198 (1980), upheld the EPA's reliance on regulations requiring parties to show relevant "material issues of fact" in denying a hearing on the issuance of a pollution permit under the Federal Water Pollution Control Act, which requires that such permits be issued after an "opportunity" for "public hearing." But the extent to which agencies can use this technique to deny adjudicatory hearings— a question that turns in large part on what constitutes a disputed material issue of fact and how far the agency can shift to private parties the burden of showing the existence of such issues—remains very much in controversy.

Page 502. Add the following after line 2:

Both Senate and House versions of regulatory reform legislation currently pending in Congress would increase the formality of the informal rule-making process. The Senate bill (recently passed in the Senate), for example, separates proposed "major rules" from other rules. A major rule is defined as a rule likely to have "an annual effect on the economy of $100,000,000 or more," or a rule likely to bring about "a substantial increase in costs or prices" for the public or to have "significant adverse

37b. The greater willingness of courts to conclude in adjudicatory cases that formal APA hearing procedures apply, plus the circumstance that APA procedures required in formal adjudication are more demanding than those required in formal rule making, can make the classification of a proceeding as adjudication or rule making quite important.

For example, in Hercules, Inc., v. EPA, 598 F.2d 91 (D.C. Cir.), the EPA used rule-making procedures to adopt two regulations limiting discharges of two specific pesticides from plants manufacturing such pesticides. The regulations were phrased in general terms, but because each of the pesticides was manufactured at only one plant, each regulation applied to only one facility. The court rejected the manufacturers' contentions that the proceeding was functionally adjudication, which must be conducted in accordance with the formal adjudicatory procedures of §§554 and 556-7 because the relevant statute provided for a "hearing" and required certain findings "on the record."

effects on competition, employment, investment, productivity, innovation, the environment, public health or safety," or ability to compete abroad. In addition to developing a "regulatory analysis" for major rules (considering costs, benefits, alternatives, etc.), the agency must provide "opportunity for oral presentation of data, views and information at informal public hearings." Those hearings "shall include an opportunity for direct and cross-examination of the principal agency employees who prepared . . . [significant] data . . . and of any other persons who present testimony, documents or other information . . . where other procedures such as the convening of public meetings, conferences or panel discussions on the presentation of staff arguments for comment and rebuttal are determined to be inadequate. . . ."

The Senate bill would also formalize *all* rule making by providing that an agency "may not rely on any factual or methodological material that was not placed in the rule making file. . . ." That file must contain, among other matters and with certain exceptions, all "data, methodologies, reports, studies, scientific evaluations, or other similar information" that "pertains directly to the rule and that the agency considered in connection with the rule making. . . ." If new, important material is developed, it must be put in the file and parties must have an opportunity to comment upon it. This file "shall constitute the rule making record for purposes of judicial review." See S. 1080, 128 Cong. Rec. S. 2713, (daily ed. March 24, 1982); H.R. 746, 97th Cong., 2d Sess. (1981). If the Senate bill becomes law, what is left of the distinction between formal and informal rule making?

Page 522. Add the following Note after line 20:

Note on Lower Court Reactions to Vermont Yankee

The developing record of lower court decisions suggests that *Vermont Yankee's*[78a] impact has been relatively modest. Lower courts have invoked *Vermont Yankee* to reject requests for trial-type procedures, such as cross-examination, in notice and comment rule making or informal adjudication.[78b] But agencies habitually prepare a record of the docu-

---

78a. For additional comment on *Vermont Yankee*, see Davis, Administrative Common Law and the *Vermont Yankee* Opinion, 1980 Utah L. Rev. 3 (1980); Nathanson, The Vermont Yankee Nuclear Power Opinion: A Masterpiece of Statutory Misinterpretation, 16 San Diego L. Rev. 183 (1979); Scalia, *Vermont Yankee:* The APA, the D.C. Circuit, and the Supreme Court, 1978 Sup. Ct. Rev. 345 (1978).

78b. See, e.g., Lead Indus. Ass'n v. EPA, 647 F.2d 1130, 1169-1171 (D.C. Cir. 1980), *cert. denied,* —U.S.— (198-) (industry had not shown "extremely compelling circumstances" to warrant requirement of cross-examination in adoption of environmental quality standards for lead pollution); United Steel Workers of America, AFL-CIO-CLC, v. Marshall, 647 F.2d 1189, 1203 n.6, 1227-1228 (D.C. Cir. 1980) (denying industry claim of right to cost-benefit analysis and cross-examination in rule making to adopt occupational health standard), *cert. denied,* 101 S. Ct. 3148 (1981). But see People of the State of Illinois v. United

ments compiled or received in connection with a rule making, and courts engage in careful scrutiny of the agency's decision, determining whether it is rationally supported by the documentary record in light of the adverse comments, analysis, and data submitted by outside parties. Courts have justified this practice as indispensable to their reviewing function.[78c] Claims that hard-look review is inconsistent with *Vermont Yankee* have thus far been largely unavailing, voiced in dissents.[78d] Where blocked by *Vermont Yankee* from imposing new procedural requirements [such as a prohibition on off-the-record communications] under the APA, some courts have interpreted the organic statute to impose such requirements.[78e]

Nonetheless, after *Vermont Yankee*, judges have shown increased caution in requiring agencies to provide further explanations for their decisions, or otherwise enforcing "hard-look" requirements with the utmost rigor.[78f] Ironically, some of the most emphatic invocations of *Vermont Yankee* have come from "activist" judges, such as J. Skelly Wright of the District of Columbia Circuit, in opinions denying industry requests for procedural protection against regulatory impositions.[78g]

Page 524. Add the following to footnote 83:

For further discussion of judicial review of rule making, two important articles are recommended: DeLong, Informal Rulemaking and the Inte-

---

States, 666 F.2d 1066 (7th Cir. 1981) ("extremely compelling circumstances" established, requiring opportunity for cross-examination of supplementary documents).

78c. See, e.g., Cotter v. Harris, 642 F.2d 700 (3d Cir. 1981); PPG Industries v. Costle, 630 F.2d 462 (6th Cir. 1980); Public Service Comm'n of New York v. FERC, 589 F.2d 542 (D.C. Cir. 1978). See also cases cited p. 47, supra. For defense of this practice see Rodgers, A Hard Look at *Vermont Yankee:* Environmental Law Under Close Scrutiny, 67 Geo. L.J. 699 (1979).

78d. Sholly v. NRC, 651 F.2d 792 (D.C. Cir. 1981) (Tamm, MacKinnon, Robb, and Wilkey, J.J., dissenting from denial of rehearing en banc), *cert. granted*, 101 S. Ct. 3004 (1981); Public Systems v. FERC, 606 F.2d 973, 983, 986 (Robb, J., dissenting).

78e. See Sholly v. NRC, 651 F.2d 792 (D.C. Cir. 1981) (en banc) *cert. granted*, 101 S. Ct. 3004 (1981) (hearing required for modification of operating license); United States Lines, Inc. v. FMC, 584 F.2d 519 (D.C. Cir. 1978) (ban on off-the-record communications in informal rule making).

78f. See Las Cruces TV Cable v. FCC, 645 F.2d 1041 (D.C. Cir. 1981) (refusing to overturn FCC's choice of alternative refund procedures); Energy Consumers & Producers Ass'n Inc. v. DOE, 632 F.2d 129 (Temp. Emer. Ct. App. 1980), *cert. denied*, 101 S. Ct. 102 (1980) (rejecting "substantial impact" test for determining whether notice and comment procedures required for assertedly "interpretive" rules); Kenworth Trucks of Philadelphia, Inc. v. NLRB, 580 F.2d 55 (3d Cir. 1978) (rejecting former Third Circuit rule that board must itself give reasons for decision rather than merely adopting those of ALJ).

78g. See United Steelworkers of America, AFL-CIO-CLC, v. Marshall, 647 F.2d 1189, 1203 n.6, 1227-1228 (D.C. Cir. 1980) (Skelly Wright, C.J.), *cert. denied*, 101 S. Ct. 3148 (1981); Lead Industries Ass'n v. EPA, 647 F.2d 1130, 1169-1171 (D.C. Cir.) (Skelly Wright, C.J.), *cert. denied*, 449 U.S. 1042 (1980); Ass'n of Nat'l Advertisers v. FTC, 617 F.2d 611, 622 (D.C. Cir. 1979) (Skelly Wright, C.J., concurring).

gration of Law and Policy, 65 Va. L. Rev. 257 (1979); Diver, Policymaking Paradigms in Administrative Law, 95 Harv. L. Rev. 393 (1981).

C. THE SCOPE OF THE RIGHT TO DECISION ON THE RECORD

Page 539. Add the following case after line 2:

Note on Seacoast Anti-Pollution League v. Costle

Seacoast Anti-Pollution League v. Costle, 572 F.2d 872 (1st Cir.), *cert. denied*, 439 U.S. 824 (1978), set aside the EPA's efforts to devise innovative ways of dealing with complex technical issues while promoting expedition of the administrative process.

Public Service Company of New Hampshire (PSCO) applied for a permit under the Federal Water Pollution Control Act to make thermal discharges from its Seabrook nuclear plant, which used ocean water for cooling. Following an adjudicatory hearing, the regional EPA administrator denied the permit, finding that PSCO had failed to establish that the discharge would not harm local marine life. PSCO appealed the decision to the EPA administrator, who assembled an in-house panel of EPA experts to assist him in evaluating the record. On advice of the panel, the administrator determined that PSCO had established an absence of harm, with the one exception of "back-flushing" operations (in which the flow of cooling water is periodically reversed to clear obstructions to the intake pipe). The administrator allowed PSCO to submit supplementary information on back-flushing effects in documentary form. He provided that the hearing would be reopened to address the back-flushing effects only if the party demanding a hearing showed that (1) there was a material disputed issue of fact; (2) that the issue could be resolved by available and specifically identified evidence; (3) that such evidence would be sufficient to resolve the factual issue in the manner sought by the demanding party; and (4) that favorable resolution of the factual issue would justify the ultimate ruling sought by the demanding party. The administrator found that environmental groups, which sought to reopen the hearing in order to deal with the back-flushing issue and PSCO's documentary submission, had failed to satisfy this threshold requirement. Relying on the advice of his panel, which found that PSCO's submission was deficient in certain respects but that such deficiencies were not material because the scientific literature provided necessary background information on such matters as species' thermal tolerances, the administrator granted the permit.

After holding that the proceeding was formal adjudication subject to APA §§554 and 556-7,[113a] the court found that the administrator had

113a. This aspect of the administrator's ruling is discussed supra, p. 75.

erred in allowing PSCO to submit additional information in documentary form. Although the APA did not prohibit such a procedure because this was a case of initial licensing subject to §556(d), the court found that it violated the "public hearing" requirement of the organic act. But such error would not be material unless there was a need for cross-examination under §556(d). Because the administrator's threshold hearing requirements were directed not to the question whether cross examination was required under §556(d), but whether any hearing should be held, the court remanded for a determination by the EPA of the desirability of cross-examination.

It also found that the administrator's reliance upon the panel's views to supplement PSCO's inadequate submission on back-flushing violated the requirement in §556(e) of decision based exclusively on the record generated below. In the court's view, the panel had not merely evaluated the record but had added to it by drawing upon the relevant literature, supplementing PSCO's submission. In such cases, the court suggested, the administrator would have to present the panel for cross-examination by the parties.

On remand, the administrator reopened the adjudicatory hearings to allow submission of new evidence by the parties and cross-examination, including cross-examination of the panel that had advised him. The administrator again decided that the permit should be issued, and this time the court upheld his decision. 597 F.2d 306 (1st Cir. 1979). Professor Scalia cites *Seacoast* (though not a D.C. Circuit decision) as an example of the sort of excessive judicial insistence on procedural formality at which *Vermont Yankee* was properly aimed. See Scalia, The APA, the D.C. Circuit, and the Supreme Court, 1978 Sup. Ct. Rev. 345, 371-372 (1978).

Page 539. Add the following to the end of footnote 113:

"Official notice" is directly relevant when a proceeding is taking place "on a record." Where informal rule making is at issue, the requirements imposed upon the agency, if any, are less severe. This may in part reflect rule making's concern with "legislative" rather than "adjudicative" facts. Or, it may reflect rule making's likely greater concern with predicting future events. Sometimes, of course, rule making can affect parties as immediately and seriously as any adjudication. In FCC v. National Citizens Committee for Broadcasting, 436 U.S. 775 (1978), the Supreme Court considered the FCC's rules prohibiting cross-ownership—common ownership of a newspaper and television station in the same community. The FCC had ordered sixteen such "egregious" combinations broken up. The D.C. Circuit Court of Appeals held that it was arbitrary not to order *more* such divestitures; the Supreme Court, in upholding the FCC on this point (and reversing the court of appeals) wrote, to "the extent that factual determinations were involved in the Commission's decision to 'grandfather' most existing combinations, they were primarily of a judgmental or predictive nature—e.g., whether a divestiture requirement would result in trading of stations with out-of-town owners; whether new owners would perform as well as existing crossowners, either in the short run or in the long run; whether losses to existing owners would result from forced sales; whether such losses would discourage future investment in quality programming; and whether new owners would have sufficient working capital to finance local programming. In such circumstances complete factual support in the record for the Commission's judgment or prediction is not possible or required; 'a forecast of the direction in which future public interest lies necessarily involves deductions based on the expert knowledge of the agency,' FPC v. Transcontinental Gas Pipe Line Corp., 365 U.S. 1, 29 (1961)."

Page 554. Add the following Note after line 17:

Note on Sierra Club v. Costle and the Problem of White House and Congressional Off-the-Record Communications in Notice and Comment Rule Making

President Reagan's Executive Order 12291, summarized at pp. 3-5 supra, is simply the most recent expression of presidential efforts to review and curb agency adoption of regulations that may threaten excessive burdens on industry and the economy. Environmentalists, unions, and consumer advocates have charged that White House and OMB review of regulations involves off-the-record "pressures" to relax regulatory stringency. They also fear that such review becomes a covert, "backdoor" conduit for submission by industry of argument, data, and analysis that are never publicly disclosed and subject to adversary testing. See the excerpt by Morrison, Casebook at p. 157.

Some of the legal issues presented by White House review of regulation were addressed in Sierra Club v. Costle, 657 F.2d 298 (D.C. Cir. 1981). The EPA adopted emission control requirements for new coal-fired electric power plants that favored high-sulfur eastern coal in comparison to low-sulfur western coal. The procedures followed by the EPA consisted of "paper hearing" procedures mandated by §307(d) of the Clean Air Act, adopted in 1977. The procedures, based in large part on the analysis and recommendations in Pederson, Formal Records and Informal Rulemaking, 85 Yale L.J. 38 (1975), require the EPA to maintain a public docket file of all documents relevant to the rule making.[130a]

130a. Section 307(d) requires the public docket file to include "[a]ll data, information and documents . . . on which [a] proposed rule relies," "all written comments and documentary information on the proposed rule received from any person for inclusion in the docket during the comment period," all written materials submitted by the EPA to the OMB for interagency review of proposed and final rules, and "all written comments thereon by other agencies."

The Environmental Defense Fund complained that extensive written and oral comments were submitted to the EPA after the close of the stated period for comment on the EPA's proposed standards, and claimed that the standards that ultimately emerged were the result of an "ex parte blitz" by eastern coal interests, senators, and White House officials.

The EPA accepted all of the nearly 300 written submissions received after the comment period and placed them in the public docket of the rule-making proceeding, but declined to reopen the comment period. The court held that this action was proper:

> Although no express authority to admit post-comment documents exists, the statute does provide that: "All documents which become available after the proposed rule has been published and which the Administrator determines are of central relevance to the rulemaking shall be placed in the docket as soon as possible after their availability.[130b] . . ."
>
> . . . Apparently it allows EPA not only to put documents into the record after the comment period is over, but also to define which documents are "of central relevance" so as to require that they be placed in the docket. . . . EPA thus has authority to place post-comment documents into the docket, but it need not do so in all instances. . . .
>
> EPA of course could have extended, or reopened, the comment period after January 15 in order formally to accommodate the flood of new documents; it has done so in other cases. But under the circumstances of this case, we do not find that it was necessary for EPA to reopen the formal comment period. In the first place, the comment period lasted over four months. . . .
>
> The case before us, moreover, does not present an instance where documents vital to EPA's support for its rule were submitted so late as to preclude any effective public comment. . . .

The court concluded that no material prejudice was shown to the EDF, which had had time to meet material documentary submissions with written rebuttal before the EPA acted.

The EDF also complained of nine off-the-record, post-comment-period meetings that involved high administration officials and, in two cases, Senator Byrd of West Virginia, Senate Majority Leader and a strong defender of eastern coal interests. Seven of the meetings were summarized in memorandum placed in the public docket file at the EPA. The failure to prepare and docket a summary of one of the remaining meetings was found by the court to be an oversight that did not prejudice the EDF. The other remaining meeting involved the president.

The court found that §307(d) did not prohibit such off-the-record meetings, and that *Vermont Yankee* precluded the court from imposing its own rule to that effect.

130b. 42 U.S.C. §7607(d)(4)(B)(i).

Under our system of government, the very legitimacy of general policymaking performed by unelected administrators depends in no small part upon the openness, accessibility, and amenability of these officials to the needs and ideas of the public from whom their ultimate authority derives, and upon whom their commands must fall. As judges we are insulated from these pressures because of the nature of the judicial process in which we participate; but we must refrain from the easy temptation to look askance at all face-to-face lobbying efforts, regardless of the forum in which they occur, merely because we see them as inappropriate in the judicial context.[130c] Furthermore, the importance to effective regulation of continuing contact with a regulated industry, other affected groups, and the public cannot be underestimated. Informal contacts may enable the agency to win needed support for its program, reduce future enforcement requirements by helping those regulated to anticipate and shape their plans for the future, and spur the provision of information which the agency needs. The possibility of course exists that in permitting ex parte communications with rulemakers we create the danger of "one administrative record for the public and this court and another for the Commission." [130d] Under the Clean Air Act procedures, however, "[t]he promulgated rule may not be based (in part or whole) on any information or data which has not been placed in the docket. . . ."[130e] Thus EPA must justify its rulemaking solely on the basis of the record it compiles and makes public.

Regardless of this court's views on the need to restrict all post-comment contacts in the informal rulemaking context, however, it is clear to us that Congress has decided not to do so. . . .

The court noted that Congress, in enacting the Sunshine Act, declined to extend to §553 notice and comment rule making the ban on ex parte communications it imposed on formal proceedings subject to §556-7.

Lacking a statutory basis for its position, EDF would have us extend our decision in Home Box Office, Inc. v. FCC to cover all meetings with individuals outside EPA during the post-comment period. Later decisions of this court, however, have declined to apply *Home Box Office* to informal rulemaking of the general policymaking sort involved here,[130f] and there is no precedent for applying it to the procedures found in the Clean Air Act Amendments of 1977.

130c. See Remarks of Carl McGowan (Chief Judge, U.S. Court of Appeals, D.C. Circuit), Ass'n of Amer. Law Schools, Section on Admin. Law (San Antonio, Texas, Jan. 4, 1981): "I think it likely that ambivalence will continue to pervade the ex parte contact problem until we face up to the question of whether legislation by informal rulemaking under delegated authority is, in terms of process, to be assimilated to lawmaking by the Congress itself, or to the adversary trial carried on in the sanitized and insulated atmosphere of the courthouse. Anyone with experience of both knows that a courtroom differs markedly in style and tone from a legislative chamber. The customs, the traditions, the mores, if you please, of the processes of persuasion, are emphatically not the same. What is acceptable in the one is alien to the other." See generally Ex Parte Communication During Informal Rulemaking, 14 Colum. J. L. & Soc. Prob. 269, 275 (1979).

130d. Home Box Office, Inc. v. FCC, 567 F.2d 9, 54 (D.C. Cir.), *cert. denied*, 434 U.S. 829, 98 S. Ct. 111, 54 L. Ed. 2d 89 (1977).

130e. 42 U.S.C. §7607(d)(6)(C).

130f. See [*Action for Children's Television*].

The court, however, held that it was a "fair inference" from §307(d)(4)(B)(i) of the act, requiring all documents of "central relevance" to the rule making be included in the public docket, that summaries of comparably important oral communications be prepared and included in the docket.

> This is so because unless *oral* communications of central relevance to the rulemaking are also docketed in some fashion or other, information central to the justification of the rule could be obtained without ever appearing on the docket, simply by communicating it by voice rather than by pen, thereby frustrating the command of section 307 that the final rule not be "based (in part or whole) on any information or data which has not been placed in the docket. . . ."
>
> EDF is understandably wary of a rule which permits the agency to decide for itself when oral communications are of such central relevance that a docket entry for them is required. Yet the statute itself vests EPA with discretion to decide whether "documents" are of central relevance and therefore must be placed in the docket; surely EPA can be given no less discretion in docketing oral communications, concerning which the statute has no explicit requirements whatsoever. . . . A judicially imposed blanket requirement that all post-comment period oral communications be docketed would, . . . contravene our limited powers of review,[130g] would stifle desirable experimentation in the area by Congress and the agencies, and is unnecessary for achieving the goal of an established, procedure-defined docket, *viz.*, to enable reviewing courts to fully evaluate the stated justification given by the agency for its final rule.

The court then considered whether in the particular circumstances of this case [a] summary of the meeting involving the president should be prepared and docketed:

> The court recognizes the basic need of the President and his White House staff to monitor the consistency of executive agency regulations with Administration policy. He and his White House advisers surely must be briefed fully and frequently about rules in the making, and their contributions to policy-making considered. The executive power under our Constitution, after all, is not shared—it rests exclusively with the President. . . . To ensure the President's control and supervision over the Executive Branch, the Constitution—and its judicial gloss—vests him with the powers of appointment and removal, the power to demand written opinions from executive officers, and the right to invoke executive privilege to protect consultative privacy. . . .
>
> [T]he desirability of such control is demonstrable from the practical realities of administrative rulemaking. Regulations such as those involved here demand a careful weighing of cost, environmental, and energy considerations. They also have broad implications for national economic policy. Our form of government simply could not function effectively or rationally if key executive policymakers were isolated from each other and from the Chief Executive.

130g. [Referring to *Vermont Yankee.*]

Single mission agencies do not always have the answers to complex regulatory problems. An overworked administrator exposed on a 24-hour basis to a dedicated but zealous staff needs to know the arguments and ideas of policymakers in other agencies as well as in the White House.

... We recognize, however, that there may be instances where the docketing of conversations between the President or his staff and other Executive Branch officers or rulemakers may be necessary to ensure due process. This may be true, for example, where such conversations directly concern the outcome of adjudications or quasi-adjudicatory proceedings; there is no inherent executive power to control the rights of individuals in such settings. Docketing may also be necessary in some circumstances where a statute like this one *specifically requires* that essential "information or data" upon which a rule is based be docketed. But in the absence of any further Congressional requirements, we hold that it was not unlawful in this case for EPA not to docket a face-to-face policy session involving the President and EPA officials during the post-comment period, since EPA makes no effort to base the rule on any "information or data" arising from that meeting. Where the President himself is directly involved in oral communications with Executive Branch officials, Article II considerations—combined with the strictures of *Vermont Yankee*—require that courts tread with extraordinary caution in mandating disclosure beyond that already required by statute.

Of course, it is always possible that undisclosed Presidential prodding may direct an outcome that *is* factually based on the record, but different from the outcome that would have obtained in the absence of Presidential involvement. In such a case, it would be true that the political process did affect the outcome in a way the courts could not police. But we do not believe that Congress intended that the courts convert informal rulemaking into a rarified technocratic process, unaffected by political considerations or the presence of Presidential power.

The court also rejected the EDF's claims that the meetings with Senator Byrd represented improper congressional pressure, distinguishing D.C. Federation of Civic Associations v. Volpe, 459 F.2d 1231 (D.C. Cir. 1971), *cert. denied*, 405 U.S. 1030 (1972), which set aside the Transportation Department's approval of a bridge across a scenic area of the Potomac River because a powerful member of Congress threatened to withhold funding for the D.C. subway system unless the bridge was built. The court noted that protection of eastern coal producers was, given the legislative background of the Clean Air Act, a statutorily legitimate consideration, unlike the subway funding in *D.C. Federation.*

In EDF v. Blum, 458 F. Supp. 650 (1978), off-the-record communications led the court to set aside the EPA's grant, through notice and comment rule making, of permission to use the pesticide ferriamicide to deal with fire ants. While the court found that the EDF had an opportunity to discover and rebut some of the off-the-record communications submitted after close of the public comment period by those favoring use of the pesticide, several such communications fell outside the "harmless error" category because they were made just before the EPA's decision and had a material impact upon it.[130h]

D. THE INTERACTION BETWEEN PROCEDURAL REQUIREMENTS AND REGULATORY POLICIES

Page 567. Add the following after line 28:

A recent estimate puts the cost for the research and development of a new drug at $70 million. It takes an average of ten years for a new drug to proceed through animal testing, clinical testing, and the FDA approval procedure. N.Y. Times, May 17, 1981, at 22, col. 4.

Page 568. Add new footnote 145a after line 2:

145a. The director of the FDA's Bureau of Drugs writes, "For nearly two decades we have seen a steady influx of new molecular entities into American medicine at a rate of 10-23 per year, more than half of which are important or modest therapeutic gains. The rate of medical advances is perhaps not as great as in the 1950s, but that is due at least in part to the success in that remarkable decade of applying new scientific techniques to what was then virgin territory. . . . No great flowering of productivity can be expected to sustain itself indefinitely, nor should any enterprise be viewed as failing simply because it is in a more mature growth phase. . . ." Crout, The Drug Regulatory System: Reflections and Predictions, March 1981 Food Drug Cosm. L.J. 106, 114.

Page 568. Add the following after line 29:

(7) Why has the FDA used procedures of so summary a nature as that described in the text? The FDA, under the "efficacy" test, had to deal with an estimated 3800 drugs and 15,000 drug "claims." The full New Drug Application procedure is highly complex. Its administrator describes it as "one of the more complex managerial operations in government, with its

130h. For discussion of the issues raised by these decisions, which will be a source of continuing controversy in the implementation of Executive Order 12291, see Bruff, Presidential Power and Administrative Rulemaking, 88 Yale L.J. 451 (1979); Nathanson, Report to the Select Committee on Ex Parte Communications in Informal Rulemaking Proceedings, 30 Ad. L. Rev. 377 (1978); Gellhorn & Robinson, Rulemaking "Due Process": An Inconclusive Dialogue, 48 U. Chi. L. Rev. 201 (1981); Preston, A Right of Rebuttal in Informal Rulemaking: May Courts Impose Procedures to Ensure Rebuttal of Ex Parte Communications and Information Derived from Agency Files After *Vermont Yankee*?, 32 Ad. L. Rev. 621 (1980). Verkuil, Jawboning Administrative Agencies: Ex Parte Contacts by the White House, 80 Colum. L. Rev. 943 (1980); Note, Due Process and Ex Parte Contacts in Informal Rulemaking, 89 Yale L.J., 94 (1979); Note, Ex Parte Communications During Informal Rulemaking, 14 Colum. J.L. & Soc. Prob. 269 (1979).

annual load of some 1,000 new INDs [Investigatorial New Drug re-quests], 100-200 original NDAs, 4,000 supplements, tens of thousands of amendments, and 35-45 advisory committee meetings. Add to this the fact that many applications require a plant inspection, a GLP (Good Laboratory Practice) or clinical investigator inspection, and validation of the analytical methods by our laboratories. Recall that the scientific staff conducting these reviews is the same group of people that handles reviews of DESI drugs and of the scientific aspects of OTC monographs. This staff also handles one of the largest loads of Freedom of Information requests in the government, assists in the review of regulations, and answers the bulk of the mail. No wonder that keeping it all straight is an abiding interest of Bureau managers." Crout, The Drug Regulatory System: Reflections and Predictions, March 1981 Food Drug Cosm. L.J. 106, 108.

Page 591. Following line 3, add:

The results of deregulation through the beginning of 1980 continued to support its proponents' predictions. Cross-country discount fares were lower in absolute terms than the lowest available fares in 1974. The fare level as a whole rose between 1976 and 1980—by 22 percent, but the Consumer Price Index in the same period rose by over 30 percent and thus real airline prices declined. In fact, since fuel and other typical airline costs rose by much more than the CPI—by 53 percent—the decline in one real airfare price level is remarkable. In general, service expanded, airlines on average filled more seats in each plane, and airline profits rose. See generally Breyer & Stein, Airline Deregulation: The Anatomy of Reform, in R. Poole, Instead of Regulation (1981); J. Meyer et al., Airline Deregulation, The Early Experience (1981); Levine, Revisionism Revised? Airline Deregulation and the Public Interest, 44 Law & Contemp. Prob. 179 (1981). At the same time, loss of service to smaller communities was not as great as feared. While the pattern of service changed in some communities, new commuter lines often replaced trunk lines, and service was sometimes expanded. See generally Havens & Heymsfeld, Small Community Air Service Under the Airline Deregulation Act of 1978, 46 J. Air Law & Commerce 641 (1981). Fares to many smaller communities (in real terms), however, have not fallen. And a few communities have undoubtedly faced declining service. See Kern County (Bakersfield) v. CAB, 633 F.2d 856 (9th Cir. 1981). But see Graham & Kaplan, Airline Deregulation Is Working, Regulation 26 (May 1982).

By early 1982, the situation was more problematic. Many new firms had entered the industry, the economy was in a serious recession, and average airline profits fell dramatically. Some airlines were threatened with bankruptcy. Cross-country fares were still very low, but very many shorter-haul fares had risen. Proponents of deregulation argued that the airline industry is cyclical and profits have always been low or nonexistent during recessions. They add that firms in other unregulated industries also face periods of low profits and threats of bankruptcy; why should airlines differ? Opponents of deregulation argue that the instability and chaos they feared will soon arrive. See Callison, Airline Deregulation—Only Partially a Hoax: The Current Status of the Airline Deregulation Movement, 45 J. Air Law & Commerce 961 (1980). But see Graham & Kaplan, Airline Deregulation Is Working, Regulation 26 (May 1982).

Page 592. Following line 34, add:

The courts have confirmed the broad authority that the act provides for deregulation and have resisted efforts to slow its pace. See, e.g., Hughes Air Corp. v. PUC, 644 F.2d 1334 (9th Cir. 1981) (state regulation of air carriers covered by the Deregulation Act is pre-empted and thus unlawful); National Small Shipments Traffic Conference v. CAB, 618 F.2d 819 (D.C. Cir. 1980); DHL Corp. v. CAB, 659 F.2d 941 (9th Cir. 1981); Nader v. CAB, 657 F.2d 453 (D.C. Cir. 1981).

Page 592. Add the following after line 38:

The airline example is often referred to as support by those who seek to deregulate the trucking industry. They argue that trucking is as competitively structured as airlines are. They add that one effect of regulation is high prices: truckers have formed rate bureaus, which in effect are price-fixing cartels that are made up of competing truckers who then propose agreed-upon rates to an ICC that lacks the ability meaningfully to supervise their reasonableness. The "deregulators" claim that regulation has also brought about high profits that have been capitalized in the form of ICC route authority or licenses. These licenses can be sold and are valuable. Deregulation, it is argued, would lead to lower prices through increased competition. See, e.g., "Federal Restraints on Competition in the Trucking Industry," Report of the Senate Committee on the Judiciary, 96th Cong., 2d Sess. (1980); see generally S. Breyer, Regulation & Its Reform (1982), ch. 12.

Congress has responded to these arguments by enacting the Motor Carrier Act of 1980, P.L. 96-296, 94 Stat. 793 (1980). This act has gone part of the way toward deregulation. The act's most important provision changes the "entry" requirements of prior law by shifting the burden of proof. Instead of the applicant having to prove that new service meets the "public convenience and necessity," the applicant now need only meet financial and safety standards; the opponent of new service must prove it is *not* consistent with the "public convenience and necessity." And, the opponent's burden of doing so is great enough to make new entry easy. The act also provides a zone of rate flexibility, within which carriers cannot be challenged as they move rates up and down. It further provides for the abolition of much antitrust immunity. Finally, it expands exemptions and removes many minor restrictions. The proponents of deregulation consider it a victory, for new entry is likely to create such pressure for competition that a return to total regulation will seem impractical. See K. Feinberg, Deregulation of the Transportation Industry, PLI No. 255 (1981).

Chapter Seven

Due Process Hearing Rights and the Positive State

B. THE EVOLUTION OF THE NEW DUE PROCESS: THE DEFINITION OF INTERESTS ENTITLED TO PROCEDURAL PROTECTION

Page 657. Add the following cases after paragraph 2:

GREENHOLTZ v. INMATES OF NEBRASKA PENAL AND CORREC-TIONAL COMPLEX

442 U.S. 1 (1979)

[Inmates of the Nebraska Penal and Correctional Complex brought a class action, claiming that denial of their parole applications by the Nebraska Board of Parole was a deprivation of liberty without due process. The challenged procedure consisted of two stages. All inmates, regardless of parole eligibility, were given an "initial parole review hearing" at least once a year. At the initial hearing, the board reviewed the inmate's file and conducted an informal interview with the inmate during which no evidence could be introduced. If the results of the initial hearing were favorable, the board would schedule a final hearing. If the decision in the initial hearing was unfavorable, parole was denied and the inmate was informed of the reasons for the denial.

At the final hearing, the inmate was permitted to present evidence, call witnesses, and be represented by private counsel. However, the inmate did not receive notice of the date and time of the final hearing until the morning of the day it took place. Prior to this notice, the inmate was informed only of the month during which the hearing would be held. If the board made a favorable decision following the final hearing, the inmate was paroled.]

MR. CHIEF JUSTICE BURGER delivered the opinion of the Court. . . .

[The district court and the court of appeals held that the parole board procedures violated due process. The court of appeals required the Board to provide each inmate eligible for parole with a "full formal hearing," including notice of the precise time of the hearing "reasonably in advance" thereof; the right (subject to security considerations) to appear and present documentary evidence (but not to call witnesses); a record; and a "full explanation" by the board of its decision.

The Court first addressed the question whether plaintiff's interest in being paroled was constitutionally protected.]

There is no constitutional or inherent right of a convicted person to be conditionally released before the expiration of a valid sentence. The natural desire of an individual to be released is indistinguishable from the initial resistance to being confined. But the conviction, with all its procedural safeguards, has extinguished that liberty right: "[G]iven a valid conviction, the criminal defendant has been constitutionally deprived of his liberty." Meachum v. Fano, 427 U.S. 215, 224, (1976). . . .

[R]espondents rely heavily on Morrisey v. Brewer. . . . They argue that the ultimate interest at stake both in a parole revocation decision and in a parole determination is conditional liberty and that since the underlying interest is the same the two situations should be accorded the same constitutional protection.

The fallacy in respondents' position is that parole *release* and parole *revocation* are quite different. There is a crucial distinction between being deprived of a liberty one has, as in parole, and being denied a conditional liberty that one desires. The parolees in *Morrissey* (and probationers in *Gagnon*) were at liberty and as such could "be gainfully employed and [were] free to be with family and friends and to form the other enduring attachments of normal life." 408 U.S., at 482, 92 S. Ct. at 2600. The inmates here, on the other hand, are confined and thus subject to all of the necessary restraints that inhere in a prison.

A second important difference between discretionary parole *release* from confinement and *termination* of parole lies in the nature of the decision that must be made in each case. As we recognized in *Morrissey*, the parole revocation determination actually requires two decisions: whether the parolee in fact acted in violation of one or more conditions of parole and whether the parolee should be recommitted either for his or society's benefit. . . . "The first step in a revocation decision thus involves a wholly retrospective factual question." . . .

The parole release decision, however, is more subtle and depends on an amalgam of elements, some of which are factual but many of which are purely subjective appraisals by the Board members based upon their experience with the difficult and sensitive task of evaluating the advisability of parole release. Unlike the revocation decision, there is no set of facts which, if shown, mandate a decision favorable to the individual. The parole determination, like a prisoner transfer decision, may be made "for a variety of reasons and often involve no more than informed predictions as to what would best serve [correctional purposes] or the safety and welfare of the inmate." Meachum v. Fano. . . . Judge Henry Friendly cogently noted that: "[T]here is a human difference between losing what one has and not getting what one wants." Friendly, Some Kind of Hearing, 123 U. Pa. L. Rev. . . .

That the state holds out the *possibility* of parole provides no more than a mere hope that the benefit will be obtained. Board of Regents v. Roth, supra, 408 U.S. 577, 92 S. Ct. at 2709. To that extent the general interest asserted here is no more substantial than the inmate's hope that he will not be transferred to another prison, a hope which is not protected by due process. . . .

Respondents' second argument is that the Nebraska statutory language itself creates a protectible expectation of parole. They rely on the section which provides in part:

> Whenever the Board of Parole considers the release of a committed offender who is eligible for release on parole, it shall order his release unless it is of the opinion that his release should be deferred because:
> (a) There is a substantial risk that he will not conform to the conditions of parole;
> (b) His release would depreciate the seriousness of his crime or promote disrespect for law;
> (c) His release would have a substantially adverse effect on institutional discipline; or
> (d) His continued correctional treatment, medical care, or vocational or other training in the facility will substantially enhance his capacity to lead a law-abiding life when released at a later date. (Neb. Rev. Stat. § 83-1,114(1) (1976).)

. . . Respondents emphasize that the structure of the provision together with the use of the word "shall" binds the Board of Parole to release an inmate unless any one of the four specifically designated reasons are found. . . .

Since respondents elected to litigate their due process claim in federal court, we are denied the benefit of the Nebraska court's interpretation of the scope of the interest, if any, its statute was intended to afford to inmates. See Bishop v. Wood, 426 U.S. 341, 345. . . . We can accept respondent's view that the expectancy of release provided in this statute is entitled to some measure of constitutional protection. However, we emphasize that this statute has unique structure and language and thus whether any other state statute provides a protectible entitlement must be decided on a case-by-case basis. We therefore turn to an examination of the statutory procedures to determine whether they provide the process that is due in these circumstances. . . .

[The Court found that Nebraska's existing procedures were constitutionally adequate, firmly rejecting the court of appeals' requirements that a formal hearing be provided to each prisoner eligible for parole, and that the board prepare a written explanation for its decision based on the evidence of record. The Court emphasized that parole decisions are essentially predictive and are based upon knowledge of the prisoner's character and history. It asserted that an automatic requirement of a formal hearing "would provide at best a negligible decrease in the risk of error."

MR. JUSTICE POWELL filed a separate opinion, concurring in part and dissenting in part, in which he argued that the existence of Nebraska's parole system, irrespective of specific statutory language, gave the inmate plaintiffs a constitutionally protected liberty interest in the opportunity to be paroled. He found the notice given by Nebraska to parole applicants constitutionally deficient. MR. JUSTICE MARSHALL, joined by MR. JUSTICE BRENNAN and MR. JUSTICE STEVENS, also dissented in part. Like Justice Powell, he would find the interest in parole constitutionally protected, regardless of the statutory details of a parole system. He found the notice given by Nebraska inadequate, and would require a written opinion based on evidence of record.]

NOTES AND QUESTIONS

1. How great is the "human difference between losing what one has and not getting what one wants"? Should the availability of due process protection turn on this difference? When should a person's eligibility for a benefit create a right to due process in deciding whether the benefit will be conferred?[56a] When eligibility criteria are quite specific, a protected "property" right in the applicant will probably be recognized. But what if the governing standards are vague or general? Does due process require that they be made more specific, thereby creating an individual entitlement? See Hornshy v. Allen, Holmes v. New York City Housing Authority, Casebook at pp. 317-319, and later decisions discussed at p. 51, supra. Should courts be readier to find that vague standards for distributing benefits create an individual entitlement in cases where such benefits are terminated than in those denying initial applications?

56a. See Griffith v. Detrich, 603 F.2d 118, *cert. denied*, 439 U.S. 551 (1979), in which the Ninth Circuit, citing *Greenholtz*, declared that applicants to San Diego County's General Relief program were entitled to due process protection because they had a "property interest" in their expectation of benefits by virtue of California statutes requiring counties to support "all incompetent, poor, indigent persons" and county regulations providing more detailed standards of eligibility.

2. Is the emphasis in *Greenholtz* on the inappropriateness of judicial procedures for parole decisions consistent with the *Roth* division of issues in due process cases into discrete inquiries into "entitlement protected" and "process due"?

VITEK v. JONES

445 U.S. 480 (1980)

MR. JUSTICE WHITE delivered the opinion of the Court, except as to Part IV-B.

The question in this case is whether the Due Process Clause of the Fourteenth Amendment entitles a prisoner convicted and incarcerated in the State of Nebraska to certain procedural protections, including notice, an adversary hearing, and provision of counsel, before he is transferred involuntarily to a state mental hospital for treatment of a mental disease or defect. . . .

III

. . . Section 83-180(1) Neb. Rev. Stats. provides that if a designated physician finds that a prisoner "suffers from a mental disease or defect" that "cannot be given proper treatment" in prison, the Director of Correctional Services may transfer a prisoner to a mental hospital. The District Court also found that in practice prisoners are transferred to a mental hospital only if it is determined that they suffer from a mental disease or defect that cannot adequately be treated within the Penal Complex. This "objective expectation, firmly fixed in state law and official Penal Complex practice," that a prisoner would not be transferred unless he suffered from a mental disease or defect that could not be adequately treated in the prison, gave Jones a liberty interest that entitled him to the benefits of appropriate procedures in connection with determining the conditions that warranted his transfer to a mental hospital. Under our cases, this conclusion of the District Court is unexceptionable.

Appellants maintain that any state-created liberty interest that Jones had was completely satisfied once a physician or psychologist designated by the director made the findings required by §83-180(1) and that Jones was not entitled to any procedural protections.[56b] But if the State grants a prisoner a right or expectation that adverse action will not be taken against him except upon the occurrence of specified behavior, "the deter-

---

[56b] A majority of the justices rejected an identical position in Arnett v. Kennedy, 416 U.S. 134. . . .

mination of whether such behavior has occurred becomes critical, and the minimum requirements of procedural process appropriate for the circumstances must be observed." Wolff v. McDonnell, 418 U.S., at 558, 94 S. Ct., at 2976. These minimum requirements being a matter of federal law, they are not diminished by the fact that the State may have specified its own procedures that it may deem adequate for determining the preconditions to adverse official action. . . .

B

The District Court was also correct in holding that independently of §83-180(1), the transfer of a prisoner from a prison to a mental hospital must be accompanied by appropriate procedural protections. The issue is whether after a conviction for robbery, Jones retained a residuum of liberty that would be infringed by a transfer to a mental hospital without complying with minimum requirements of due process.

We have recognized that for the ordinary citizen, commitment to a mental hospital produces "a massive curtailment of liberty," Humphrey v. Cady, 405 U.S. 504, 509. . . . The loss of liberty produced by an involuntary commitment is more than a loss of freedom from confinement. It is indisputable that commitment to a mental hospital "can engender adverse social consequences to the individual" and that "[w]hether we label this phenomena 'stigma' or choose to call it something else . . . we recognize that it can occur and that it can have a very significant impact on the individual." Addington v. Texas, (441 U.S. 418, 425.) Also, "[a]mong the historic liberties" protected by the Due Process Clause is the "right to be free from, and to obtain judicial relief for, unjustified intrusions on personal security." Ingraham v. Wright. . . . Compelled treatment in the form of mandatory behavior modification programs, to which the District Court found Jones was exposed in this case, was a proper factor to be weighed by the District Court. . . .

Were an ordinary citizen to be subjected involuntarily to these consequences, it is undeniable that protected liberty interests would be unconstitutionally infringed absent compliance with the procedures required by the Due Process Clause. We conclude that a convicted felon also is entitled to the benefit of procedures appropriate in the circumstances. . . .

Appellants maintain that the transfer of a prisoner to a mental hospital is within the range of confinement justified by imposition of a prison sentence, at least after certification by a qualified person that a prisoner suffers from a mental disease or defect. We cannot agree. . . . Such consequences visited on the prisoner are qualitatively different from the punishment characteristically suffered by a person convicted of crime. . . .

IV

The District Court held that to afford sufficient protection to the liberty interest it had identified, the State was required to observe the following minimum procedures before transferring a prisoner to a mental hospital:

A. Written notice to the prisoner that a transfer to a mental hospital is being considered;

B. A hearing, sufficiently after the notice to permit the prisoner to prepare, at which disclosure to the prisoner is made of the evidence being relied upon for the transfer and at which an opportunity to be heard in person and to present documentary evidence is given;

C. An opportunity at the hearing to present testimony of witnesses by the defense and to confront and cross-examine witnesses called by the state, except upon a finding, not arbitrarily made, of good cause for not permitting such presentation, confrontation, or cross-examination;

D. An independent decisionmaker;

E. A written statement by the fact-finder as to the evidence relied on and the reasons for transferring the inmate;

F. Availability of legal counsel, furnished by the state, if the inmate is financially unable to furnish his own; and

G. Effective and timely notice of all the foregoing rights.

We recognize that the inquiry involved in determining whether or not to transfer an inmate to a mental hospital for treatment involves a question that is essentially medical. . . . The medical nature of the inquiry, however, does not justify dispensing with due process requirements. It is precisely "the subtleties and nuances of psychiatric diagnoses" that justify the requirement of adversary hearings. Addington v. Texas, 441 U.S., at 430. . . .

In view of the nature of the determinations that must accompany the transfer to a mental hospital, we think each of the elements of the hearing specified by the District Court was appropriate. The interests of the State in avoiding disruption was recognized by limiting in appropriate circumstances the prisoner's right to call witnesses, to confront and cross examine. The District Court also avoided unnecessary intrusion into either medical or correctional judgments by providing that the independent decisionmaker conducting the transfer hearing need not come from outside the prison or hospital administration. . . .

B[56c]

The District Court did go beyond the requirements imposed by prior cases by holding that counsel must be made available to inmates facing transfer hearings if they are financially unable to furnish their own. We

56c. This part is joined only by MR. JUSTICE BRENNAN, MR. JUSTICE MARSHALL, and MR. JUSTICE STEVENS.

have not required the automatic appointment of counsel for indigent prisoners facing other deprivations of liberty, but we have recognized that prisoners who are illiterate and uneducated have a greater need for assistance in exercising their rights. . . . A prisoner thought to be suffering from a mental disease or defect requiring involuntary treatment probably has an even greater need for legal assistance, for such a prisoner is more likely to be unable to understand or exercise his rights. In these circumstances, it is appropriate that counsel be provided to indigent prisoners whom the State seeks to treat as mentally ill.

V

Because Mr. Justice Powell, while believing that Jones was entitled to competent help at the hearing, would not require the State to furnish a licensed attorney to aid him, the judgment below is affirmed as modified to conform with the separate opinion filed by Mr. Justice Powell.

So ordered.

MR. JUSTICE POWELL, concurring in part.

I join the opinion of the Court except for Part IV-B. . . .

The essence of procedural due process is a fair hearing. I do not think that the fairness of an informal hearing designed to determine a medical issue requires participation by lawyers. Due process merely requires that the State provide an inmate with qualified and independent assistance. Such assistance may be provided by a licensed psychiatrist or other mental health professional. Indeed, in view of the nature of the issue involved in the transfer hearing, a person possessing such professional qualifications normally would be preferred. . . . I would not exclude, however, the possibility that the required assistance may be rendered by competent laymen in some cases. The essential requirements are that the person provided by the State be competent and independent, and that he be free to act solely in the inmate's best interest.

[JUSTICES STEWART, BURGER, REHNQUIST, and BLACKMUN dissented on the ground that the case was moot.]

QUESTIONS

Can *Vitek* be reconciled with *Meachum*? Is the difference between transfer to a maximum security prison and transfer to a state mental hospital one of constitutional significance? Do you suspect that the court in *Vitek* was swayed by the "behavior modification" programs to which Nebraska subjected its mental patients, or does the case signify a more fundamental doctrinal shift? If the latter, does the Court give any indications of new criteria for the identification of liberty interests?

Logan v. Zimmerman Brush Co., 102 S. Ct. 1148 (1982), held that a state administrative agency may in some circumstances be constitutionally required to redress violations of a regulatory statute. An Illinois statute prohibiting discrimination against the handicapped in employment required the Illinois Fair Employment Practices Commission to hold a fact-finding conference on complaints of discrimination within 120 days. Upon a finding of "substantial evidence" of illegal conduct, the commission was required to eliminate the violation by informal negotiation or institute formal enforcement proceedings. Logan, a handicapped worker who had been discharged, filed a complaint with the commission. Through apparent inadvertence, the commission failed to schedule a hearing on the complaint within the 120-day period. The Illinois Supreme Court held that the failure to observe the 120-day period deprived the commission of jurisdiction to hear Logan's claim.

In an opinion by Justice Blackmun that was joined by five other justices, (Burger, Brennan, White, Marshall, and Stevens), the Court held that due process required the commission to hear Logan's claim. It found that the Illinois statutes gave Logan a "property" entitlement to have his complaint heard by the commission and to obtain a remedy if the claim were meritorious. While indicating that the state might choose not to provide such an entitlement, just as it might choose not to provide a right to welfare or continued employment, once it had done so the entitlement was protected by due process.

The Court went on to find that due process had been violated because Logan's right to an administrative hearing had been totally cut off in "a random manner" that "necessarily presents an unjustifiably high risk that meritorious claims will be terminated." The Court also held that private actions by Logan against his employer, or against responsible commission officials for negligent deprivation of his hearing right, were speculative and inadequate remedies that could not relieve the state of its obligation to provide an administrative hearing on Logan's complaint.

Six justices (Blackmun, Brennan, Marshall, and O'Connor in one opinion, Powell and Rehnquist in another) found that there was no rational basis for the commission's failure to consider claims such as Logan's within the 120-day period, and that such failure violated equal protection.

QUESTION

Does *Logan* establish a general right on the part of beneficiaries of regulatory programs to require administrative agencies to enforce regulatory controls? Shortly after the *Logan* litigation was instituted, the Illinois legislature amended the relevant statutes to give enforcement agencies apparently complete discretion in hearing and proceeding on handicapped discrimination cases. Does this amendment wipe out all due process claims to regulatory protection by the handicapped? Is the vesting of total enforcement discretion in regulatory agencies constitutional in light of decisions such as Holmes v. New York City Housing authority, Casebook at p. 318? For discussion of these and related issues, see Stewart & Sunstein, Public Programs and Private Rights, 95 Harv. L. Rev. 1293 (1982).

C. DETERMINING WHAT PROCESS IS DUE

Page 682. Add the following at the end of the page:

VITEK v. JONES

445 U.S. 480 (1980)

Review this case, supra, p. 95.

NOTES AND QUESTIONS

1. Matthews v. Eldridge is not cited anywhere in the *Vitek* opinion. Does this imply a departure from the *Eldridge* standards for determining "process due"? Note the majority's assertions that "the medical nature of the inquiry . . . does not justify dispensing with due process requirements" (this seems contrary to the arguments in *Eldridge*), and its claim that "notice is essential to afford the prisoner an opportunity to challenge the contemplated action and understand the nature of what is happening to him." Does this indicate that the Court is concerned with values distinct from the interest in accuracy emphasized in *Eldridge*?

Note in this connection Justice Stevens's dissent in Lassiter v. Department of Social Services of Durham County, N.C., 101 S. Ct. 2153 (1981), a case involving an indigent parent's right to counsel in proceedings in which a state seeks to take custody of a child on grounds of the parent's neglect. The majority treated the parent's right to custody as a liberty interest and the right to counsel as a "process due" question, appropriately decided under *Eldridge*. Justice Stevens had the following to say: "Without so stating explicitly, the Court appears to treat this case as though it merely involved the deprivation of an interest in property that is less worthy of protection than a person's liberty. The analysis employed in Mathews v. Eldridge, 424 U.S. 319, . . . in which the Court balanced the costs and benefits of different procedural mechanisms for allocating a finite quantity of material resources among competing claimants, is an appropriate method of determining what process is due in property cases. . . .

In my opinion the reasons supporting the conclusion that the Due Process Clause of the Fourteenth Amendment entitles the defendant in a criminal case to representation by counsel apply with equal force to a case of this kind. The issue is one of fundamental fairness, not of weighing the pecuniary costs against the societal benefits. Accordingly, even if the costs to the State were not relatively insignificant but rather were just as great as the costs of providing prosecutors, judges, and defense counsel to ensure the fairness of criminal proceedings, I would reach the same result in this category of cases. For the value of protecting our liberty from deprivation by the State without due process of law is priceless."

Is the *Vitek* majority in agreement with Justice Stevens's argument that there are certain important liberty interests that merit more procedural protection than the *Eldridge* calculus would yield? What might these liberty interests be?

2. If, as suggested above, the cost-benefit approach of *Eldridge* is inappropriate in certain situations, what other standards are available for determining the process due in such cases? A number of commentators have suggested that, even in those cases where the Supreme Court purports to follow *Eldridge*, its analysis is not consistent with a cost-benefit approach.[93a] To what extent is it possible to draw on the APA and on administrative law doctrines and precedent developed by the courts in reviewing regulatory decisions as a source of standards for the definition of constitutional due process in the "new property" context?[93b]

93a. See Mashaw, Conflict and Compromise between Models of Administrative Justice, 1981 Duke L. Rev. 181; Note, Due Process, Due Politics and Due Respect: Three Models of Legitimate School Government, 94 Harv. L. Rev. 1106 (1981). Both argue that, despite frequent citation of *Eldridge*, the Court has forsaken the quantitative analysis mandated in that case in favor of the application of qualitative "models" of appropriate processes. Mashaw suggests that these models may be generalized as one of "bureaucratic rationality" focusing on "error costs," one stressing the "therapeutic" and "clinical" values inherent in the relationship between service professionals and their clients, and one of "fairness" and "justice" based on the ideal of trial-type judicial proceedings.

93b. See, e.g., Mackey v. Montrym, 443 U.S. 1 (1979). *Mackey* involved a challenge to a Massachusetts statute that provided for a 90-day suspension of the driver's license of any person who refused a breathalyzer test following his arrest for drunk driving. A post-suspension hearing was available, limited to the issues of (1) whether the arresting officer had "reasonable grounds to believe" that the suspended licensee was under the influence, (2) whether the licensee had been arrested, and (3) whether he had refused a breathalyzer test. The Court held, citing *Eldridge*, that a pre-suspension hearing was unnecessary, arguing that "the predicates for a driver's suspension under the Massachusetts scheme are objective facts either within the personal knowledge of a government official or readily ascertainable by him. . . .

"The summary and automatic character of the suspension sanction available under the statute is critical to the attainment of [legitimate statutory] objectives. A pre-suspension hearing would substantially undermine the state interest in public safety by giving drivers significant incentive to refuse the breathalyzer test and demand a pre-suspension hearing as a dilatory tactic." 443 U.S. Is this an extention into the due process field of the reasoning of FPC v. Texaco and American Airlines v. CAB, Casebook at pp. 492-499, which held that an agency may properly specify its standards through objective rules applied in summary adjudication?

Page 686. Add the following case at the end of the page:

O'BANNON v. TOWN COURT NURSING CENTER

447 U.S. 773 (1980)

MR. JUSTICE STEVENS delivered the opinion of the Court. . . .

[Town Court Nursing Center was certified by HEW as eligible to care for Medicare and Medicaid patients and receive reimbursement from HEW for such care. HEW later notified Town Court that it no longer met standards of eligibility established by statute and regulation, and that it would be decertified and deprived of eligibility for reimbursement payments. Town Court and six of the Medicaid patients in the facility filed suit in federal district court to enjoin decertification. The complaint alleged that termination of the payments would require Town Court to close and would cause the individual plaintiffs to suffer both a loss of benefits and "immediate and irreparable psychological and physical harm," caused by the trauma inflicted by moving elderly patients from familiar surroundings.

The Third Circuit held that the patients had a right to an evidentiary hearing before Town Court was decertified. The court based its opinion on the language[94a] of the Medicaid statute and regulations, and on the theory that decertification of a nursing home is equivalent to a government-ordered transfer of the home's residents, which the court held would trigger due process protections under the cited provisions. The Supreme Court reversed, finding that the residents had no constitutionally protected interest in remaining in Town Court.]

Whether viewed singly or in combination, the Medicaid provisions relied upon by the Court of Appeals do not confer a right to continued residence in the home of one's choice. 42 U.S.C. §1396a(a)(23) gives

---

94a. 42 U.S.C. §1396a(a)(23) (1976 ed., Supp. II) provides, in relevant part: . . . any individual eligible for medical assistance (including drugs) may obtain such assistance from any institution, agency, community pharmacy, or person, qualified to perform the service or services required (including an organization which provides such services, or arranges for their availability, on a prepayment basis), who undertakes to provide him such services. . . . "

The same "free choice of providers" is also guaranteed by 42 CFR §431.51 (1979).

42 CFR §405.1121(k)(4) (1979) requires skilled nursing facilities that are licensed either as Medicaid or Medicare providers to establish written policies and procedures to ensure that each patient admitted to the facility "[i]s transferred or discharged only for medical reasons, or for his welfare or that of other patients, or for nonpayment of his stay (except as prohibited by titles XVIII or XIX of the Social Security Act), and is given reasonable advance notice to ensure orderly transfer or discharge. . . . "

45 CFR §305.10(a)(5) (1979) provides, in relevant part, that an ". . . opportunity for a hearing shall be granted to any applicant who requests a hearing because his or her claim for financial assistance . . . or medical assistance is denied, . . . and to any recipient who is aggrieved by any agency action resulting in suspension, reduction, discontinuance, or termination of assistance."

recipients the right to choose among a range of *qualified* providers, without government interference. By implication, it also confers an absolute right to be free from government interference with the choice to remain in a home that continues to be qualified. But it clearly does not confer a right on a recipient to enter an unqualified home and demand a hearing to certify it, nor does it confer a right on a recipient to continue to receive benefits for care in a home that has been decertified. Second, although the regulations do protect patients by limiting the circumstances under which a *home* may transfer or discharge a Medicaid recipient, they do not purport to limit the Government's right to make a transfer necessary by decertifying a facility. Finally, since decertification does not reduce or terminate a patient's financial assistance, but merely requires him to use it for care at a different facility, regulations granting recipients the right to a hearing prior to a reduction in financial benefits are irrelevant. . . .

This case does not involve the withdrawal of direct benefits. Rather, it involves the Government's attempt to confer an indirect benefit on Medicaid patients by imposing and enforcing minimum standards of care on facilities like Town Court. When enforcement of those standards requires decertification of a facility, there may be an immediate, adverse impact on some residents. But surely that impact, which is an indirect and incidental result of the Government's enforcement action, does not amount to a deprivation of any interest in life, liberty or property.

Medicaid patients who are forced to move because their nursing home has been decertified are in no different position for purposes of due process analysis than financially independent residents of a nursing home who are forced to move because the home's state license has been revoked. . . .

The simple distinction between government action that directly affects a citizen's legal rights, or imposes a direct restraint on his liberty, and action that is directed against a third party and affects the citizen only indirectly or incidentally, provides a sufficient answer to all of the cases on which the patients rely in this Court. Thus, Memphis Light, Gas & Water Division v. Craft . . . involved the direct relationship between a publicly-owned utility and its customers; the utility had provided its customers with a legal right to receive continued service as long as they paid their bills. . . .[94b]

94b. We of course need not and do not hold that a person may never have a right to a hearing before his interests may be indirectly affected by government action. Conceivably, for example, if the Government were acting against one person for the purpose of punishing or restraining another, the indirectly affected individual might have a constitutional right to some sort of hearing. But in this case the Government is enforcing its regulations against the home for the benefit of the patients as a whole and the home itself has a strong financial incentive to contest its enforcement decision; under these circumstances the parties suffering an indirect adverse effect clearly have no constitutional right to participate in the enforcement proceedings.

MR. JUSTICE BLACKMUN, concurring in the judgment. . . .

[Justice Blackmun found that the residents had a protected "property" interest in remaining at Town Court, disagreeing with the Court's view that their transfer was only an "indirect" result of decertification. However, he found that their interest was validly qualified by the decertification procedures provided by federal law. The interests of the residents, he found, would be protected by Town Court, which had every incentive to fight decertification.]

That the asserted deprivation of property extends in a nondiscriminatory fashion to some 180 patients also figures in my calculus. . . . "[W]here a rule of conduct applies to more than a few people, it is impracticable that every one should have a direct voice in its adoption. The Constitution does not require all public acts to be done in town meeting or an assembly of the whole." Bi-Metallic Co. v. Colorado, 239 U.S. 441, . . . When governmental action affects more than a few individuals, concerns beyond economy, efficiency and expedition tip the balance against finding that due process attaches. We may expect that as the sweep of governmental action broadens, so too does the power of the affected group to protect its interests outside rigid constitutionally imposed procedures. Moreover, "the case for due process protection grows stronger as the identity of the persons affected by a government choice becomes clearer; and the case becomes stronger still as the precise nature of the effect on each individual comes more determinately within the decisionmaker's purview. For when government acts in a way that singles out identifiable individuals—in a way that is likely to be premised on suppositions about specific persons—it activates the special concern about being personally *talked to* about the decision rather than simply being *dealt with.*" L. Tribe, American Constitutional Law, §10-7, pp. 503-504 (1978) (emphasis in original). I agree with this general statement and find its "flipside" informative here.

[MR. JUSTICE BRENNAN dissented; MR. JUSTICE MARSHALL did not participate.]

QUESTIONS

1. Do you find the majority's distinction between "direct" and "indirect" harm persuasive? How much difference do you think it makes to the residents of Town Court? Should the direct/indirect distinction have been used in deciding Hahn v. Gottlieb, casebook at p. 683.

2. What of Justice Blackmun's treatment of the rule-making/adjudication problem? Are the concerns that animated the *Bi-Metallic* decision present on the facts of *O'Bannon*? Why do you think the majority in *O'Bannon* declined to employ the rule-making/adjudication distinction?

Pg. 688. Add the following problem after line 4:

3. Thomas Winsett is serving a sentence of life imprisonment imposed upon his conviction for the felony murder of a Delaware state trooper in 1964. The killing aroused public outrage throughout the state. During the years since his commitment to the Delaware Correctional Center, Winsett has been a model prisoner. In 1974, Winsett applied for work-release status under a program established under a Delaware statute and Department of Corrections regulations that give the prison authorities a substantial measure of discretion.98a Evaluation of a work-release application takes place in three stages, the final one being approval or disapproval by the office of the Delaware Superintendant of Corrections.

Winsett was successful in obtaining favorable determinations at the first two levels of the application process, both of which produced strong recommendations in favor of granting work-release status. However, public opposition to work-release status for Winsett soon became evident. Before Winsett's application had reached Superintendant Raymond Anderson for final approval, Delaware State Senator Cicione, chairman of the legislature's Joint Finance Committee, sent a letter to Anderson strongly opposing work-release status for Winsett. Anderson sent Senator Cicione a reply stating that "as long as I am Superintendant of the institution, I shall never be able to entertain any requests from [Winsett] in regards to work release." Anderson subsequently denied Winsett's application.

Winsett then sued Anderson and his fellow administrators of the Department of Corrections, alleging that their actions had violated due process protections to which Winsett was entitled. Between the filing of the complaint and the trial of the suit, Winsett filed a new application for work release, which again succeeded in the first two stages of evaluation but was denied at the highest administrative level, this time by the acting commissioner of corrections, Paul Keve. Winsett's complaint was amended to reflect these events.

At trial, Anderson testified that the rejection of Winsett's first applica-

98a. The work-release program in Delaware is governed by 11 Del. C. §6533(a). That section, at the time of Winsett's initial application, provided: "The Department may adopt rules and regulations governing the employment or education of trustworthy inmates outside the institutions. . . . "

The Department's rules in effect at that time were entitled "Criteria and Procedure for Statewide Work Education Release." They provided: "I. Basic Criteria, All Institutions: (1) Within one year of release or parole eligibility date. (2) Demonstrated interest in personal improvement; progress toward increased maturity and self-understanding. This will be evaluated on basis of inmate's work habits, program participation and general adjustment. II. Basic Procedures: (1) Written application is submitted by inmate, following which it is considered by and must be approved successively by: a. Classification team b. Work/education release staff c. Superintendent. . . . "

tion had been influenced by "public pressure in general and the complaints of the State Police and certain State Senators in particular." Anderson also acknowledged that he had been aware that acting commissioner Keve had been seeking confirmation by the state legislature during the pendancy of both applications and that a decision in favor of Winsett might have jeopardized Keve's confirmation.

Keve testified that the rejection of Winsett's second application "had nothing at all to do with existing eligibility criteria" and was the result of "intense legislative pressure." Had it not been for this pressure, Keve testified, Winsett would have gone on work release. Keve added that he saw his role as one of "protecting the inmate population as a whole," whose privileges might be threatened by legislative retaliation for a decision in favor of Winsett.

Assume that the testimony of Anderson and Keve is a correct statement of the facts. What relief, if any, should Winsett obtain on the basis of his due process claim?[98b]

D. DUE PROCESS IN PARTICULAR CONTEXTS

Page 690. Add the following after line 16:

Is a statewide reduction in welfare benefits, uniformly imposed on a large class of recipients, subject to a prior hearing requirement? The lower federal courts have split on this question. Those courts that deny hearings emphasize the distinction between the "facts" involved in individual reductions and the "policy" that a state implements through across-the-board reductions, holding that due process is not appropriate in the latter context. The courts that favor hearings reject the fact/policy distinction as being too vague to be meaningful and detect factual issues in what appear at first glance to be policy decisions.[101a]

In addition to the magnitude of particular benefit levels, the *structure* of different levels of assistance supplied to different groups of recipients may also be subject to review under due process standards. In Griffin v. Harris, 571 F.2d 767 (3rd Cir. 1978), the plaintiffs, recipients of rent

98b. See Winsett v. McGinnis, 617 F.2d. 966 (3rd Cir. en banc, 1980), *cert. denied*, 101 S. Ct. 891 (1981).

101a. Courts denying hearings: Provost v. Betit, 326 F. Supp. 920 (D. Vt., 1971) (changes in Vermont welfare program affecting 4 percent of recipients); Whitfield v. King, 364 F. Supp. 1296 (M.D. Ala. 1973), *aff'd mem. sub nom.* Whitfield v. Barns, 431 U.S. 910 (1977) (change in method of calculating payments under welfare program affecting almost all recipients). Courts favoring hearings: Turner v. Walsh, 435 F. Supp. 707 (W.D. Mo. 1977), *aff'd*, 574 F.2d 456 (8th Cir. 1978) (change in calculation of benefits); Becker v. Blum 464 F. Supp. 152 (S.D. N.Y. 1978) (statute altering payment levels for medical assistance). See generally Note, Welfare, Due Process and "Brutal Need": The Requirement of a Prior Hearing in State Wide Benefit Reductions, 34 Vand. L. Rev. 173 (1981).

subsidies from HUD, challenged the benefit structure prescribed in the department's "rent supplement handbook." The handbook provided that no more than 25 percent of the tenants in any project would receive more than 60 percent of their total rent as a supplement under the program. HUD defended this rule as designed to ensure a tenant mix including tenants capable of paying a substantial portion of their rents, as well as the completely destitute families requiring more than a 60 percent supplement. The court found as a fact, however, that in the program as administered there was no discernible difference between the favored 25 percent of families receiving relatively high supplements, and the remaining 75 percent. Stating that HUD's rule amounted to distribution of benefits "on an arbitrary, irrational, *ad hoc* basis," the court invalidated the rate structure. A due process entitlement in the tenants was found on the grounds that they had been "induced" by HUD's promise of rent supplements to take apartments in the projects involved. To what extent is *Griffin* a revival or expansion of the theory of Holmes v. New York City Housing Authority, Casebook at p. 318, to the effect that *all* public benefits must be distributed in a rational manner?

Page 691. Add the following at the end of page:

The controversy over hearing rights before recoupment of overpayed social security disability benefits was resolved by the Supreme Court in Califano v. Yamasaki, 442 U.S. 682 (1979). The Court declined to reach the constitutional issue and decided that, as a matter of statutory interpretation, a prerecoupment hearing is required.

Page 698. Add the following after line 12:

b.1. *Dismissal for Constitutionally Impermissible Reasons*

In Elrod v. Burns, 427 U.S. 347 (1976), the Court held, on First Amendment grounds, that state and local governments may not dismiss "non-policy-making" officials on solely political or "patronage" grounds. The plaintiffs in *Elrod* were three process servers and a juvenile court bailiff in the employ of the Cook County, Illinois, Sheriff's Office. Branti v. Finkle, 445 U.S. 507 (1980), significantly expanded the class of "non-policymaking" officials to whom *Elrod* applies. The plaintiffs in *Branti* were two assistant public defenders for Rockland County, New York. They had been hired by a Republican public defender. Upon the appointment of a Democratic public defender by a newly Democratic legislature, the plaintiffs were dismissed, the district court found, on purely political grounds. In holding that the First and Fourteenth Amendments protected the plaintiffs from such a discharge, the majority opinion by Justice Stevens stated that "[t]he ultimate inquiry [under *Elrod*] is not whether the label 'policymaking' or 'confidential' fits a particular position; rather, the question is whether the hiring authority can demonstrate that party affiliation is an appropriate requirement for the effective performance of the public office involved." 445 U.S., at 518-519. The Court went on to hold that partisan considerations were irrelevant to the duties of an assistant public defender, and that the dismissals in *Branti* were therefore unconstitutional.

Mr. Justice Powell dissented forcefully in *Branti*, as he had in *Elrod*, stating that "with scarcely a glance at 200 years of American political tradition, the Court further limits the relevance of political affiliation to the selection and retention of public employees. Many public positions . . . now must be staffed in accordance with a constitutionalized civil service standard." 445 U.S. at 521.

QUESTIONS

1. Are *Elrod* and *Branti* correct in their elevation of a public employee's freedom of thought and political affiliation above considerations of partisan loyalty? Do the decisions represent the bias of elitist "reformers" ignorant or disdainful of the practice of majoritarian democracy?

2. Is it institutionally appropriate for the federal courts to impose the extensive restrictions on local government hiring and firing that result from *Elrod* and *Branti*? Note that in cases involving "property" entitlements in public employment, the language of state and local law is crucial, giving localities substantial control over the extent of an employee's entitlement. *Elrod* and *Branti*, in contrast, hold that the First Amendment imposes restrictions similar to those of civil service legislation without regard to the law or policy of the political unit involved. Does this mean that if all civil service legislation were repealed, the federal courts would nonetheless be empowered to review all governmental hiring and firing to ensure that decisions were made on grounds other than loyalty to a particular party or political figure?

Page 716. Add the following after line 3:

The legislation discussed in the last paragraph of page 715 of the Casebook has become law as 42 U.S.C. §§1997e et seq.

In Parrat v. Taylor, 101 S. Ct. 1908 (1981), an inmate claimed he had been denied due process through the negligent loss by state prison officials of hobby materials that the prisoner had ordered by mail. The Supreme Court, in an opinion by Justice Rehnquist, held that the state's post-deprivation claims procedure satisfied the requirements of due process and rejected the inmate's §1983 claim. The Court's opinion did not rule out the possibility that a negligent deprivation of property might support a due process claim under §1983. But it expressed concern over "federalizing" state tort law, echoing a similar concern in the Court's opinion in Paul v. Davis. It invoked this concern in holding the state's claims procedure adequate even though it did not provide the full range of remedies available under §1983 (such as punitive damages).

Chapter Eight

Organizing and Managing a Bureaucratic Agency: The FTC and Its Reform

B. PROBLEMS ARISING FROM THE COMBINATION OF CONFLICTING FUNCTIONS WITHIN AN AGENCY

Page 737. Add the following after line 29:

HERCULES INC. v. EPA

598 F.2d 91 (D.C. Cir. 1971)

TAMM, CIRCUIT JUDGE. . . .

[Petitioners challenged the EPA's regulations limiting discharges of toxaphene and endrin into rivers and other waterways. These regulations grew out of rule-making proceedings, though it is doubtful that the "rule" applied to anyone other than petitioners. One portion of the case concerned "separation of functions." The petitioners argued that there had been impermissible contacts between EPA's staff and the EPA judicial officer who promulgated the rules.

Before 1976 the EPA's internal procedural rules governing rule making barred "the Administrator or the presiding officer [from] consult[ing] with any person or party on a fact at issue." In 1976 EPA changed those rules, deleting this "ex parte" contact rule as unnecessary. Instead, the new EPA rule stated that "the administrator with such staff assistance as he deems necessary and appropriate, shall review the entire record and prepare and file a tentative decision based thereon." The agency wrote:

The promulgated standards in turn are to be based solely on that record. Cf., Administrative Procedure Act, 5 U.S.C. Section 556(e). With respect to discussions between the Administrator and Agency staff involved in the presentation of evidence at the hearing, the rule requiring separation of functions which applies in cases of adjudication, 5 U.S.C.

Section 554(b), is inapplicable to rulemaking. Hoffmann-La Roche, Inc. v. Kleindienst, 478 F.2d 1 (3rd Cir. 1973).

[At the time this new procedure was being considered, commentators in opposition cited] . . . K. Davis, Administrative Law Treatise, Section 13.00 at 453 (1970 Supp.). Davis is at the point discussing the separation of prosecutorial and decision-making functions within an administrative Agency, which is closely related to the ex parte question since the issue with respect to Agency personnel is whether the staff who presents the evidence should be precluded from discussing the regulation with the Administrator out of the presence of the objector's representatives. Although Professor Davis equivocates on what the policy should be, he leaves no doubt about the law: "The conclusion seems to be rather solid that no law requires the Commissioner [of FDA] to separate functions in rulemaking for which on-the-record hearings are required". Id. p. 443.

The rationale for not imposing separation of functions, and the attendant prohibition on communication between those responsible for developing and presenting the proposed rule or standard and the person ultimately charged with promulgation, lies with the nature of rulemaking. The development of a proposed rule or standard includes a number of policy decisions in which many program offices within the agency participate. The Administrator relies on the advice and recommendations of these offices in developing and proposing the standards. At the same time, persons within these offices may well present evidence at rulemaking hearings including information on which the proposed standard was based. It would be counterproductive to reasoned rulemaking if, at the stage of final decision and promulgation, the administrator were isolated from those within the Agency whom he normally consults on policy determinations and whose offices will be charged with implementation and enforcement of the regulations. The institutional nature of the Administrator's decision, as noted previously, is inherent in the very nature of rulemaking, and is normally absent from adjudication.

Because the law clearly does not require the prohibition on ex parte discussions contained in Section 104.16 as originally promulgated, and because nothing in the rulemaking process warrants its retention, it is deleted as proposed.

EPA conducted the proceeding now on review under the new procedural rules. Its chief judicial officer, Ms. Harriet B. Marple, was assigned to aid the Administrator in preparing his final decision. Ms. Marple was confronted with a loosely organized rulemaking record of enormous detail and staggering complexity—thousands of pages of highly technical testimony, affidavits, and studies from a variety of sources—to be considered against an uncertain scientific and legal background. The record had been closed on Oct. 12, 1976. . . . Under the deadline imposed by Section 307(a) (2), the Administrator had two months or less to issue his final standards. . . .

[Ms. Marple described her intra-agency contacts as follows: (1) consultation with the administrator, Russell Train; (2) consultation with several EPA attorneys in the Water Quality Division and other EPA attorneys working on the case, for help in locating documents in the record; (3) consultation with an EPA section chief to discuss "toxicological issues . . . raised by the record;" (4) consultation with an EPA expert to discuss "record evidence regarding species diversity"; (5) discussion with Russell Train's executive assistant, in order to explain the issues to him. Ms. Marple stated that all these consultations were "for the sole and limited purpose of properly understanding and interpreting . . . the record."] . . .

Petitioners' contention that the contacts between the judicial officer and the agency staff were improper is most troubling. Recently, this court has twice held that particular ex parte contacts between private parties and agency decisionmakers in rulemaking were improper. United States Lines, Inc. v. FMC (Euro-Pacific), 189 U.S. App. D.C. 361, 584 F.2d 519 (1978); Home Box Office, Inc. v. FCC, 185 U.S. App. D.C. at 142, 567 F.2d at 9. This Court has held that *other* ex parte contacts between private parties and agency decisionmakers in rulemaking were *not* improper. Action for Children's Television v. FCC, 183 U.S. App. D.C. 437, 564 F.2d 458 (1977). None of these cases concerned intra-agency staff contacts.

At the outset, we reject any notion that the Administrator or the judicial officer proceeded in bad faith. The contacts here in no way involved a cabal-like arrangement within the agency. To the contrary, the contacts were permissible under procedural rules adopted by EPA in 1976 after public comment and legal debate. . . .

[We also note that] the administrator and the judicial officer [Ms. Marple] did not consider or rely on any evidence presented outside the record. . . .

In *Home Box Office,* this court held that the wide-ranging *private* contacts with the FCC decisionmakers that had occurred were impermissible. . . . Petitioners contend that staff contacts offend the principles underlying the *Home Box Office* decision no less than private contacts. In their view, staff contacts deprive the reviewing court of the full and accurate administrative record, . . . foreclose the opportunity for genuine adversarial discussion among the parties, . . . and, most importantly, are inconsistent with fundamental notions of fairness implicit in due process and with the ideal of reasoned decisionmaking. . . . They stress that this proceeding was more adversarial and formal than the informal rulemaking proceeding reviewed in *Home Box Office.*

EPA responds that, in the APA, Congress expressly sanctioned staff contacts, in contrast to private contacts, because of the quasi-legislative nature of the rulemaking process and the necessities of implementation of administrative policy. 5 U.S.C. §554(d) prohibits staff contacts in adjudication; 5 U.S.C. §§553, 556 & 557[8a] do not express a similar prohibition in rulemaking.

These statutory provisions are discussed in the legislative history, which demonstrates that Congress decided that the strictures of 5 U.S.C. §554(d) should not extend to rulemaking proceedings. . . . Senate Report for the APA, S. Rep. No. 752, 79th Cong., 1st Sess. 17-18 (1945). . . . House Report for the APA, H.R. Rep. No. 1980, 79th Cong., 2d Sess. 14 (1946) U.S. Code Cong. Serv. 1946, p. 1202.[8b] . . . This legislative history has been construed consistently to allow the agency's rulemaking staff to assist agency administrators in interpreting the rulemaking record. Further, the Supreme Court's decision in *Vermont Yankee Nuclear Power Corp.* counsels restraint in imposing procedural requirements beyond the letter of the APA. . . .

For two reasons, we have determined that EPA's standards must be upheld in this particular context. . . .

First, both the adoption by EPA of its procedural rules and the issuance of the final decision preceded *Home Box Office*. . . .

Second, the administrative history under section 307(a) created a peculiar context wherein the necessity for staff contacts existed with unusual and compelling force. As we have noted, section 307(a) sets forth rigid and compressed timetables. . . . In view of the extraordinary bulk and complexity of the administrative record, a judicial officer attempting to digest the record and prepare a decision in a matter of weeks would face, at the least, great difficulty in proceeding without staff assistance. Thus, this context invokes the rule of ancient origin that expedition in protecting the public health justifies less elaborate procedure than may be required in other contexts. . . .

. . . Accordingly, we uphold EPA because the contacts only concerned assistance in understanding the record, EPA proceeded in good faith, section 554(d) is clearly inapplicable, *Home Box Office* does not apply retroactively, and the particular statutory and administrative context

8a. 5 U.S.C. §557(d) (1976) generally prohibits ex parte communications between agency decisionmaking officials and interested persons outside the agency during formal, "on-the-record" proceedings. Intra-staff contacts are clearly exempt from the strictures of this section. As both the Senate and House Reports state: "Communications solely between agency employees are excluded from the section's prohibition." S. Rep. No. 354, 94th Cong., 1st Sess. 36 (1975). . . .

8b. Further, the Attorney General, in a letter to the Senate Judiciary Committee, noted that rulemaking exempt from 5 U.S.C. §554(d) "includes a wide variety of subject matters, and within the scope of those matters it is not limited to the formulation of rules of general applicability but includes also the formulation of agency action whether of general or particular application. . . ." See S. Rep. No. 752, supra note 59, at 41.

Because the statutory language and legislative history are so unambiguous, we reject petitioners' assertion that 5 U.S.C. §554(d) applies to the decisionmaking stage of the instant proceedings merely because 5 U.S.C. §556(e) requires the decision to be on the record.

made rapid action by EPA necessary to carry out congressional mandates for the protection of public health and the environment.

Notwithstanding our decision, however, we feel compelled to record our uneasiness with one aspect of this case—the communication between Ms. Marple and EPA staff legal advocates. . . . The fact that the attorneys who represented the staff's position at the administrative hearing were later consulted by the judicial officer who prepared the final decision possibly gives rise to an appearance of unfairness, even though the consultations did not involve factual or policy issues. During congressional deliberation on the APA, the flexibility of rulemaking procedures was of concern, as the bill's sponsor indicated. . . .

"The exemption of rule making and determining applications for licenses, *from provisions of sections 5(c)* [5 U.S.C. §554(d)], 7(c), and 8(a) *may require change if, in practice, it develops that they are too broad."* . . . 92 Cong. Rec. 2159 (1946) (remarks of Sen. McCarran) (emphasis added); S. Rep. No. 752, supra, at 30; accord, id. at 5652 (remarks of Rep. Walter).

Amendatory legislation may be justified if agencies do not themselves proscribe post-hearing contacts between staff *advocates* and decisionmakers in formal rulemaking proceedings, lest there be an erosion of public trust and confidence in the administrative process. As we have discussed, until 1976, EPA banned intra-agency contacts in hearings such as these. EPA lifted this ban in 1976 in response to a peculiar situation of past failure and current necessity. Now might be a particularly propitious time for Congress or the agencies to limit or provide disclosure of post-hearing contacts between staff advocates and decision makers. . . .

Professor Davis has criticized the "APA separation of functions" provisions as being both too broad and too narrow. See 3 K. Davis, Administrative Law Treatise, ch. 18 (1980). Indeed, one might wonder at the complete exemptions for all rule making and for commissioners or agency heads. Are there not some rule-making occasions, as the *Hercules* court wonders, when agency decision makers ought to be forbidden to consult off the record, say, a staff lawyer directly involved in the case? Are there not other occasions, involving adjudication, when internal communication even with prosecutors is desirable for the agency to discuss, say, a proposed settlement? How is a commissioner to keep control of a case, to narrow its charges or to drop it where appropriate, unless he can communicate with the staff about it? Yet should he be totally free to talk to all those involved in the adjudication? The considerations are different for the hearing examiner, but should he not, at least, be able to communicate with his law clerk? What about uninvolved, expert, staff? See generally Pederson, The Decline of Separation of Functions in Regulatory Agencies, 64 U. Va. L. Rev. 991 (1978).

The Administrative Conference of the United States has recently been considering proposals for reform based on a study by Professor Michael Asimow, The Curtain Falls: Separation of Functions in the Federal Administrative Agencies, 81 Colum. L. Rev. 759 (1981). Asimow surveys current practice in the agencies; we recommend his study.

Page 741. Add the following after line 19:

As of 1953, the 294 hearing examiners were distributed broadly among five grade levels, from GS-11 to GS-15. . . . As of 1979, all 1134 ALJs were GS-15s or -16s. The accompanying elimination of promotional opportunities, along with discharge only for "cause" and mechanical systems of selection and of work assignment is, in the view of one experienced student of the subject, "a horror story of personnel management which should come to an end. It . . . prevents intelligent selection and adequate compensation of the finest judges, deters voluntary departure of the worst, and erodes incentive all along the way." Scalia, The ALJ Fiasco— A Reprise, 47 U. Chi. L. Rev. 57 (1979).

Recent legislative proposals would reform the selection process, making it easier for agencies to choose the ALJs they wish, providing fixed terms of ten years, allowing review of the quality of the ALJ's work at the expiration of the term, and making removal easier. See, e.g., S. 262, 96th Cong., 2d Sess. (1980). However, the ALJs organized politically and opposed these provisions strongly; the provisions have been dropped from current versions. Some notion of the emotions that are aroused when one begins to examine the "quality of work" is provided by an affidavit of Robert Trachtenberg, director of the Social Security Administration's Bureau of Hearings and Appeals, that was given to a House Subcommittee in 1980. He wrote that "[u]pon my appointment as Director in January 1979 I discovered the most lethargic, indifferent, unresponsive and unaccountable organization that I have ever seen in 15 years as a federal employee." In response, a different agency official wrote that Mr. Trachtenberg "grossly exaggerates and flagrantly distorts the truth in his self-serving sworn statement. He appears intoxicated by his own press releases; thereby deluding himself in believing he is the Messiah. . . ." Lubbers, Federal Administrative Law Judges: A Focus on Our Invisible Judiciary, 33 Ad. L. Rev. 108 (1981). See also Mans, Selecting the "Hidden Judiciary," 63 Judicature 60, 131 (1976).

Page 741. Add the following at the end of footnote 21:

For recent proposals to revive this notion and for variations on the "administrative court" idea, see Marquardt & Wheat, The Developing Concept of an Administrative Court, 33 Ad. L. Rev. 301 (1981); The Central Penal System: A New Framework for the Use of Administrative Law Judges, 65 Judicature 233 (1981).

Page 742. Add the following after line 7:

The controversy over the title of Social Security examiners ended in 1978 when Congress enacted a law replacing the words "hearing examiner" with the words "administrative law judge" wherever they appeared in the United States Code. P.L. 95-251, 92 Stat. 183.

The current number of ALJs and their assignment is given by Lubbers, as follows. (Lubbers, Federal Administrative Law Judges: A Focus on Our Invisible Judiciary, 33 Ad. L. Rev. 108 (1981)):

NUMBER OF ADMINISTRATIVE LAW
JUDGES SERVING, BY AGENCY

	Number of ALJs	
Agency or Department	Jan. 1979[a]	June 1980[b]
Agriculture, Department of	5	5
Alcohol, Tobacco and Firearms, Bureau of (Dept. of the Treasury)	1	1
Civil Aeronautics Board	17	11
Commodity Futures Trading Commission	4	4
Consumer Product Safety Commission	1	0[c]
Drug Enforcement Administration (Dept. of Justice)	1	1
Environmental Protection Agency	6	7
Federal Communications Commission	14	13
Federal Energy Regulatory Commission	23	22
Federal Labor Relations Authority	4	10[d]
Federal Maritime Commission	7	7
Federal Mine Safety and Health Review Commission	12	18
Federal Trade Commission	12	12
Food and Drug Administration (Dept. of H.E.W.)	1	1
Housing and Urban Development, Department of	1	1
Interior, Department of the	8	13[e]
Interstate Commerce Commission	61	55
Labor, Department of	49	66
Maritime Administration (Dept. of Commerce)	3	3
Merit Systems Protection Board	1	1[f]
National Labor Relations Board	98	115
National Transportation Safety Board	6	6
Nuclear Regulatory Commission	1	1
Occupational Safety and Health Review Commission	47	48
Postal Rate Commission	0	0[g]
Securities and Exchange Commission	8	7

Agency or Department	Number of ALJs	
	Jan. 1979[a]	June 1980[b]
Social Security Administration		
(Dept. of H.E.W.)	660	698
U.S. Coast Guard (Dept. of Transportation)	16	16
U.S. International Trade Commission	2	2
U.S. Postal Service	2	2
TOTAL	1070	1146

[a]Data derived from "Management Improvements in the Administrative Law Process: Much Remains to be Done," Report by the Comptroller General of the U.S., FPCD-79-44, May 23, 1979 (Appendix III).

[b]Information obtained from Office of Administrative Law Judges, OPM, June 1980.

[c]Position is temporarily vacant due to a retirement.

[d]The FLRA was created in 1979 by the Civil Service Reform Act.

[e]Does not include 11 GS-14 Indian Probate Judges.

[f]The MSPB was created in 1979 by the Civil Service Reform Act. This position was formerly located in the Civil Service Commission.

[g]The position allotted to the Postal Rate Commission has been vacant since 1977.

Page 752. Add the following after line 35:

ASSOCIATION OF NATIONAL ADVERTISERS, INC. v. FTC

627 F.2d 1151 (D.C. Cir. 1979), cert. denied, 100 S. Ct. 3011 (1980)

TAMM, CIRCUIT JUDGE. . . .

[In 1977, Michael Pertschuk, a new chairman of the Federal Trade Commission, gave a speech in which he strongly suggested that advertising aimed at children harms them. He argued that children do not understand commercials, will fail to distinguish them adequately from other information, and in particular fail to understand how harmful to them advertised sugared foods may be. He outlined a theory under which children's advertising might be legally "deceptive" because it suggests that sugared foods are desirable without explaining the health risks. He suggested that the commission might take action but concluded that it must be "rigorous and open-minded in our analysis of both law and fact." He subsequently repeated these views—often in strong anti-advertising language—in television interviews and in press releases.

In April 1978 the commission issued a notice of Proposed Rulemaking that considered, among other things, banning televised advertising of sugared products on children's programs. Various advertising associations moved that Pertschuk disqualify himself and sought court review of his refusal to do so. The district court held that, under the standards of *Cinderella*, Pertschuk should be disqualified. The court first held that, although Section 18 of the Magnusen-Moss Act requires hearings with cross-examination for "specific" facts in FTC rule-making proceedings, these are not "adjudicative" facts. Hence, what is at issue here is "rule making," not "adjudication."] . . .

Had Congress amended section 5 of the FTC Act to declare certain types of children's advertising unfair or deceptive, we would barely pause to consider a due process challenge. . . Indeed, any suggestion that congressmen may not prejudge factual and policy issues is fanciful. A legislator must have the ability to exchange views with constituents and to suggest public policy that is dependent upon factual assumptions. Individual interests impinged upon by the legislative process are protected, as Justice Holmes wrote, "in the only way that they can be in a complex society, by [the individual's] power, immediate or remote, over those who make the rule." Bi-Metallic Investment Co. v. State Board of Equalization, 239 U.S. 441, 445, 36 S. Ct. 141, 142, 60 L. Ed. 372 (1915).

Congress chose, however, to delegate its power to proscribe unfair or deceptive acts or practices to the Commission because "there were too many unfair practices for it to define." S. Rep. No. 597, 63d Cong., 2d Sess. 13 (1914). In determining the due process standards applicable in a section 18 proceeding, we are guided by its nature as rulemaking. When a proceeding is classified as rulemaking, due process ordinarily does not demand procedures more rigorous than those provided by Congress. See Vermont Yankee Nuclear Power Corp. v. NRDC, 435 U.S. 519, 524 & n.1, 542 & n.16, 98 S. Ct. 1197, 55 L. Ed. 2d 460 (1978). Congress is under no requirement to hold an evidentiary hearing prior to its adoption of legislation, and "Congress need not make that requirement when it delegates the task to an administrative agency." Bowles v. Willingham, 321 U.S. 503, 519, 64 S. Ct. 641, 649, 88 L. Ed. 892 (1944) (citing Bi-Metallic Investment Co. v. State Board of Equalization, 239 U.S. 441, 36 S. Ct. 141, 60 L. Ed. 372 (1915)). . . .

We never intended the *Cinderella* rule to apply to a rulemaking procedure such as the one under review. The *Cinderella* rule disqualifies a decisionmaker if " 'a disinterested observer may conclude that [he] has in some measure adjudged the facts as well as the law of a particular case in advance of hearing it.' " . . . [L]egislative facts adduced in rulemaking partake of agency expertise, prediction, and risk assessment. In *Cinderella*, the court was able to cleave fact from law in deciding whether Chairman Dixon had prejudged particular factual issues. In the rulemaking context, however, the factual component of the policy decision is not easily assessed in terms of an empirically verifiable condition. Rulemaking involves the kind of issues "where a month of experience will be worth a year of hearings." Application of *Cinderella's* strict law-fact dichotomy would necessarily limit the ability of administrators to discuss policy questions.

The legitimate functions of a policymaker, unlike an adjudicator, demand interchange and discussion about important issues. We must not impose judicial roles upon administrators when they perform functions very different from those of judges. . . . The *Cinderella* view of a neutral and detached adjudicator is simply an inapposite role model for an administrator who must translate broad statutory commands into concrete social policies. If an agency official is to be effective he must engage in debate and discussion about the policy matters before him. . . .

Accordingly, a Commissioner should be disqualified only when there has been a clear and convincing showing that the agency member has an unalterably closed mind on matters critical to the disposition of the proceeding. The "clear and convincing" test is necessary to rebut the presumption of administrative regularity. . . . The "unalterably closed mind" test is necessary to permit rulemakers to carry out their proper policy-based functions while disqualifying those unable to consider meaningfully a section 18 hearing. . . .

[Reversed.] . . .

LEVENTHAL, CIRCUIT JUDGE, concurring. . . .

The ultimate test announced by Judge Tamm as to the merits is that disqualification from a rulemaking proceeding results "only when there has been a clear and convincing showing that [the agency member] has an unalterably closed mind on matters critical to the disposition of the [proceeding]." The test reflects a Supreme Court ruling as to administrative agencies.

It is not far removed from the test used in considering challenges to those considered for the duty as jurors quintessentially engaged in specific fact-finding. It is similar to a standard articulated as to recusal of judges.

The application of this test to agencies must take into account important differences in function and functioning between the agencies and court systems. In fulfilling the functions of applying or considering the validity of a statute, or a government program, the judge endeavors to put aside personal views as to the desirability of the law or program, and he is not disqualified because he personally deems the program laudable or objectionable. In the case of agency rulemaking, however, the decisionmaking officials are appointed precisely to implement statutory programs, and with the expectation that they have a personal disposition to enforce them vigilantly and effectively. They work with a combination rather than a separation of functions, in legislative modes, and take action on the basis of information coming from many sources, even though that provides a mind-set before a proceeding is begun, subject to reconsideration in the light of the proceeding. . . .

Consider, for example, the assertions of an agency head that he discerns abuses that may require corrective regulation. One can hypothesize beginning an adjudicatory proceeding with an open mind, indeed a blank mind, a tabula rasa devoid of any previous knowledge of the matter. In sharp contrast, one cannot even conceive of an agency conducting a rulemaking proceeding unless it had delved into the subject sufficiently to become concerned that there was an evil or abuse that required regulatory response. It would be the height of absurdity, even a kind of abuse of administrative process, for an agency to embroil interested parties in a rulemaking proceeding, without some initial concern that there was an abuse that needed remedying, a concern that would be set forth in the accompanying statement of the purpose of the proposed rule.

In its administrative setting an agency's effort is not limited to one type of activity. Investigation and policy-making are integral to the total function just as much as decisionmaking. It is appropriate and indeed mandatory for agency heads and staff to maintain contacts with industry and consumer groups, trade associations and press, congressmen of various persuasions, and to present views in interviews, speeches, meetings, conventions, and testimony. The agency gathers information and perceptions in a myriad of ways and must use it for a myriad of purposes. With capacity and willingness to reconsider there is no basis for disqualification.

The tests of disqualification cannot be applied identically for judges and agency heads, for reasons already identified. Yet even judges are not disqualified merely because they have previously announced their positions on legal issues, even as to announcements outside the course of written decisions. Judicial disqualification cannot be based on general frame of reference, attitudes or assumptions as to the processes of society. And even a judge's public comment giving a general impression of a state of facts does not present a rigidity against refinement and reflection that disqualifies him from sitting in judgment on a particular fact issue. . . .

MACKINNON, J., (dissenting). [Judge Mackinnon wrote in part that Pertschuk's comments show bias even under the majority's test. He quoted some of those comments:]

[I]n his speech to the Action for Children's Television Research Conference at Boston on November 8, 1977, [Chairman Pertschuk] referred to the *"moral myopia* of children's television advertising." (Emphasis added). He also stated that "advertisers *seize* on the child's trust and *exploit* it as a weakness for their gain." (Emphasis added). . . . Later he stated: "using sophistication [*sic*] techniques like fantasy and animation, they [TV advertisers] *manipulate* children's attitudes". (Emphasis added). . . .

He then argued: "Why isn't [the] . . . principle [that those responsible for children's well being are entitled to the support of laws designed to aid discharge of that responsibility] applicable to television advertising directed at young children? Why shouldn't established legal precedents embodying this public policy be applied to protect children from this *form of exploitation*? In short, why isn't such advertising unfair within the meaning of the Federal Trade Commission Act and, hence, unlawful?" (Emphasis added) Can any reasonable person contend that such remarks do not indicate that he has prejudged TV Advertising and decided that it *exploits* children? . . .

In a 1978 Newsweek article the Chairman is quoted as follows: "Commercialization of children has crept up on us without scrutiny or action," says Michael Pertschuk, the agency's new chairman. *"It is a major, serious problem. I am committed to taking action."* (Emphasis added) . . .

[Pertschuk also sent several letters to heads of other agencies and to a senator. In content they resembled the following:]

MEMORANDUM
TO: Coleman [*sic*] McCarthy
FROM: Mike Pertschuk

Coleman, I know you share my concern in raising public consciousness to the part we play as a society for permitting children to be made commercial objects. I thought you'd want to see this statement in which I've tried to establish underpinings [*sic*] for a *fundamental assault* on television advertising directed toward young children. (Emphasis added).

November 17, 1977

Honorable Donald Kennedy
Food and Drug Administration
Parklawn Building
5600 Fishers Lane
Rockville, Maryland 20852

Dear Don:

Setting legal theory aside, the truth is that we've been drawn into this issue because of the *conviction,* which I know you share, that one of the *evils* flowing from the *unfairness* of children's advertising is the resulting distortion of children's perceptions of nutritional values. I see, at this point, our logical process as follows: children's advertising is inherently unfair. [The letter then sets out a plan for an attack on the advertising].

Sincerely yours,
Michael Pertschuk

(Emphasis added).

These letters indicate that by November 17, 1977, the Chairman had a *"conviction"* that there are *"evils"* flowing from the *unfairness* of children's advertising . . ." and he had been vigorously marshalling sentiment throughout the nation for a "fundamental assault on television advertising directed toward young children." . . .

Thus, if the Notice of Rulemaking were truthful, so far as Chairman Pertschuk's views were concerned, it would have stated in substance: "The Commission has decided to make a fundamental assault upon Children's Advertising on TV because we are convinced that it is *evil,* unfair and allowed solely because of the moral myopia of the public and the industry. We solicit comments as to whether it should be prohibited entirely or to some lesser degree."

Do you believe that the bias standards to be applied to the FTC chairman ought to be the same as those applied to a congressman or other legislator? Note the very fundamental issue at stake here—an issue with ramifications well beyond the narrow area of the "law of bias." A legislator has broad authority to act on the basis of her own views, prejudices, or on any other basis. But a legislator is *elected*—she is held accountable by the voter—and she must persuade a majority of each of two houses of Congress and the president to agree with her. The FTC chairman is not elected and he need persuade only two other commissioners to go along. As chapters 2 and 3 suggest, it used to be argued that this vast power would be held in check by the "canons" of the discipline—i.e., expertise. That is to say, setting rates (or regulating business?) was a "scientific" matter; therefore experts will carry it out scientifically and will not wield unchecked power. This view is discredited.

More recently, it has been argued that the regulator's power will be checked by the requirement that decisions are to be made after *public proceedings*, in which a wide range of interest groups participate. This effort—illustrated by hybrid rule-making requirements—"judicializes" the agency's rule making (i.e., its "legislative" activity). But, if that effort fails to hold the regulator in check—if major legislative decisions are, in fact, made in advance and the record is manipulated—what then is to limit the legislative power of these few appointed officials, who are operating under a broad statutory mandate? It is clear that their powers are not minor or interstitial, for very few laws of Congress in any given session are likely to have as broad an impact as the "children's TV" proposals. Is it then so surprising that in 1980 Congress took matters back into its own hands, limited the FTC's rule-making powers, imposed a legislative veto, and curtailed the children's TV proceedings? See FTC Improvements Act of 1980, described at the end of this supplement's notes on chapter 8.

Page 756. Add the following at the end of footnote 37:

In Marshall v. Jerrico, 446 U.S. 238 (1980), the Supreme Court made clear that *Tumey* did not forbid a regional administrator to assess fines for violations of child labor laws simply because the fines collected (after administrative hearings) were used to finance some of the enforcement costs. The administrator is not a judge and the possibility of bias is too remote.

Page 756. Add the following at the end of footnote 38:

In Friedman v. Rogers, 440 U.S. 1 (1979), the Supreme Court rejected an "equal protection" challenge to the make-up of the Texas Optometry

Board, four of the six members of which were required by statute to belong to the Texas Optometric Association, a professional organization. The Court found the membership rule reasonable in light of "experience with the commercial and professional optometrists preceding the passage of the Act." Although the plaintiff "does have a right to a fair and impartial hearing in any disciplinary proceeding," he was not being disciplined, so that issue was not before the Court.

D. REVITALIZING THE FTC: THE PROBLEM OF FALSE ADVERTISING

Page 804. Add the following after line 23:

The substantive and statutory law related to the FTC's power to regulate advertising is continually changing. We shall note certain major developments here, but for more extensive treatment we refer you to G. Robinson & E. Gellhorn, The Administrative Process (2d ed. 1980); S. Kanwit, The Federal Trade Commission (1979 & Supp. 1981). For purposes of analyzing the commission's bureaucratic problems—and generalizing from them to problems of managing other bureaucracies—it is important to begin with the state of the law as it was in the early to mid-1970s. This supplement will help bring you up to date. But, providing you with the details of "advertising law" is only a subsidiary purpose of this chapter. Its main purpose is to lead you to think through Pitofsky's problems, to determine in what way he succeeded, and why. If you do so, you will learn something, not just about the FTC, but about agencies and bureaucratic political life in general.

Page 804. Add the following after line 29:

The Magnusen-Moss Warranty—FTC Improvements Act, 88 Stat. 218 (1975), broadened the FTC's jurisdiction. Section 5(a)(1) now reads: "unfair methods of competition in or affecting commerce, and unfair or deceptive acts or practices in or affecting commerce, are declared unlawful." 15 U.S.C. §45(a)(1).

Section 5(a)(2) states that the commission "is empowered and directed to prevent persons, partnerships or corporations [with exceptions] . . . from using unfair methods of competition in or affecting commerce."

The Magnusen-Moss Act also explicitly provided the commission with authority to "prescribe . . . rules which define with specificity acts or practices which are unfair or deceptive acts or practices on or affecting commerce" (trade regulation rules) 15 U.S.C. §5a. And, the FTC can obtain a $10,000 civil penalty for each knowing violation of any such rule. 15 U.S.C. §45(m). The Magnusen-Moss Act also provides for "hybrid rulemaking" procedures. See chapter 6, supra.

Page 806. Add the following after line 21:

The advertisement must be "in or affecting commerce." The Magnusen-Moss Act overturned FTC v. Bunte Bros. Inc., 312 U.S. 349 (1941).

Page 813. Add the following to footnote 93:

, aff'd, 532 F.2d 107 (2d Cir. 1976).

Page 814. Add the following to footnote 97:

But see ABA Distributors, Inc. v. Adolph Coors Co., 496 F. Supp. 1149, 1199 (W.D. Mo. 1980) ("We do not believe *Guernsey* accurately states the applicable law."); and see footnote 97a.

Page 814. Add the following to line 9:

But it appears as a general matter to be well settled that private rights of action are not available under the act.[97a]

Page 818. Add the following after line 23:

The Circuit Court in *Warner Lambert*, 562 F.2d 749, quoted with approval the following language of the commission setting out the "corrective advertising" test: "[I]f a deceptive advertisement has played a substantial role in creating or reinforcing in the public's mind a false and material belief which lives on after the false advertising ceases, there is clear and continuing injury to competition and to the consuming public as consumers continue to make purchasing decisions based on the false belief. Since this injury cannot be averted by merely requiring respondent to cease disseminating the advertisement, we may appropriately order respondent to take affirmative action designed to terminate the otherwise continuing ill effects of the advertisement."

Precisely what "affirmative action" might be ordered is still an open question. The FTC staff, for example, has suggested requiring the company to obtain a specified level of consumer awareness any way it wishes rather than having the FTC prescribe specific advertising language. See FTC Briefing Book on Consumer Information Remedies (July 1979). Commissioner Pitofsky has suggested having independent third parties control the advertising, presumably on the ground that the commission does not have sufficient sophistication to prevent subversion of the "corrective ad's" purpose. See his speech to the American Advertising Federation, June 12, 1979. The commission has also begun to ask advertisers to pay for public service announcements to counteract allegedly unfair advertising. Thus a bicycle manufacturer has agreed (in a consent order)

97a. Halloway v. Bristol-Myers Corp., 485 F.2d 986 (D.C. Cir. 1973); Carlson v. Coca-Cola Co., 483 F.2d 279 (9th Cir. 1973).

to pay for ads about safe bicycle riding to counteract ads depicting unsafe practices. See AMF, Inc., 3 CCH Trade Reg. Rep. ¶31,589 (1979). And, a doctor agreed not to advertise hair implants and (if he continued to perform them) to place $8,000 worth of advertising in Los Angeles newspapers specifying that "hair implants are unsafe." Terrence D. Lesko, M.D., 3 CCH Trade Reg. Rep. ¶21,670 (1980).

All this may reflect some uncertainty about the actual effects of corrective advertising. As a result of the FTC's order, Warner Lambert ran, in its television advertising from September 1978 through January 1980, the following corrective ad: "Listerine will not help prevent colds or sore throat or lessen their severity." In October 1981 the FTC released a mail survey taken before and then after the corrective advertising campaign. The number of people who, when buying, considered a mouthwash's ability to prevent colds or sore throats dropped from 31 percent to 25 percent. There was a drop in the extent to which people said that they used mouthwash for that purpose; but at the end of the campaign 39 percent of Listerine's users still reported using mouthwash for colds and sore throats. BNA Antitrust & Trade Reg. Rep. No. 1037 A-23 (Oct. 29, 1981).

The commission has announced that in deciding whether to seek corrective ads it will apply four factors: (1) the amount of exposure consumers have had to the claim, (2) the claim's persuasive characteristics, (3) how the claim was presented, and (4) how persuadable the audience was. 936 BNA Antitrust & Trade Reg. Rep. A-7 (Oct. 25, 1979).

Page 827. Add the following to footnote 111:

The Federal Trade Commission Improvements Act of 1980, P.L. 96-252, 94 Stat. 374, narrowed the information-gathering power of the commission. It amended section 10 so that it requires "an order of a district court of the United States directing compliance" before a respondent can be found guilty of noncompliance with a commission subpoena. See 15 U.S.C. §50 (1981). The act also states that information gathering under §6 and §9—if it concerns "investigations . . . with respect to unfair or deceptive acts or practices in or affecting commerce"—must take the form of "civil investigative demands." These demands "shall state the nature of the conduct constituting the alleged violation which is under investigation" and shall, for example, "describe each class of documentary material to be produced under the demand with such definiteness and certainty as to permit such material to be fairly identified." 15 U.S.C. §57b-1 (1981). The purpose of the provision is to require the FTC to be more specific about the information it needs for its investigations. See S. Rep. No. 96-500, 96th Cong., 1st Sess. (1979).

Page 834. Add the following to footnote 118:

In *Barlow* Justice White wrote for the Court: "Whether the Secretary proceeds to secure a warrant or other process, with or without prior notice, his entitlement to inspect will not depend on his demonstrating probable cause to believe that conditions in violation of OSHA exist on the premises. Probable cause in the criminal law sense is not required. For purposes of an administrative search such as this, probable cause justifying the issuance of a warrant may be based not only on specific evidence of an existing violation but also on a showing that 'reasonable legislative or administrative standards for conducting an . . . inspection are satisfied with respect to a particular [establishment].' Camara v. Municipal Court, 387 U.S., at 538. A warrant showing that a specific business has been chosen for an OSHA search on the basis of a general administrative plan for the enforcement of the Act derived from neutral sources such as, for example, dispersion of employees in various types of industries across a given area, and the desired frequency of searches in any of the lesser divisions of the area, would protect an employer's Fourth Amendment rights. We doubt that the consumption of enforcement energies in the obtaining of such warrants will exceed manageable proportions."

Page 837. Add the following after line 27:

The commission's advertising substantiation program was criticized as moving far too slowly by a House of Representatives committee in 1977. Only a few industries had been asked for data, and the FTC took years before taking any final action. See H.R. Rep. No. 95-472, 95th Cong., 1st Sess. (1977). In 1975, however, the FTC set out an elaborate protocol for use in selecting advertising substantiation targets.[126a] It investigated "energy saving" claims in 1977.[126b] And, it also promulgated an "exclusionary" rule of practice under which an advertiser is forbidden to introduce substantiating information in response to a specific FTC complaint against it, say, for false advertising, if the information was not disclosed to the FTC in response to compulsory process during the investigation. 16 C.F.R. §3.40 (1977).

In response to various FTC rule-making activities, in 1980 Congress limited the FTC's powers. It prohibited the FTC from promulgating any rule that "prohibits or otherwise regulates any commercial advertising on the basis of a determination . . . that [it] . . . constitutes an unfair act or practice. . . ." for the life of the current FTC appropriation (fiscal 1980, 1981, and 1982). Pub. L. 96-252 §11, 94 Stat. 374 (1980). James Miller, the new FTC chairman, has also criticized the "advertising substantiation" program as possibly too burdensome in light of its effectiveness. BNA Antitrust & Trade Reg. Rep. No. 1037 at A-4, No. 1039 at A-20. He has also, however, indicated that the 1975 protocol is to be used for examining advertising cases. BNA Antitrust & Trade Reg. Rep. No. 1043 at A-8. (The FTC staff has published an evaluation of the program from

126a. See S. Kanwit, The Federal Trade Commission (1979), ch. 22, for a description.
126b. See Kanwit, note 126a supra, at 22-5.

1971 to 1977. See Evaluation and Evaluation of the Ad Substantiation Program Since 1971 (available at the FTC).)

Page 841. Add the following after line 17:

CENTRAL HUDSON GAS & ELECTRIC CORP. v. PUBLIC SERVICE COMMISSION OF NEW YORK

447 U.S. 557 (1980)

[In December, 1973, the PSC ordered electric utilities in New York State to cease all advertising that promotes the use of electricity. It continued to allow advertising that encourages shifts in consumption from peak to off-peak periods. In striking down the order as contrary to the First Amendment, the Supreme Court set forth a four-part test for considering the constitutionality of rules regulating "commercial speech":]

BLACKMUN, J. . . .

The First Amendment's concern for commercial speech is based on the informational function of advertising. . . . Consequently, there can be no constitutional objection to the suppression of commercial messages that do not accurately inform the public about lawful activity. . . .

If the communication is neither misleading nor related to unlawful activity, the government's power is more circumscribed. The State must assert a substantial interest to be achieved by restrictions on commercial speech. Moreover, the regulatory technique must be in proportion to that interest. The limitation on expression must be designed carefully to achieve the State's goal. Compliance with this requirement may be measured by two criteria. First, the restriction must directly advance the state interest involved; the regulation may not be sustained if it provides only ineffective or remote support for the government's purpose. Second, if the governmental interest could be served as well by a more limited restriction on commercial speech, the excessive restrictions cannot survive. . . .

. . . In commercial speech cases, then, a four-part analysis has developed. At the outset, we must determine whether the expression is protected by the First Amendment. For commercial speech to come within that provision, it at least must concern lawful activity and not be misleading. Next, we ask whether the asserted governmental interest is substantial. If both inquiries yield positive answers, we must determine whether the regulation directly advances the governmental interest asserted, and whether it is not more extensive than is necessary to serve that interest. . . .

[The Court struck down the PSC regulation primarily because it violated the last—the "less restrictive alternative"—test.]

Appellant insists that but for the ban, it would advertise products and services that use energy efficiently. . . .

The Commission's order prevents appellant from promoting electric services that would reduce energy use by diverting demand from less efficient sources, or that would consume roughly the same amount of energy as do alternative sources. In neither situation would the utility's advertising endanger conservation or mislead the public. To the extent that the Commission's order suppresses speech that in no way impairs the State's interest in energy conservation, the Commission's order violates the First and Fourteenth Amendments and must be invalidated.

The Commission also has not demonstrated that its interest in conservation cannot be protected adequately by more limited regulation of appellant's commercial expression. To further its policy of conservation, the Commission could attempt to restrict the format and content of Central Hudson's advertising. It might, for example, require that the advertisements include information about the relative efficiency and expense of the offered service. . . . In the absence of a showing that more limited speech regulation would be ineffective, we cannot approve the complete suppression of Central Hudson's advertising.[130a]

Page 855. Add the following after line 28:

[The FCC's Fairness Report was upheld by the courts in National Citizens Committee for Broadcasting v. FCC, 567 F.2d 1095 (D.C. Cir. 1977). As the text points out, this report repudiated the *Banzhaf* doctrine. The court noted that the report divides advertisements into three general categories: editorial advertising (direct and substantial commentary on controversial issues of public importance), standard product commercials (such as the cigarette advertising in *Banzhaf*), and product claims alleged to be false and misleading. The "fairness doctrine" henceforth applies *only* to the first, namely, editorial advertising.

On review, the D.C. Circuit held that the Fairness Report was constitutional, i.e., the Constitution does not *compel* a "standard commercial" fairness doctrine. In holding that the report was not arbitrary and within the FCC's statutory power, the court first reviewed the prior cases in which it had been applied, emphasizing the practical difficulties of deciding whether a public issue is "implicitly" raised. See, e.g., Neckritz v. FCC, 502 F.2d 411 (D.C. Cir. 1974) (ad for gasoline additive that reduces auto emissions does *not* raise the auto pollution issue as only "efficacy" of product is at issue). The court added]:

As we have demonstrated, two of the greatest uncertainties in administration of the [*Banzhaf*] approach were (1) ascertaining what issues were "implicitly" raised by standard product commercials and institutional advertising, and (2) determining when a view on a controversial issue of

---

130a. [See also Metromedia v. City of San Diego, 49 U.S.L.W. 4925 (July 2, 1981), in which the Court applied the four-part test to invalidate a city ban on outdoor billboard advertising—Ed.]

public importance was expressed so elliptically that it could not be said to have been "raised" for purposes of the fairness doctrine. The policies announced in the Fairness Report seem to us to be a straightforward attempt to remove these uncertainties by all-but-completely removing "implicit" advocacy from the confines of the fairness doctrine. As long as the Commission strictly enforces the . . . fairness obligation to present opposing points of view whenever there is direct, obvious, or explicit advocacy on one side of a controversial issue of public importance, it will be acting consistently with the public interest standard [in addition.] . . . Three major arguments are presented by the Commission. First, the Commission made the judgment that the [*Banzhaf*] approach to the fairness doctrine and standard product commercials at most informed the public about only one side of a controversial issue. . . .

Certainly it must be admitted that counter-commercials are of a very different genre than are the product commercials themselves. They do not simply state, "Do not buy X; it is not desirable," but rather argue one side of the issues underlying the debate over desirability. Given this fundamental asymmetry, we do not think it was unreasonable for the Commission to conclude that application of the fairness doctrine to standard product commercials does not further the objective of presenting all viewpoints on controversial issues of public importance.

The second major argument put forth by the Commission is that application of the fairness doctrine to noneditorial advertisements would "divert the attention of broadcasters from their public trustee responsibilities in aiding the development of an informed public opinion." . . . [E]ven if enforcement of fairness doctrine obligations with respect to commercial advertisements might marginally contribute to an informed public opinion, these benefits are outweighed by the reduction in public information which results from the decreased attention that broadcasters will afford to other aspects of the fairness doctrine. Given the wide range of controversial products to which the [*Banzhaf*] approach could be applied and the difficulties, discussed above, in determining which issues implicitly addressed give rise to fairness obligations, it is indeed quite possible that the effort broadcasters would have to devote to enforcing the fairness doctrine with respect to commercial advertisements would contribute relatively little to the overall objectives of the doctrine. We caution, however, that it is doubtful that the new FCC policy will substantially lessen the difficulties of drawing the line between advertisements which do and those which do not incur fairness obligations. The difference between obvious and unobvious advocacy is not obvious.

Finally, the Commission suggested in the Fairness Report, though not in its arguments to this court, that application of the fairness doctrine to commercial advertisements could undermine the economic base of commercial broadcasting. It is possible that sponsors would be discouraged from broadcasting advertisements subject to mandatory counter-commercials, and that broadcasters could suffer additional losses through operation of the *Cullman* principle under which they must bear the cost of presenting opposing views where paid sponsorship is not available. Yet no evidence has been presented which indicates that the [*Banzhaf*] policy had an adverse effect on commercial broadcasters, though admittedly this may be due to the rather unvigorous and confused enforcement of that policy. While we do not think this economic argument is conclusive standing alone, the other two arguments put forth by the Commission provide adequate and substantial support for its decision.

The fairness doctrine itself—as applied in noncommercial contexts— has also increasingly come under attack. It is not simply that bills have been introduced in Congress to repeal it, see, e.g., S. 2, 94th Cong., 1st Sess.; S. 622, 96th Cong., 1st Sess.; but, more importantly, a growing body of opinion rejects the "scarcity" rationale as a basis for distinguishing between the written press and television. CATV, satellites, and currently unused channels make any claim of spectrum space scarcity difficult to maintain. Of course, there is economic scarcity; it is difficult to establish a major television channel in a large market capable of drawing a large audience. But precisely the same is true of the newspaper business. Some have argued that the greater impact of television may warrant a different First Amendment approach. But others have warned of the intrusive effects of government regulation based on content, urging instead a *structural* approach seeking to encourage more entry into, or competition within, the business. See Judge Bazelon's interesting article, The First Amendment and "New Media"—New Directions in Regulating Telecommunications, 31 Fed. Comm. L.J. 201 (1979); Coyne, The Future of Content Regulation in Broadcasting, 69 U. Calif. L. Rev. 555 (1981).

Page 855. Add the following after line 13:

As should be apparent by now, the effort to revitalize the FTC *did* succeed. The Magnusen-Moss Act of 1975, 88 Stat. 2183, was in part a result of this FTC revival. Among other things, it explicitly granted the commission power to issue trade regulation rules in the consumer protection area. It also strengthened the FTC's powers of enforcement.

The FTC eagerly embraced its new-found rule-making powers. And by 1977, when Michael Pertschuk was appointed chairman, it had begun seventeen rule-making proceedings, concerning such diverse industries, markets, and practices as funeral homes, used cars, credit practices, over-the-counter drugs, eyeglasses, mobile homes, hearing aids, food advertising, health spas, vocational schools, flammable plastics, appliance labeling, protein supplements, core labeling, franchises, home insulation materials, and gasoline station lotteries. Because of the long period of time needed to complete a rule-making proceeding, hardly any such proceedings were concluded prior to his becoming chairman.150a Moreover, certain of the notices of proposed rule making relating to these proceedings suggested possible remedies that the relevant industries viewed as "extreme" (e.g., depriving funeral homes of profits on the sale of flowers).

Congress then reacted strongly against the FTC's efforts. The causes of this reaction are subjects of debate and speculation: a changing political mood, powerful interest groups, tactlessness on the part of the chairman or staff, ill-advised press conferences and speeches, and bad public relations. All or none of these may have helped reinforce a popular image of the FTC as an agency "out of control." The catalyst, however, was probably Chairman Pertschuk's effort to regulate children's television advertising, discussed in Association of National Advertisers, supra. This effort led the Washington Post to write an editorial entitled "The FTC as National Nanny" (March 1, 1978). See generally Gellhorn, The Wages of Zealotry: The FTC Under Seige, Regulation Jan.-Feb. 1980, at 33. Congress responded with the FTC Improvements Act of 1980, 94 Stat. 374, which (1) limited the FTC's power to disclose certain collected business information; (2) prohibited the FTC from investigating the insurance industry; (3) required the FTC to go to court to enforce its subpoenas; (4) curtailed the FTC's "unfair practice" rule-making proceeding dealing with industry standards and certifications; (5) curtailed the children's television rule-making proceeding; (6) removed "unfairness" as a basis for new advertising rule making in 1980, 1981, and 1982; (7) required publication of the text of a proposed rule at the beginning of a rule-making proceeding; (8) limited the FTC's information-gathering powers; (9) restricted the FTC's power to issue a "funeral practices" rule; (10) restricted the FTC's authority to investigate agricultural cooperatives; (11) required the FTC to prepare elaborate statements of costs, other impacts, and alternative for any major proposed rules (see this supplement, ch. 3); (12) provided for a "two house" legislative veto of future FTC rules (see chapters 3 and 4).

The new chairman of the FTC, James Miller, has suggested that he favors a more limited "consumer protection" role for the FTC and a larger role for the competitive market than that implied by many of the highly controversial rule-making proceedings that took place between 1976 and 1980.

150a. One of the few that was completed—a rule applying to vocational schools—was reversed: Katherine Gibbs School v. FTC, 612 F.2d 685 (2d Cir. 1979).

Chapter Nine

The Availability and Timing of Judicial Review

A. JURISDICTION AND THE FORMS OF ACTION

Page 867. Add the following after line 3:

A plaintiff might also find that the agency action of which he complains is not final enough to warrant review in a court of appeals under a specific statute requiring a "final order" but that he can obtain review in a district court on the basis of a statute of general jurisdiction.[37a]

Page 868. Add the following after line 7:

Section 1331 was amended in 1980 to eliminate the amount-in-controversy requirement. 94 Stat. 2369 (1980). That section now reads: "The district courts shall have original jurisdiction of all civil actions arising under the Constitution, laws, or treaties of the United States."

Page 873. Add the following after line 4:

Despite the wide range of choice provided by the 1962 venue amendments, many critics claim that too many agency review cases are brought in the District of Columbia Circuit, perhaps because many such cases involve institutional plaintiffs who, along with the agency, "reside" there. They charge that this forum is too distant from those in the country directly affected by many agency decisions. Some of those critics have introduced legislation that would (1) require an agency review proceeding to be brought only in a judicial district where the agency's action "would substantially affect the residents" and (2) require both circuit and

---

37a. See Westinghouse Broadcasting Co., Inc. v. NTSB, No. 82-1095 (1st Cir. Jan. 28, 1982) (decision of local official of National Transportation Safety Board limiting media access to crash site likely to be reviewable in district, but not circuit, court).

district courts to transfer such actions (upon request) to a circuit or district "in which the action would have a substantially greater impact" (unless the interests of justice require retention).[57a]

Page 878. Add the following after line 12:

Two recent Supreme Court cases may have significantly expanded a plaintiff's ability to sue state and, in particular, *municipal* governments for violations of federal law. One of them, Maine v. Thiboutot, 448 U.S. 1 (1980), interprets the Civil Rights Act, 42 U.S.C. §1983, to create a cause of action based on violation by state or local officials or governments of most federal laws. The other, Owen v. City of Independence, 445 U.S. 622 (1980), eliminates any immunity by municipal governments for many violations of §1983.

In Maine v. Thiboutot, the Supreme Court considered 42 U.S.C. §1983, which states: "Every person who, under color of any statute, ordinance, regulation, custom, or usage, of any State or Territory, subjects, or causes to be subjected, any citizen of the United States or other person within the jurisdiction thereof to the deprivation of any rights, privileges, or immunities secured by the Constitution *and laws,* shall be liable to the party injured in an action at law, suit in equity, or other proper proceeding for redress." (Emphasis added.) In an opinion written by Justice Brennan, the Supreme Court held that the words "and laws" mean what they say: they are not limited to "some subset of laws," but rather, include virtually *all* federal laws. Thus, the act encompasses respondents' claim that they were denied rights granted under the Federal Social Security Act. The Court wrote that the legislative history of §1983 shows that Congress did *not* want to limit these words to "civil rights or equal protection laws." Moreover, the Civil Rights Attorney's Fees Awards Act of 1976 specifically allows a "court in its discretion . . . [to] allow the prevailing party, other than the United States, a reasonable attorney's fee" in §1983 actions. Thus, attorney's fees are in principle available should respondents prevail in their Social Security Act claim.

Justice Powell, joined by the Chief Justice and Justice Rehnquist, dissented, reading the relevant legislative history differently. While we leave the merits of the opinion to courses on federal courts, we include here several excerpts from the dissent and the dissenters' Appendix:

"The Court's opinion does not consider the nature or scope of the litigation it has authorized. In practical effect, today's decision means that state and local governments, officers, and employees[68a] now may face

---

57a. Amendment No. 1267 to S. 1080 (Senators DeConcini, Hatch, and Simpson). 128 Congressional Record (daily ed. Feb. 9, 1982). S. 658-59; id., Feb. 10, 1982, S. 755-61.

68a. "Section 1983 actions may be brought against States, municipalities and other subdivisions, officers, and employees. Although I will refer to all such potential defendants

liability whenever a person believes he has been injured by the administration of *any* federal-state cooperative program, whether or not that program is related to equal or civil rights.[68b] . . .

"Even a cursory survey of the United States Code reveals that literally hundreds of cooperative regulatory and social welfare enactments may be affected. The States now participate in the enforcement of federal laws governing migrant labor, noxious weeds, historic preservation, wildlife conservation, anadromous fisheries, scenic trails, and strip mining. Various statutes authorize federal-state cooperative agreements in most aspects of federal land management. In addition, federal grants administered by state and local governments now are available in virtually every area of public administration. Unemployment, Medicaid, school lunch subsidies, food stamps, and other welfare benefits may provide particularly inviting subjects of litigation. Federal assistance also includes a variety of subsidies for education, housing, health care, transportation, public works, and law enforcement. Those who might benefit from these grants now will be potential §1983 plaintiffs.

"No one can predict the extent to which litigation arising from today's decision will harass state and local officials; nor can one foresee the number of new filings in our already overburdened courts. But no one can doubt that these consequences will be substantial. And the Court advances no reason to believe that any Congress—from 1874 to the present day—intended this expansion of federally imposed liability on state defendants. . . .

"Even when a cause of action against federal officials is available, litigants are likely to focus efforts upon state defendants in order to obtain attorney's fees under the liberal standard of 42 U.S.C. §1988. There is some evidence that §1983 claims already are being appended to complaints solely for the purpose of obtaining fees in actions where 'civil rights' of any kind are at best an afterthought.

APPENDIX TO OPINION OF POWELL, J., DISSENTING

"A small sample of statutes that arguably could give rise to §1983 actions after today may illustrate the nature of the 'civil rights' created by the Court's decision. . . .

---

as 'state defendants' for purposes of this opinion, there may be a notable difference among them. States are protected against retroactive damages awards by the Eleventh Amendment, and individual defendants generally can claim immunity when they act in good faith. Municipalities, however, will be strictly liable for errors in the administration of complex federal statutes. See Owen v. City of Independence, 445 U.S. 622 (1980)."

68b. "The only exception will be in cases where the governing statute provides an exclusive remedy for violations of its terms. See Adickes v. Kress & Co., 398 U.S. 144, 150-151, n.5 (1970). . . ."

A. Joint regulatory endeavors

1. Federal Insecticide, Fungicide, and Rodenticide Act, 86 Stat. 973, as amended, 7 U.S.C. §136 et seq. (1976 ed. and Supp. III); see, e.g., §§136u, 136v (1976 ed., Supp. III).
2. Federal Noxious Weed Act of 1974, 88 Stat. 2148, 7 U.S.C. §§2801-2813; see §2808.
3. Historic Sites, Buildings, and Antiquities Act, 49 Stat. 666, as amended, 16 U.S.C. §§461-467 (1976 ed. and Supp. III); see §462(e).
4. Fish and Wildlife Coordination Act, 48 Stat. 401, as amended, 16 U.S.C. §§661-666c; see §661.
5. Anadromous Fish Conservation Act, 79 Stat. 1125, as amended, 16 U.S.C. §§757a-757d (1976 ed., Supp. III); see §757a(a) (1976 ed., Supp. III).
6. Wild Free-Roaming Horses and Burros Act, 85 Stat. 649, as amended, 16 U.S.C. §§1331-1340 (1976 ed. and Supp. III); see §1336.
7. Marine Mammal Protection Act of 1972, 86 Stat. 1027, as amended, 16 U.S.C. §§1361-1407 (1976 ed. and Supp. III); see §1379.
8. Wagner-Peyser National Employment System Act, 48 Stat. 113, 29 U.S.C. §49 et seq.; see §49g (employment of farm laborers).
9. Surface Mining Control and Reclamation Act of 1977, 91 Stat. 447, 30 U.S.C. §§1201-1328 (1976 ed., Supp. III); see §1253 (1976 ed., Supp. III).
10. Interstate Commerce Act, 49 Stat. 548, as amended, 49 U.S.C. §11502(a)(2) (1976 ed., Supp. III) (enforcement of highway transportation law).

B. Resource management

1. Laws involving the administration and management of national parks and scenic areas: e.g., Act of May 15, 1965, §6, 79 Stat. 111, 16 U.S.C. §281e (Nez Perce National Historical Park); Act of Sept. 21, 1959, §3, 73 Stat. 591, 16 U.S.C. §410u (Minute Man National Historical Park); Act of Oct. 27, 1972, §4, 86 Stat. 1302, 16 U.S.C. §460bb-3(b) (Muir Woods National Monument).
2. Laws involving the administration of forest lands: e.g., Act of Mar. 1, 1911, §2, 36 Stat. 961, 16 U.S.C. §563; Act of Aug. 29, 1935, 49 Stat. 963, 16 U.S.C. §§567a-567b.
3. Laws involving the construction and management of water projects: e. g., Water Supply Act of 1958, §301, 72 Stat. 319, 43 U.S.C. §390b; Boulder Canyon Projects Act, §§4, 8, 45 Stat. 1058, 1062, as amended, 43 U.S.C. §§617c, 617g; Rivers and Harbors Appropriation Act of 1899, §9, 30 Stat. 1151, 33 U.S.C. §401.
4. National Trails System Act, 82 Stat. 919, as amended, 16 U. S. C. §§1241-1249 (1976 ed. and Supp. III); see §1246(h) (1976 ed., Supp. III).

5. Outer Continental Shelf Lands Act Amendment of 1978, §208, 92 Stat. 652, 43 U.S.C. §1345 (1976 ed., Supp. III) (oil leasing).

C. Grant programs

In addition to the familiar welfare, unemployment, and medical assistance programs established by the Social Security Act, these may include:

1. Food Stamp Act of 1964, 78 Stat. 703, as amended, 7 U.S.C. §§2011-2026 (1976 ed. and Supp. III); see e.g., §§2020(e)-2020(g) (1976 ed., Supp. III).
2. Small Business Investment Act of 1958, §602(d), 72 Stat. 698, as amended, 15 U.S.C. §636(d) (1976 ed., Supp. III).
3. Education Amendments of 1978, 92 Stat. 2153, as amended, 20 U.S.C. §2701 et seq. (1976 ed., Supp. III); see, e.g., §§2734, 2902.
4. Federal-Aid Highway Act legislation, e.g., 23 U.S.C. §§128, 131 (1976 ed. and Supp. III).
5. Comprehensive Employment and Training Act Amendments of 1978, 92 Stat. 1909, 29 U.S.C. §801 et seq. (1976 ed., Supp. III); see, e.g., §§823, 824.
6. United States Housing Act of 1937, as added, 88 Stat. 653, and amended, 42 U.S.C. §1437 et seq. (1976 ed. and Supp. III); see, e.g., §§1437d(c), 1437j.
7. National School Lunch Act, 60 Stat. 230, as amended, 42 U.S.C. §1751 et seq. (1976 ed. and Supp. III); see, e.g., §1758 (1976 ed. and Supp. III).
8. Public Works and Economic Development Act of 1965, 79 Stat. 552, as amended, 42 U.S.C. §3121 et seq.; see, e.g., §§3132, 3151a, 3243.
9. Justice System Improvement Act of 1979, 93 Stat. 1167, 42 U.S.C. §3701 et seq. (1976 ed., Supp. III); see, e.g., §§3742, 3744(c).
10. Juvenile Justice and Delinquency Prevention Act of 1974, 88 Stat. 1109, as amended, 42 U.S.C. §5601 et seq. (1976 ed. and Supp. III); see, e.g., §5633 (1976 ed. and Supp. III).
11. Energy Conservation and Production Act, 90 Stat. 1125, as amended, 42 U.S.C. §6801 et seq. (1976 ed. and Supp. III); see, e.g., §§6805, 6836 (1976 ed. and Supp. III).
12. Developmentally Disabled Assistance and Bill of Rights Act, §125, 89 Stat. 496, as amended, 42 U.S.C. §6000 et seq. (1976 ed. and Supp. III); see, e.g., §§6011, 6063 (1976 ed. and Supp. III).
13. Urban Mass Transportation Act of 1964, 78 Stat. 302, as amended, 49 U.S.C. §1601 et seq. (1976 ed. and Supp. III); see, e.g., §§1602, 1604(g)-(m) (1976 ed. and Supp. III)."

More recently, the Supreme Court, using the theory mentioned by Justice Powell in note 68b, drew back from the implications of *Thiboutot* drawn by Justice Powell. The Court held that Congress did not create a private right of action to enforce the Federal Water Pollution Control Act and the Marine Protection Research and Sanctuaries Act of 1972. The court deduced this conclusion from Congressional creation of other mechanisms to enforce the statutory scheme, and it used the same facts to infer a congressional intent *not* to have §1983 apply to these statutes. Middlesex County Sewerage Authority v. National Sea Clammers Ass'n, 49 U.S.L.W. 4783 (1981). If one has a §1983 action founded on statute only when one *also* has a private right of action derived directly from the statute, what does §1983 add? Attorney's fees? One district court has held that §1983 *cannot* be used solely to secure attorney's fees. Tatro v. Texas, 49 U.S.L.W. 2773 (N.D. Tex. June 9, 1981). Or must Congress be "clearer" to indicate a desire to make §1983 inapplicable than to indicate a desire not to bestow a private right of action?

In Owen v. City of Independence, 445 U.S. 622 (1980), the Supreme Court held that municipal governments were not entitled to any form of official immunity when sued under the Civil Rights Acts, e.g., 42 U.S.C. §1983. Monroe v. Pape, 365 U.S. 167 (1961), had given local governments near absolute immunity. Monell v. City of New York Dept. of Social Services, 436 U.S. 658 (1978), overruled *Monroe*, making it clear that immunity was not absolute. And *Owen* expands *Monell*, leaving municipalities immune only if the injury was inflicted "solely" by employees or agents, that is to say, when the injury is *not* caused by the "execution of a government's policy or custom, whether made by its lawmakers or by those whose edicts or acts may fairly be said to represent official policy."

Justice Brennan, writing for the Court, noted that by its language, §1983 applies to "every person." Moreover, previously existing immunity for municipalities rested either on doctrines of sovereign immunity, now outmoded, or on the courts' hesitancy to substitute "their own judgment on matters within the lawful discretion of the municipality. But a municipality has no 'discretion' to violate the Federal Constitution. . . . [And a court] looks only to whether the municipality has conformed to the requirements of the Federal Constitution and statutes." Further, given the qualified immunity enjoyed by most officials [see Butz v. Economou, Casebook at p. 883], were the city to have a "good faith" defense, many victims would have no remedy. Finally, the fear of possible liability will not deter officials from exercising discretion despite the risk of later being found to have acted unreasonably, for they themselves would not be liable. Only the city would have to pay.

Justice Powell, joined by the Chief Justice, Justice Stewart, and Justice Rehnquist, wrote a dissent, in which the four took issue with Justice Brennan's assessment of the holding's likely effect upon the conduct of city officials. They argued that fear of suit against the city—including numerous unfounded suits—would deter many officials from choosing a discretionary action that they considered to be most in the public interest. They further argued that unqualified liability was often unfair to the city.

Page 883. Delete the citation for Butz v. Economou and substitute:

438 U.S. 478 (1978).

Page 891. Add the following after line 4:

1. You should recall that Civil Rights Act §1983 applies only to *state* officials (those who act "under color of state law or custom"), not to federal officials. Yet, *federal* officials were held potentially liable for violating a plaintiff's Fourth Amendment rights in Bivens v. Six Unknown Fed. Narcotics Agents, 403 U.S. 388 (1971), because the Supreme Court implied a cause of action *from the Constitution itself*. The Court extended *Bivens* in Davis v. Passman, 442 U.S. 228 (1979), where it held that a former congressional employee could sue a congressman for sex discrimination, directly implying a cause of action from the Fifth Amendment (i.e., from the Fifth Amendment's due process clause, if it is read to forbid sex discrimination by a federal official). Then, in Carlson v. Green, 446 U.S. 14 (1980), the Court found that the Eighth Amendment implies a cause of action. And the Court went on to indicate that there is a private right of action against federal officials for *any* Constitutional violation, drawn from the Constitution itself—unless (1) there are "special factors counseling hesitation" or (2) "an alternative remedy" is provided by Congress and "explicitly declared to be a *substitute* for recovery directly under the Constitution and viewed as equally effective." 446 U.S. at 18-19. The Court interpreted these exceptions narrowly. Thus, despite §1983's limitation to *state* actions, it ought not to be difficult to sue federal officials for violations of the federal Constitution. This fact makes the scope of the immunity that those officials enjoy of particular importance.

2. The dissenters' concern in *Economou* that high level executive branch officials would be deprived of absolute immunity for discretionary acts appears to have been well-founded.

HALPERIN v. KISSINGER

606 F.2d 1192 (D.C. Cir. 1979), aff'd by an equally divided Court, 101 S. Ct. 3132 (1981)

J. SKELLY WRIGHT, CHIEF JUDGE. . . .
[Morton Halperin, a former member of the National Security Council staff, sued ten federal officials for damages, claiming that a wiretap on his home telephone violated his Fourth Amendment, and certain statutory, rights. The defendants included former president Nixon, former attorney general Mitchell, Henry Kissinger, Robert Haldeman, and several other presidential aides. The district court found for Halperin and awarded one

dollar as nominal damages. Defendants Nixon, Mitchell, and Haldeman appealed the district court's denial of absolute immunity.

The court of appeals affirmed the district court on this issue, discussing it in part as follows:]

All individual defendants claim an absolute immunity from civil damage suits for actions undertaken in their official capacities. The District Court rejected these claims, and we agree with that ruling. Defendants, including former President Nixon, are entitled to a qualified immunity on both the Fourth Amendment and the Title III claims if they can show that they had reasonable grounds for believing their actions were legal (the "objective" basis) and that there was no malice or bad faith in either the initiation or the conduct of the wiretapping (the "subjective" basis). Because former President Nixon advances particular arguments in support of his own absolute immunity, we will consider his status separately. . . .

Officials making adjudicative and prosecutorial decisions are absolutely immune from civil suit based on such actions. This doctrine assumes that the initiation of a prosecution and the resolution of a dispute are especially likely to incite individualized wrath, and that the review processes of the judicial system provide an automatic safeguard against improper actions. Absolute immunity is not available, however, for those same officials for acts not involving adjudication or prosecution.

In Butz v. Economou, 438 U.S. 478, . . . the Supreme Court outlined two bases for qualifying the immunity from suit enjoyed by Executive officials: (1) without such qualification the damage actions contemplated by *Bivens* would be "drained of meaning" and many constitutional violations would go unremedied; and (2) since state officials may be held liable for such violations, it would "stand the constitutional design on its head" if the courts established "a system in which the Bill of Rights monitors more closely the conduct of state officials than it does that of federal officials. . . ."

The *Economou* Court adopted for federal officials the objective and subjective standards for qualified immunity of Wood v. Strickland: "[An official is] not immune . . . [A] if he knew or reasonably should have known that the action he took . . . would violate the constitutional rights of the [person] affected, or [B] if he took the action with the malicious intention to cause a deprivation of constitutional rights or other injury. . . ." We stress that only one of these two standards need be satisfied in order for a defendant to lose his immunity from suit.

To reduce the potential for harassment of Executive officials, the Supreme Court has recommended resolution of the immunity issue, when possible, on summary judgment. This course is best suited for handling the objective basis for qualified immunity. Courts should be able to determine at the pretrial stage whether there is a genuine issue of material fact as to the reasonableness of a defendant's belief that he was acting legally. On the subjective criterion—which "turns on officials' knowledge and good faith belief"—summary action may be more difficult. Questions of intent and subjective attitude frequently cannot be resolved without direct testimony of those involved. . . .

[The court upheld the district court's finding that Mitchell and Haldeman failed to meet either the subjective or objective test.]

In order to accept defendant Nixon's argument that he, as a former President, is absolutely immune from this suit, we would have to hold that his status as President sets him apart from the other high Executive officials named as defendants to this action. Such a distinction would have to rest on a determination either that the Constitution impliedly exempts the President from all liability in cases like this or that the repercussions of finding liability would be drastically adverse. Because we are unable to make that distinction, we do not believe he is entitled to absolute immunity to a damage action by a citizen subjected to an unconstitutional or illegal wiretap.

1. The constitutional scheme betrays no indication that any kind of immunity was intended for the President or the Executive Branch. While congressmen enjoy the privileges of the Speech and Debate Clause of Article I, "[t]he Constitution makes no mention of special presidential immunities. . . ."

2. The doctrine of separation of powers wisely counsels the judiciary to act with care when reviewing actions by other branches, but the courts may not evade their constitutional responsibility to delineate the obligations and powers of each branch. Thus, although courts lack power to grant injunctive relief against prospective presidential actions that may be discretionary, Presidents are scarcely immune from judicial process. Courts have intervened in defense of congressional lawmaking prerogatives to block improper presidential exercise of emergency powers and to assert the President's duty to execute mandatory legislative instructions. They have also ordered production of presidential documents needed for orderly functioning of the criminal justice system. Clearly, a proper regard for separation of powers does not require that the courts meekly avert their eyes from presidential excesses while invoking a sterile view of three branches of government entirely insulated from each other. Such an abdication of the judicial role would sap the vitality of the constitutional rights whose protection is entrusted to the judiciary.

3. We also find no basis for absolute presidential immunity on what might be termed prudential grounds. We do not believe that any inhibiting effect such suits might have on the presidential will to act should hinder effective governance of the nation. To some extent, of course, the denial of absolute immunity is intended to affect Executive behavior that threatens to violate constitutional rights. We believe, however, that suits that may successfully be pursued against a President will be quite rare.

And if we are serious about providing a remedy for constitutional violations, there can be no rational basis, as the *Economou* Court emphasized, for holding inferior officials liable for constitutional violations while immunizing those higher up. "Indeed, the greater power of such [higher] officials affords a greater potential for a regime of lawless conduct. Extensive Government operations offer opportunities for unconstitutional action on a massive scale. . . ."

In addition, the doctrine of qualified immunity, as elaborated by the Supreme Court in Scheuer v. Rhodes and by this court in Apton v. Wilson, makes allowance for the additional demands on the time and attention of a Chief Executive. The President, like all citizens, must be held to know the relevant law, but he "may be entitled to consult fewer sources and expend less effort inquiring into the circumstances of a localized problem." This sliding scale would apply with even greater force if the President were acting in an emergency situation. The President would lose his immunity only if plaintiffs could show that he acted with "actual malice" or that he failed to meet a statutory or constitutional obligation that was clear under the circumstances as understood at the time. Under this approach plaintiffs would have substantial difficulty in defeating a President's claim of immunity, an outcome that helps satisfy our concern that suits like this one would place major and unwarranted demands on a President's time. In considering the case to be made out by plaintiffs before trial, District Courts should be sensitive to the extraordinary practical difficulties confronting a President who is charged in such a suit.

4. We do not think that the personal burden on the President of having to answer civil suits like this one is so great as to justify absolute immunity. Like other Executive officials, he is represented by the Government if he is sued for his official actions; and there seems to be no basis for greater solicitude for the personal finances of a President ordered to pay damages for his constitutional violations than for a governor or a cabinet officer.

[As the Supreme Court stated in *Economou*] . . . "No man in this country is so high that he is above the law. No officer of the law may set that law at defiance with impunity. All officers of the government, from the highest to the least, are creatures of the law, and are bound to obey it."

The Supreme Court decided (too late for inclusion here) Nixon v. Fitzgerald, 50 U.S.L.W. 4797 (June 24, 1982) (President has absolute immunity), and Harlow v. Fitzgerald, 50 U.S.L.W. 4815 (June 24, 1982) ("qualified" immunity means immunity unless official's conduct violates "clearly established statutory or constitutional rights of which a reasonable person would have known").

The Supreme Court has not made serious inroads in the immunity granted to legislators, prosecutors, and judges. In Davis v. Passman, 442 U.S. 228 (1979), the Court held that the fired female employee, alleging sex discrimination, had a cause of action derived from the Fifth Amendment, but it expressly did not consider whether the congressman nonetheless had immunity based upon the Speech and Debate Clause of the Constitution. Previously, in Lake Country Estates v. Tahoe Regional Planning Agency, 440 U.S. 391 (1979), the Court held that members of a regional planning board, as well as state and federal legislators, have absolute immunity when "acting in a legislative capacity."

The Court has recently held that a defense attorney appointed to represent an indigent defendant does not enjoy the immunity that cloaks judges, grand jurors, and prosecutors. Ferri v. Ackerman, 444 U.S. 193 (1979). And, private persons who conspire with a judge do not receive the benefit of his or her immunity, Dennis v. Sparks, 449 U.S. 24 (1980). But the Court took care to reaffirm "the rule that judges defending against §1983 actions enjoy absolute immunity from damages liability for acts performed in their judicial capacity." 449 U.S. at 27.

3. To what extent do these cases allow disgruntled employees to sue high officials—cabinet members or the president—alleging, for example, a malicious effort to deprive them of jobs, or disciplinary action, without due process? To what extent will answering ill-founded complaints, appearing in court, and so forth, burden the government official? Will it interfere with his or her ability to exercise judgment as he or she believes the public interest requires?

The Supreme Court in *Economou* may have been overly optimistic in its claim that "summary judgments" can dispose of many such cases. To survive a motion for summary judgment, a plaintiff need only come up with affidavits showing there is a genuine and material issue of fact. It is frequently not too difficult for a plaintiff to do so, for the plaintiff's version of what occurred may simply be different from that of the defendant. Moreover, it is up to a jury, not a judge, to decide which of different witnesses to believe. See, e.g., Hanrahan v. Hamilton, 446 U.S. 754 (1980), where, after sixteen months of trial, a district court dismissed a civil rights suit as to some, but not all, government officials, only to be reversed by a divided court of appeals. Justice Powell, dissenting from a Supreme Court affirmance of the court of appeals, points out how burdensome the defense of such a suit may be, even where the evidence suggests it is most unlikely that the plaintiffs have a valid claim.[57b]

57b. See the recent legislative proposals aimed at "rationalizing the law concerning officers' immunity." E.g., H.R. 24, 97th Cong., 1st Sess. (1981) (Sen. Grassley); testimony by Deputy Attorney General Edward Schmultz on S. 1775 before the Senate Committee on the Judiciary, Nov. 13, 1981. See generally the article by former attorney general Griffin Bell, Proposed Amendments to the Federal Tort Claims Act, 16 Harv. J. on Leg. 1 (1979); and P. Schuck, Suing our Servants: The Court, Congress, and the Liability of Public Officials for Damages, 1980 Supreme Court Review 281.

4. In commenting upon the difference between the immunity granted judges and the lack of immunity provided other officials, Justice Rehnquist is reported to have said, "If one were to hazard an informed guess as to why such a distinction in treatment between judges and prosecutors, on the one hand, and other public officials on the other, obtains, mine would be that those who decide the common law know through personal experience the sort of pressures that might exist for such decision-makers in the absence of absolute immunity, but may not know or may have forgotten that similar pressures exist in the case of nonjudicial public officials to whom difficult decisions are committed." (Quoted in Administrative Conference of U.S., Project Outline "Advice on Official Immunity" at 11 (1981).)

B. REVIEWABILITY

Page 900. Add the following after line 11:

While cases finding *non*reviewability in the face of Congressional silence are rare, they still exist. In Southern Railway v. Seaboard Allied Milling Co., 442 U.S. 444 (1979), the Supreme Court considered whether courts could review an ICC decision *not* to investigate seasonal rate increases proposed by a group of railroads. Shippers, challenging the rate increases, noted that Interstate Commerce Act §15(8)(a) says that "[t]he Commission may, upon the complaint of an interested party, or on its own initiative, order a hearing concerning the lawfulness of some of [a proposed] rate. . . ." The shippers argued that some of the proposed rates violated antidiscrimination sections of the act and that the ICC abused its discretion in failing to investigate.

Justice Stevens, for the Court, wrote that the federal courts are without power to review ICC actions (or inaction) under §15(8)(a). He noted that "the ultimate analysis is always one of Congress' intent, and in this case, there is persuasive reason to believe that [nonreviewability] was the purpose of Congress." (1) A shipper can always secure review of an individual rate in effect under Act §13(1), though compared with §15(8)(a), the shipper suffers certain procedural disadvantages (e.g., he has the burden of proving the rate "unreasonable"). (2) The statute uses the word "may," giving the commission broad discretion and leaving the courts with "no law to apply." (3) When Congress wanted review, it put the word "shall" into the act. (4) If the commission can be forced to use §15(8)(a), shippers will almost always make them use it, for there is likely to be some unlawful rate somewhere in any proposed general rate change, which typically involves thousand of individual rates. Section 13(1) would then become superfluous. (5) The commission typically makes its investigation decisions within thirty days of filing. It receives about 50,000 filings per year, and each filing embodies thousands of individual rates. It is administratively impossible to consider the likely lawfulness of all these rates in so short a time. (6) The effect of review here would be to curtail experimentation with seasonal (peak and off-peak) rates, despite a specific new law aimed at encouraging them. (7) The power to investigate rates and the power to suspend them are interlinked, but it has long been held that the "merits of a suspension decision are not reviewable. . . . Aberdeen & Rockfish R. Co. v. SCRAP," 422 U.S. 289, 311. (Is this to say more than that the "merits" are "committed to agency discretion"?) (8) Judicial review would disrupt orderly commission procedure "by bringing the courts into the adjudication of the lawfulness of rates in advance of administrative consideration." It would undermine the commission's primary jurisdiction and would create hazards to uniformity all shown by the act's legislative history to be undesirable.

"In short," said the Court, "the necessary 'clear and convincing evidence' that Congress meant to prohibit all judicial review of the Commission's limited decision not to initiate an investigation under §15(8)(a) is provided by the language of the statute, as well as its place within the statutory design of the Act, its legislative history, and the light shed on it by our case law concerning analogous statutes."

More normally, of course, silence is interpreted to mean "review." There must be "clear and convincing" evidence of a congressional intent to preclude review. Commonwealth of Virginia ex rel. Commission v. Marshall, 599 F.2d 588, 592 (4th Cir. 1979); Sunter Dairy v. Bergland, 591 F.2d 1063 (5th Cir. 1979).

Page 900. At the end of line 14, add new callout 102a and the accompanying footnote:

102a. Cf. Graham v. Coston, 568 F.2d 1092 (5th Cir. 1978).

Page 906. Add to footnote 112 the following:

See, e.g., Commonwealth of Virginia ex rel. Commissioner v. Marshall, 599 F.2d 588, 592 (4th Cir. 1979).

Page 916. At the end of footnote 131, add the following:

As is true of "questions of law" (see chapter 4), Saferstein's factors may be viewed through the lens of congressional intent. The D.C. Circuit writes, "the judicial role is to determine the extent of the agency's delegated authority and then determine whether the agency has acted within that authority." National Association of Postal Supervisors v. United States Postal Service, 602 F.2d 420, 432 (D.C. Cir. 1979) (issue of relative rates of pay of managerial and other postal employees mostly within discretion of agency).

C. STANDING TO SECURE JUDICIAL REVIEW

Page 958. Add the following at the end of the page:

Notes and Questions on Recent Developments in the Law of Standing

1. Valley Forge Christian College v. Americans United for Separation of Church and State Inc., 102 S. Ct. 752 (1982), denied taxpayer and citizen standing to object to the Department of Health, Education and Welfare's donation, pursuant to federal statute, of a US military hospital to a church-related college, as violating the Establishment Clause.

Distinguishing Flast v. Cohen, Justice Rehnquist's opinion for the majority denied standing to the members of the plaintiff organization in their capacity as taxpayers because the transfer of property did not represent a congressional exercise of the Article I §8 spending power, but an administrative exercise of the Article IV §3 power to administer and dispose of government property. Standing was denied them in their capacity as citizens on the authority of Schlesinger v. Reservists Committee to Stop the War and United States v. Richardson. Asserting that Article III requires plaintiffs to establish "injury in fact" and to show that the injury is "fairly traceable to the challenged action" and "is likely to be redressed by a favorable decision" (quoting from Simon v. Eastern Kentucky Welfare Rights Org.) the Court denied that a government violation of the Establishment Clause causes "injury in fact" to a citizen. It stated that ". . . the Establishment Clause does not provide a special license to roam the country in search of governmental wrongdoing. . . . The federal courts were simply not constituted as ombudsmen of the general welfare." The Court also warned of "the conversion of the courts of the United States into judicial versions of college debating forums."

Justice Brennan, joined by Justices Marshall and Blackmun, issued a strong dissent. He argued that the members of the plaintiff organization would clearly have taxpayer standing under Flast v. Cohen if the government had given funds directly to the college, and that they should not lose standing simply because the government, in a two-step transaction, used taxpayer funds to purchase property, and then turned the property over to the college. Justice Stevens also dissented.

2. One of the important questions raised by recent Supreme Court statements on standing is the continued vitality of the "zone of interests" test. Professor Davis states that "[p]robably the Court is allowing the test to die, for the Court might be expected to mention it when it is relevant if it is still alive." K. Davis, Administrative Law §22.02-11 (Supp. 1980).

Yet the Court did mention the zone test, albeit in a footnote and as dictum, in Gladstone, Realtors v. Village of Bellwood, 441 U.S. 91 (1979). The Court, in discussing constitutional and certain prudential limitations on standing, stated: "There are other nonconstitutional limitations on standing to be applied in appropriate circumstances. See, e.g., Simon v. Eastern Kentucky Welfare Rights Org., . . . ('the interest of the plaintiff, regardless of its nature in the absolute, [must] at least be arguably within the zone of interests to be protected or regulated by the statutory framework within which his claim arises.')" And in *Valley Forge*, the Court referred to the *Data Processing* zone test as a "prudential" limitation on standing, as contrasted with the Article III requirement of injury in fact being fairly traceable to the challenged action and likely to be redressed by a favorable decision.

3. Following the Court's failure to apply the zone test in *Duke Power*, there was speculation that the test would be applied only when the plaintiff's claim was based on nonconstitutional grounds. Lower courts, however, have generally not responded to this suggestion. See, e.g., Moore v. Tangipahoa Parish School Board, 625 F. 2d 33 (5th Cir. 1980) (white female not within the zone of interests of the constitutional protections against racial discrimination); Haring v. Blumenthal, 471 F. Supp. 1172 (D.D.C. 1979) (IRS agent challenging constitutionality of tax exemption for immoral religious group not within the zone of interests protected by the First Amendment).

4. One court has claimed that the zone test is confined to cases arising under the APA. See Sneaker Circus, Inc. v. Carter, 457 F. Supp. 771 (E.D.N.Y. 1978).

Two courts have equated the zone test with the issue of causation. See Loewen v. Turnipseed, 488 F. Supp. 1138 (N.D. Miss. 1980); American Friends Service Comm. v. Webster, 485 F. Supp. 222 (D.D.C. 1980).

5. Whatever the current state of the law, it appears that lower courts lack a coherent vision of Supreme Court standing doctrine:

a. Many courts have simply continued to apply the injury-in-fact and zone-of-interests test of *Data Processing*. See, e.g., American Federation of Government Employees, AFL-CIO, v. Stetson, 640 F. 2d 642 (5th Cir. 1981).

b. Other courts have attempted to incorporate more recent Supreme Court cases. The most common test is the three-pronged test suggested in *Duke Power* and reiterated in *Valley Forge:* plaintiffs must demonstrate injury in fact, a causal connection between the injury and the action of the defendant, and a substantial likelihood that the relief requested will remedy the injury. See, e.g., Theriault v. Brennan, 641 F.2d 28, 31 (1st Cir. 1981); Dowling v. United States, 476 F. Supp. 1018 (D. Mass. 1979); Hall v. Equal Employment Opportunity Comm., 456 F. Supp. 695 (N.D. Cal. 1978).

c. Still other courts have adopted two of the three prongs stated in *Duke Power*. See McCoy-Elkhorn Coal Corp. v. United States Environmental Protection Agency, 622 F. 2d 260 (6th Cir. 1980) (injury in fact and substantial probability that relief would redress the injury); Chamber of Commerce of the United States v. United States Department of Agriculture, 459 F. Supp. 216 (D.D.C. 1978) (injury in fact and fairly traceable causal connection).

d. A new development is various four-pronged tests that have been used to test standing. The most common is simply the three-pronged test suggested by *Duke Power* combined with the zone of interests test. See, e.g., Theriault v. Brennan, 488 F. Supp. 286 (D. Me. 1980), *aff'd*, 641 F.2d 28 (1st Cir. 1981).

e. Another four-pronged test was suggested in Wright v. Miller, 480 F. Supp. 790, 793 (D.D.C. 1979). In addition to the three-pronged test suggested by *Duke Power*, the court imposed a new condition—that "there must exist a sufficient degree of concrete adverseness between the plaintiff and defendant."

f. Finally, two courts have tried to win the hearts of administrative law students by eliminating all multipronged tests. In United States v Professional Air Traffic Controllers Organization, 504 F. Supp. 442, 445 (N.D. Ill. 1980), the court stated that to establish standing "it is necessary that a complaining party be able to demonstrate injury to a legally protected interest (Perkins v. Lukins Steel Co.)." In Tasby v. Estes, 643 F.2d 1103, 1105 (5th Cir. 1981), the court upheld standing on the ground that "[t]here is no doubt that within the context of this litigation the plaintiffs here have the personal stake and interest that impart the concrete adverseness required by Article III."

To what extent do you feel that these different standards are functionally equivalent?

Is it time to start all over again? If so, how would you avoid the problems that developed with the *Data Processing* test? What degree of specificity is desirable? Is it possible to develop a test that would not be subject to as great a degree of judicial manipulation?

6. Gladstone, Realtors, v. Village of Bellwood, 441 U.S. 91 (1979), and Havens Realty Corp. v. Coleman, 102 S. Ct. 1114 (1982), sustained the standing of various plaintiffs to sue realtors engaged in "racial steering" (steering blacks to predominantly black neighborhoods and whites to predominantly white neighborhoods) in violation of the Fair Housing Act. *Gladstone* held that four residents of a "target" integrated area from which whites were steered could bring suit, as well as the town in which the target area was located. *Haven Realty* allowed suit by "testers" who purposely sought information about housing in order to detect violations of the act, and were steered; by a nonprofit organization dedicated to promoting interracial housing and providing information to house buyers; and by two residents of the area, provided that they showed that their neighborhoods were affected by the practice.

Although both cases involved private litigation, the opinions in *Gladstone* and *Haven Realty* invoked "injury in fact" and related decisions of standing developed in decisions, such as *Duke Power, Simon,* and Warth v. Seldin, involving judicial review of governmental action. Are the considerations involved in the two situations the same? Should standing doctrines governing judicial review of administrative action be used to determine when one private party may bring suit in federal court against another private party for violation of a statute?

D. THE TIMING OF JUDICIAL REVIEW

Page 977. Add the following after line 27:

5. The relaxation of the "finality" rule and of "ripeness" requirements for reviewing regulations and informal agency actions does not imply any such relaxation when adjudications are at issue. The appellate courts readily understand the resemblance between agency and court adjudications and recognize how any such relaxation of finality rules would bring about the harms and delays that accompany piecemeal appeals from district courts.

Thus, the Supreme Court firmly rejected the Standard Oil Company's (SoCal) appeal from an FTC decision not to dismiss its complaint against SoCal. SoCal had argued that there was no evidence to warrant bringing a proceeding that would subject it to millions of dollars of defense costs.

FTC v. STANDARD OIL CO. OF CALIFORNIA

449 U.S. 232 (1980)

MR. JUSTICE POWELL delivered the opinion of the Court. . . .

The Commission averred in its complaint that it had reason to believe that Socal was violating the Act. That averment is subject to judicial review before the conclusion of administrative adjudication only if the issuance of the complaint was "final agency action" or otherwise was "directly reviewable" under §10(c) of the APA, 5 U.S.C. §704. We conclude that the issuance of the complaint was neither.

The Commission's issuance of its complaint was not "final agency action." The Court observed in Abbott Laboratories v. Gardner, 387 U.S. 136, 149 (1967), that "[t]he cases dealing with judicial review of administrative actions have interpreted the 'finality' element in a pragmatic way.". . .

By its terms, the Commission's averment of "reason to believe" that Socal was violating the Act is not a definitive statement of position. It represents a threshold determination that further inquiry is warranted and that a complaint should initiate proceedings. To be sure, the issuance of the complaint is definitive on the question whether the Commission avers reason to believe that the respondent to the complaint is violating the Act. But the extent to which the respondent may challenge the complaint and its charges proves that the averment of reason to believe is not "definitive."; . . . [It is] a determination only that adjudicatory proceedings will commence. . . .

Serving only to initiate the proceedings, the issuance of the complaint averring reason to believe has no legal force comparable to that of the regulation at issue in *Abbot Laboratories*, [Casebook, at p. 965] nor any comparable effect upon Socal's daily business. The regulations in *Abbott Laboratories* forced manufacturers to "risk serious criminal and civil penalties" for noncompliance, . . . or "change all their labels, advertisements, and promotional materials; . . . destroy stocks of printed matter; and . . . invest heavily in new printing type and new supplies." . . . Socal does not contend that the issuance of the complaint had any such legal or practical effect, except to impose upon Socal the burden of responding to the charges made against it. Although this burden certainly is substantial, it is different in kind and legal effect from the burdens attending what heretofore has been considered to be final agency action.

In contrast to the complaint's lack of legal or practical effect upon Socal, the effect of the judicial review sought by Socal is likely to be interference with the proper functioning of the agency and a burden for the courts. Judicial intervention into the agency process denies the agency an opportunity to correct its own mistakes and to apply its expertise. . . . Intervention also leads to piecemeal review which at the least is inefficient and upon completion of the agency process might prove to have been unnecessary. . . .

Furthermore, unlike the review in *Abbott Laboratories*, judicial review to determine whether the Commission decided that it had the requisite reason to believe would delay resolution of the ultimate question whether the Act was violated. Finally, every respondent to a Commission complaint could make the claim that Socal had made. Judicial review of the averments in the Commission's complaints should not be a means of turning prosecutor into defendant before adjudication concludes.

In sum, the Commission's issuance of a complaint averring reason to believe that Socal was violating the Act is not a definitive ruling or regulation. It had no legal force or practical effect upon Socal's daily business other than the disruptions that accompany any major litigation. And immediate judicial review would serve neither efficiency nor enforcement of the Act. These pragmatic considerations counsel against the conclusion that the issuance of the complaint was "final agency action.". . .

[SoCal argues] that it will be irreparably harmed unless the issuance of the complaint is judicially reviewed immediately. Socal argues that the expense and disruption of defending itself in protracted adjudicatory proceedings constitutes irreparable harm. As indicated above, we do not doubt that the burden of defending this proceeding will be substantial. But "the expense and annoyance of litigation is 'part of the social burden of living under government.' ". . .

As we recently reiterated: "Mere litigation expense, even substantial and unrecoupable cost, does not constitute irreparable injury.". . .

Socal further contends that its challenge to the Commission's averment of reason to believe can never be reviewed unless it is reviewed before the Commission's adjudication concludes. As stated by the Court of Appeals, the alleged unlawfulness in the issuance of the complaint "is likely to become insulated from any review" if deferred until appellate review of a cease-and-desist order. . . . Socal also suggests that the unlawfulness will be "insulated" because the reviewing court will lack an adequate record and it will address only the question whether substantial evidence supported the cease-and-desist order, [not whether the FTC had sufficient ground to *begin* the proceeding.]

We are not persuaded by this speculation. The Act expressly authorizes a court of appeals to order that the Commission take additional evidence. . . . Thus, a record which would be inadequate for review of alleged unlawfulness in the issuance of a complaint can be made adequate. We also note that the APA specifically provides that a "preliminary, procedural, or intermediate agency action or ruling not directly reviewable is subject to review on the review of the final agency action," 5 U.S.C. §704, and that the APA also empowers a court of appeals to "hold unlawful and set aside agency action . . . found to be . . . without observance of procedure required by law." 5 U.S.C. §706. Thus, assuming that the issuance of the complaint is not "committed to agency discretion by law," a court of appeals reviewing a cease-and-desist order has the power to review alleged unlawfulness in the issuance of a complaint. We need not decide what action a court of appeals should take if it finds a cease-and-desist order to be supported by substantial evidence but the complaint to have been issued without the requisite reason to believe. It suffices to hold that the possibility does not affect the application of the finality rule. . . .

[JUSTICE STEVENS, concurring separately, argued that a decision to issue a complaint was not "agency action." Hence, it was never reviewable.]

Page 984. Add the following after line 25:

In a recent case, the Fifth Circuit, en banc, rejected the Supreme Court's suggestion, derived from Monroe v. Pape, 365 U.S. 167 (1961) (among other cases), that "exhaustion" does not apply to §1983 actions. Patsy v. Florida International University, 634 F.2d 900 (5th Cir. 1981), *cert. granted*, 50 U.S.L.W. 3244 (Oct. 5, 1981). The opinion contains an interesting analysis of the exhaustion doctrine. It suggests that prior Supreme Court holdings on the subject are no longer good law. And, it states that the "exhaustion" doctrine applies in a §1983 case like any other case. Is this result inevitable given the expansion of §1983 to cover jurisdictionally so many violations of federal law? See the supplement to Chapter 9,B, supra.

Page 984. Add the following after line 27:

For an effort to apply a "functional" analysis of the exhaustion doctrine, see Ezratty v. Commonwealth of Puerto Rico, 684 F.2d 770 (1st Cir. 1981).

Page 984. At the end of line 27 add the new callout and accompanying footnote:

191a. In Social Security Act cases the Supreme Court has held that the secretary may waive the act's exhaustion requirements. Mathews v. Eldridge, 424 U.S. 319, 328. In fact, a court might itself find a waiver over the secretary's opposition "where a claimant's interest in having a particular issue resolved promptly is so great that deference to the agency's judgment is inappropriate." 424 U.S. at 330. Such compulsory waivers, which amount to a court's refusal to require exhaustion, have been found as to members of a class *other* than a named plaintiff in a suit, when the named plaintiff has itself exhausted its remedies. The courts have stated that the secretary in such cases has taken a final position on the merits of their argument. See Jones v. Califano, 568 F.2d 333 (3d Cir. 1977). See also Wilson v. Secretary of HHS, No. 81-1188 (1st Cir. March 8, 1982).

E. PRIMARY JURISDICTION

Page 1011. Add the following after line 20:

The analysis developed in the antitrust area has been used elsewhere. The First Circuit Court of Appeals, for example, has generalized three factors to be used for determining whether a court should invoke the doctrine: "(1) whether the agency determination lay at the heart of the task assigned the agency by Congress; (2) whether agency expertise was required to unravel intricate, technical facts; and (3) whether, though perhaps not determinative, the agency determination would materially aid the court." Mashpee Tribe v. New Seabury Corp., 592 F.2d 575, 580-581 (1st Cir.), *cert. denied,* 444 U.S. 866 (1979).

* Some courts have believed that agency expertise argues for allowing the agency to *decide* the issue first, rather than simply submit an amicus brief. If so, the nature of the legal issue, whether it calls for a legal or technical judgment, would be highly relevant to a decision about whether to require exhaustion. See United States Tour Operators Association v. Trans World Airlines, 556 F.2d 126 (2d Cir. 1977); Lubrizol Corp. v. EPA, 562 F.2d 807 (D.C. Cir. 1977).

Chapter Ten

"Public Interest" Administrative Law: Representation and Disclosure

Page 1013. Add the following to footnote 1:

See also Note, In Defense of an Embattled Mode of Advocacy: An Analysis and Justification of Public Interest Practice, 90 Yale L.J. 1436 (1981).

In recent years, business-oriented "public interest" groups, funded by corporations and business executives, have been created to challenge environmental and social regulations as unduly restrictive or costly. See, e.g., Costle v. Pacific Legal Foundation, 445 U.S. 198 (1980); Mountain States Legal Foundation v. Andrus, 499 F. Supp. 383 (D. Wyo. 1980).

A. THE JUDICIAL DEVELOPMENT OF AN INTEREST REPRESENTATION MODEL OF ADMINISTRATIVE LAW

Page 1039. Add the following after paragraph 6:

7. The failure of the secretary of the interior to act upon applications for oil and gas leases on public lands in Wyoming, Idaho, and Montana was successfully challenged in Mountain States Legal Foundation v. Andrus, 499 F. Supp. 383 (D. Wyo. 1980). The secretary had declined to process applications for oil and gas leases on lands administered by the Forest Service, pending its completion of an extended study of areas that might be recommended to Congress for inclusion in the National Wilderness Preservation System. The court found that the secretary's inaction amounted to a de facto withdrawal from leasing of the lands in question, in violation of the Mineral Leasing Act and other relevant statutes. The court also held that the Interior Department was required to promulgate

rules and regulations stating the terms upon which oil and gas lease applications would be approved or rejected. Relying upon Environmental Defense Fund, Inc. v. Ruckleshaus, the court rejected the Interior Department's argument that inaction is not reviewable: ". . . At some point administrative delay amounts to a refusal to act, with sufficient finality and ripeness to permit judicial review. . . . When administrative inaction has precisely the same effect on the rights of the parties as denial of the requested agency action, an agency may not prevent judicial review by masking agency policy in the form of inaction rather than an order denying the action requested. . . . The Administrative Procedure Act requires every agency to conclude any matter presented to it within a reasonable time, and provides that the reviewing court shall compel agency action unlawfully withheld or unreasonably delayed. 5 U.S.C. §§555(b) and 706."

Page 1040. Add the following after line 4:

In recent years the Court has become even more hostile to private rights of action, creating a strong presumption against allowing them unless specifically authorized by Congress. See e.g., Middlesex City Sewage Auth. v. National Sea Clammers, 101 S. Ct. 2615 (1981) (Federal Water Pollution Control Act); California v. Sierra Club, 101 S. Ct. 1775 (Rivers and Harbors Act); Kissinger v. Reporters Comm. for Freedom of the Press, 445 U.S. 136, 148-49 (1980) (Federal Records Act); Transamerica Mortgage Advisers, Inc. v. Lewis, 444 U.S. 11 (1979) (securities laws). The question whether a statute creates a private right of action is now solely "one of congressional intent, not whether this Court thinks that it can improve upon the statutory scheme that Congress enacted in law." Touche Ross & Co. v. Redington, 442 U.S. 560, 578 (1979) (securities laws).

This hostility reflects judicial concern with the complexities and costs involved in private litigation of asserted regulatory violations, particularly where damages are sought. Large damage awards, especially in class-action cases, may also create serious risks of overdeterrence. The Court is also sensitive to concerns that judicial creation of private remedies usurps Congress's power to structure and oversee regulatory programs and their implementation. For a comprehensive discussion of these and related issues, see Stewart & Sunstein, Public Programs and Private Rights, 95 Harv. L. Rev. 1293 (1982). This article examines the comparative advantages and disadvantages of private rights of initiation (judicial review proceedings by regulatory beneficiaries seeking a court order requiring the responsible administrative agency to enforce controls on regulated firms) and private rights of action by beneficiaries directly against regulated firms as remedies for deficient agency performance.

Page 1057. Add the following after line 11:

3a. In Copeland v. Marshall, 641 F.2d 880 (1980), an important en banc decision, the D.C. Circuit Court of Appeals sought to establish general guidelines for statutory attorney's fees awards against the government. The case involved an award under Title VII of the Civil Rights Act, authorizing suits against the government for sex discrimination. The attorney's fees provision, 42 U.S.C. §2000e-5(k), authorizes the court, "in its discretion," to "allow the prevailing party . . . a reasonable attorney's fee as part of the costs, and the United States shall be liable for costs the same as a private person." The case had produced equitable relief and back pay awards of $31,345 for twenty-four women employees.

The court authorized an award of $160,000 for 3,606 hours worked on the case. Over a strong dissent by Judges Wilkey and Tamm, the court held that attorneys should be compensated at prevailing hourly commercial rates for attorneys of similar experience. It firmly rejected the government's contention that attorneys should be compensated on a "cost-plus" basis, consisting of the actual cost to the attorney's firm or organization of his or her services, plus a reasonable allowance for profit or overhead. The difference between the two approaches is particularly significant in the case of "public interest" attorneys, whose salaries are typically much lower than prevailing commercial rates, and whose organizations make no profit. Judges Wilkey and Tamm complained that much of the work on the case, handled by a large D.C. law firm, was performed by junior associates with little experience or concern to minimize costs, for whom high hourly fees were charged. They also complained that the majority's approach gave plaintiffs' lawyers an incentive to engage in massive discovery and refuse settlement in order to run up fee awards.

Copeland went on to hold that attorney's fees should be determined by multiplying appropriate hourly rates times the number of hours "reasonably expended" on the litigation, in order to arrive at a basic "lodestar" total. The lodestar might then be adjusted upward to reflect the contingent nature of victory and accompanying fee awards, and any unusual skill or creativity on the part of the attorneys not already reflected in the hourly rate.

The application of *Copeland* guidelines to cases where the plaintiff does not prevail or is only partially successful was considered in three recent decisions by the D.C. Circuit. Environmental Defense Fund v. EPA, No. 79-1580 (D.C. Cir. Feb. 5, 1982), granted the EDF's application for attorney's fees for its largely successful challenge to the EPA's failure to regulate most uses of PCB chemicals. The award was sought pursuant to Section 19(d) of the Toxic Substances Control Act, 15 U.S.C. §2618(d), which provides that a reviewing court's decision "may include an award of the costs of suit and reasonable attorneys' fees for attorneys and expert witnesses if the court determines such an award is appropriate." The appropriateness standard is found in many attorney's fees provisions in environmental statutes.

The EDF court applied the *Copeland* standards for fee awards. It found that 825.4 hours were a reasonable expenditure by the EDF attorneys on the case, and calculated a lodestar fee, based on hourly rates ranging from $55 to $110 an hour, of $76,804. It rejected the EPA's claim that the lodestar should not include the EDF's work on issues on which it did not prevail, concluding that the appropriateness standard in TSCA, as contrasted with the "prevailing party" language in the *Copeland* statute, authorized the court to make awards to nonprevailing parties. It further concluded that the litigation involved important and difficult issues of first impression, that "the outcome of the litigation greatly served the public interest," and that there should be no discount "simply because EDF failed to prevail on one of three closely-related issues." It rejected the EPA's claim that no allowance should be made for the hours spent by the EDF on issues raised by industry intervenors or on postdecision negotiations.

The court rejected the EDF's argument that the lodestar figure should be doubled, concluding that the public benefits from the suit and the delay in receiving compensation warranted a 17.18 percent increase, for a total of $90,000. In rejecting the EDF's claim, the court pointed out that the contingency risk of not winning the case was eliminated or greatly reduced by the appropriateness standard for the awards; and that the admitted difficulty of the case was reflected in the hourly rates, which were set by reference to current commercial rates rather than to those prevailing at the time of the original litigation.

In a "fees on fees" award, the court also awarded $9534.50 for the hours expended on the EDF's behalf in litigating its right to fee awards in the basic case.

In Alabama Power Co. v. Gorsuch, No. 78-1006 (D.C. Cir. Feb. 5, 1982), and Sierra Club v. Gorsuch, No. 79-1580 (D.C. Cir. Feb. 5, 1982), the court held that attorney's fees and costs should be awarded to environmental groups who had challenged EPA regulations. In *Alabama Power* they had won only half the issues that they raised and in *Sierra Club* they had not won on any issue.

The fee awards were made pursuant to §307(f) of the Clean Air Act, authorizing such awards "whenever . . . appropriate." *Alabama Power* made awards on issues on which the environmental groups had not prevailed, or which had been withdrawn before decision on the merits. In doing so, it relied on Metropolitan Washington Coalition for Clean Air v. District of Columbia, 639 F.2d 802, 804 (D.C. Cir. 1981), which held that the test was not the hindsight determination whether plaintiff had won on the merits or had caused the government to comply with the law simply by instituting the litigation, but an "inducement" test: whether "the underlying suit was a prudent and desirable effort to achieve an unfulfilled objective of the Act." This rationale was followed in *Sierra Club* to award fees even though the environmental groups had not prevailed on any issue. The court found that the case, involving the adoption of control requirements for new coal-fired power plants, was an important one; that the Sierra Club had asserted important claims, none of which was "remotely frivolous"; and that the Sierra Club had contributed to the court's understanding and resolution of novel and difficult substantive and procedural issues. The two decisions also held that the amount of the fee awarded should be determined in accordance with the lodestar technique endorsed in *Copeland.*

Judge Wilkey entered a lengthy dissent in *Alabama Power,* sharply disagreeing with the appropriateness test employed in *Alabama Power* and *Sierra Club.* He argued that while an appropriateness standard could be used to justify attorney's fees awards to parties who *prevailed* on their claims, it did not provide judicially manageable criteria for determining when awards should be made to *nonprevailing* parties. He derided *Sierra Club's* efforts to give content to the appropriateness standard, pointing to some sixteen formulations of different criteria in the opinion. These included "encourag[ing] litigation which will ensure proper implementation and administration of the [Clean Air Act]"; the "benefits conferred by the litigation"; whether it was of "the type Congress intended to encourage"; the desirability of encouraging "the participation of 'public interest' groups in resolving complex technical questions"; the need for economic incentives not otherwise available; and allocating "the costs of litigation equitably, to encourage the achievement of statutory goals." Judge Wilkey concluded that "these multifarious and diffuse 'standards' amount to no standard at all" unless the standard was to award fees to *any* party asserting a nonfrivolous claim—a result Congress plainly had not intended.

Judge Wilkey conceded that in enacting §307(f), Congress had intended to go beyond the "prevailing party" approach in the Civil Rights statutes. But given the impossibility of developing judicially manageable "public interest" criteria for awards to nonprevailing parties, Judge Wilkey would apparently conclude that the statute would be unconstitutional if read to authorize such awards, because it would then represent an invalid delegation of legislative powers to courts, which are limited by Article III to the exercise of "judicial" powers.

Accordingly, Judge Wilkey would read §307(f) as authorizing fee awards if, and only if, a party prevails on at least some part of its claims. Applying this approach to the case at hand, Judge Wilkey concluded that eligibility for awards should be determined on an issue-by-issue basis. He also repudiated intimations by the *Alabama Power* majority that industrial firms that had not applied for fee awards would not be entitled to such awards because they have an independent economic incentive to bring suit. Judge Wilkey asserted that "we ought not to require the court to look into the heart of the petitioner to determine whether his motivations were in the public interest only."

QUESTIONS

Is it plausible to read §307(f), as Judge Wilkey apparently would, to require automatic fee awards to any prevailing party (including, apparently, industry)? Even the civil rights statutes, which limit awards to parties who prevail, authorize the court to make such awards "in its discretion." See, e.g., 42 U.S.C. §2000e-5(k). Would Judge Wilkey hold this "discretion" provision invalid? On the other hand, what standard *should* courts apply in the exercise of such discretion or in determining whether fee awards are "appropriate"?

B. PUBLIC DISCLOSURE OF AGENCY INFORMATION AND DECISION MAKING

Page 1061. Add the following after line 10:

a1. Agency Records Subject to Disclosure

The FOIA, 5 U.S.C. §552(a)(4)(B), empowers federal courts to enjoin an "agency from withholding agency records and to order the production of any agency records improperly withheld." Kissinger v. Reporters Committee for Freedom of the Press, 445 U.S. 136 (1980), presented the question whether this provision may be used to require agencies to obtain and disclose records no longer in their possession.

While national security advisor to President Nixon and while secretary of state during the Nixon and Ford administrations, Henry Kissinger caused summaries or verbatim transcripts of his telephone conversations to be prepared. Acting upon an opinion from the State Department's legal adviser that the telephone notes were Kissinger's personal papers and were not agency records, Kissinger removed the notes before leaving office and donated them to the Library of Congress, under conditions limiting access to the notes.

New York Times columnist William Safire, the Military Audit Project, the Reporters Committee for Freedom of the Press, the American Historical Association, the American Political Science Association, and several journalists requested production by the State Department of the notes under the FOIA. The lower courts required production of the notes prepared while Kissinger was secretary of state, finding that they had been improperly removed by Kissinger from the State Department's custody and that the district court's equitable powers could be used to require their return by the Library of Congress even though it is not an "agency" subject to the FOIA. The State Department was required to recover the notes and disclose those not exempt from disclosure to plaintiffs.

The Court reversed, holding that the FOIA does not empower private plaintiffs to obtain recovery of documents wrongfully removed from agency custody.[29a] The Court held that an agency does not "withhold" a document in violation of FOIA when it fails to produce a document that is no longer in its possession, basing its result on the statutory language and the fear that a contrary result would burden agencies with the task of searching for and retrieving documents no longer in their possession. Since all of the requests except Safire's had been made after the notes had been removed from the State Department, the Department's failure to honor those requests did not violate the act. The Court held Safire's request was not covered by FOIA because it was directed to notes prepared by Kissinger when he was national security advisor to the president. Although FOIA applies to the "Executive Office of the President," 5 U.S.C. §552(e), the Court invoked legislative history to the effect that FOIA was not intended to apply to the president's immediate personal staff or those in the executive office whose sole function is to advise or assist the president.

Justices Brennan and Stevens dissented from the Court's ruling that FOIA does not require production of documents wrongfully removed from an agency.

Page 1066. Add the following after line 24:

The limits of this exemption have been tested in a number of cases involving requests for enforcement manuals employed by federal law enforcement agencies. Such information certainly is used by the agencies to instruct their personnel in the "practices of [the] agency," and thus falls within the rubric of the exemption. For members of the public, however, these manuals resemble the "secret law" that FOIA was designed to open to public scrutiny; information concerning enforcement practices can inform the public of the effective limits of the law by revealing the way the law will be enforced. None of the courts of appeals have allowed these manuals to be released. For a summary of the case law, see Cooke v. Bureau of Alcohol, Tobacco & Firearms, —F.2d—(D.C. Cir. 1981) (en banc). In Cooke the D.C. Circuit ruled that the manual had been developed and used for predominantly "internal purposes," and noted that disclosure could lead to circumvention of agency regulations.

29a. The Court also held that no private action lies under the Federal Records Act of 1950 and the Records Disposal Act to obtain return of wrongfully removed documents. The Court did not reach the question whether the telephone notes had been wrongfully removed from the State Department.

Page 1072. Add the following cases after line 25:

TAXATION WITH REPRESENTATION FUND v. INTERNAL REVENUE SERVICE

646 F.2d 666 (D.C. Cir. 1981)

[This decision involved the application of Exemption 5 to internal IRS memoranda examining and explaining the rationale for various IRS rulings and decisions. While originally prepared as part of the agency's deliberative process on those rulings and decisions, once the rulings and decisions have been made these memoranda are indexed and used by IRS officials in future administrative decisions on tax policy and the resolution of particular controversies with taxpayers. The court of appeals, in a decision by Judge Harry Edwards, sustained the district court's ruling that the memoranda were not exempt. The court summarized the requested material as follows:]

The records in dispute in this case fall under three general headings: General Counsel's Memoranda ("GCMs"), Technical Memoranda ("TMs"), and Actions on Decisions ("AODs"). After carefully considering the evidence before it, the District Court found that none of the disputed documents were covered by Exemption 5. . . .

. . . As to the GCMs, the trial court found that these documents "contain the reasons behind the adoption of revenue rulings, private letter rulings, and technical advice memoranda," and that they are "indexed and have important precedential value in determining future tax questions."

. . . As to AODs, the trial court found that the documents "contain the reasons behind the acquiescence or nonacquiescence of the IRS in court decisions," and that the documents are "made available to IRS personnel and are cited and applied by IRS personnel in later AOD's, and TM's to promote the consistent application of the tax laws." . . . As to the TMs, the trial court found that these documents "explain the reasons behind the adoption of [a] Treasury Decision" and that "[t]hey are used by IRS personnel in determining the tax status of taxpayers."

II. Analysis of the Relevant Case Law

A GENERAL DEFINITION OF THE DELIBERATIVE PROCESS PRIVILEGE

. . . Given the literal language of Exemption 5, it is not surprising that the courts have construed this exemption to encompass the protections traditionally afforded certain documents pursuant to evidentiary privileges in the civil discovery context.

The courts have recognized that Exemption 5 protects, as a general rule, materials which would be protected under the attorney-client privilege, . . . the attorney work-product privilege, . . . or the executive "deliberative process" privilege. . . .

. . . Of these privileges recognized under section (b)(5) of FOIA, *the only privilege claimed by appellants,* and considered by the court below, was the "deliberative process" privilege, sometimes called the "executive" or "governmental" privilege.

The deliberative process privilege protects "confidential intra-agency advisory opinions . . . disclosure of which would be injurious to the consultative functions of government.". . .

As was recently noted by Judge Wald in [Coastal States Gas Corp. v. DOE, 617 F.2d 854 (D.C. Cir. 1980,] the deliberative process privilege is "unique to government" and has a number of purposes: it serves to assure that subordinates within an agency will feel free to provide the decision-maker with their uninhibited opinions and recommendations without fear of later being subject to public ridicule or criticism; to protect against premature disclosure of proposed policies before they have been finally formulated or adopted; and to protect against confusing the issues and misleading the public by dissemination of documents suggesting reasons and rationales for a course of action which were not in fact the ultimate reasons for the agency's action. 617 F.2d at 866. . . .

. . . Thus, the privilege protects documents reflecting advisory opinions, recommendations, and deliberations comprising part of a process by which governmental decisions and policies are formulated, as well as other subjective documents that reflect the personal opinions of the writer prior to the agency's adoption of a policy. . . .

"PREDECISIONAL" VERSUS "POST-DECISIONAL" DOCUMENTS AND INQUIRIES CONCERNING THE "WORKING LAW OF THE AGENCY"

Exemption 5 does not apply to final agency actions that constitute statements of policy or final opinions that have the force of law, or which explain actions that an agency has already taken.

. . . Nor does Exemption 5 protect communications that implement an established policy of an agency. . . .

Predecisional documents are thought generally to reflect the agency "give-and-take" leading up to a decision that is characteristic of the deliberative process; whereas *post-decisional* documents often represent the agency's position on an issue, or explain such a position, and thus may constitute the "working law" of an agency. Accordingly, the courts have recognized little public interest in the disclosure of "reasons supporting a policy which an agency has rejected, or . . . reasons which might have supplied, but did not supply, the basis for a policy which was actually adopted on a different ground." [Quoting NLRB v. Sears, Roebuck & Co., 421 U.S. 132 (1975).]

However, the courts have recognized a strong public interest in the disclosure of reasons that *do* supply the basis for an agency policy actually adopted. As noted by the Supreme Court in *Sears:* "Exemption 5, properly construed, calls for 'disclosure of all "opinions and interpretations" which embody the agency's effective law and policy, and the withholding of all papers which reflect the agency's group thinking in the process of working out its policy and determining what its law shall be.' " Davis, The Information Act: A Preliminary Analysis, 34 U. Chi. L. Rev. 761, 797 (1967). . . .

FUNCTION AND SIGNIFICANCE OF THE DOCUMENT IN THE AGENCY DECISIONMAKING PROCESS

In Sterling Drug, Inc. v. FTC, 450 F.2d 698 (D.C. Cir. 1971), this court [required disclosure of] memoranda "prepared, or at least issued, by the Commission itself." [T]he court noted that: . . . These are *not the ideas and theories which go into the making of the law,* they are the law itself, and as such should be made available to the public. Thus, to prevent the development of secret law within the Commission, we must require it to disclose *orders and interpretations which it actually applies in cases before it.* Sterling, 450 F.2d at 708 (emphasis added).

FLOW OF DOCUMENTS FROM SUPERIORS TO SUBORDINATES, OR VICE VERSA

In *Coastal States,* this court . . . [observed that] a document from a subordinate to a superior official is more likely to be predecisional, while a document moving in the opposite direction is more likely to contain instructions to staff explaining the reasons for a decision already made. 617 F.2d at 868. . . .

. . . As will be indicated below, this factor—along with the others heretofore discussed—is important in this case because all of the disputed documents are used and relied upon by agency personnel after being reviewed and approved by superiors with decisionmaking authority.

[Applying these criteria, the court of appeals affirmed, with limited exceptions, the district court's ruling that the documents requested were subject to disclosure. It found that GCMs, for example, are memoranda originally prepared by the office of IRS Chief Counsel for the Commissioner, providing legal and policy background on proposed revenue rulings, private letter rulings, and technical advice memoranda. Once those rulings or advice memoranda are adopted and issued by the IRS, the GCMs are widely used within the service for legal research and guidance on relevant issues of tax law and policy. They are used by IRS officials in determining what position to take in conferences or negotiations with taxpayers. TMs (background memoranda prepared in connection with treasury decisions) and AODs (memoranda prepared in connection with IRS decisions whether to appeal adverse court rulings) had a similar history. Originally prepared for internal deliberative purposes, they were subsequently indexed and used within the service as precedent and policy for dealing with current tax controversies. The court held that they should accordingly be disclosed.]

QUESTION

Is this decision consistent with Cooke v. Bureau of Alcohol, Tobacco & Firearms, p. 159, supra?

Federal Open Market Committee of the Federal Reserve System v. Merrill, 443 U.S. 340 (1979), extended the section 5 exemption to include commercially sensitive financial information. The Open Market Committee of the Federal Reserve meets monthly to determine appropriate monetary policy for the coming month, and to implement its decision through instructions to the Federal Reserve Account Manager, who is responsible for market purchases and sales of government securities that help determine the growth of the money supply. The committee's determinations and instructions are incorporated in a Domestic Policy Directive, which is not made public until the end of the month whose operations it determines, at which time it has been superseded by a new directive.

Plaintiff, a law student, sought to require disclosure of Domestic Policy Directives immediately after their formulation. The courts below required immediate disclosure, finding that directives are "statements of general policy" that the Federal Reserve must, as required by 5 U.S.C. §552(a)(1)(D), "currently [publish] in the Federal Register for the guidance of the public,"[40a] and that Exemption 5 did not apply.

The Supreme Court reversed. It found that a directive, containing instructions from the committee to the account manager, is an "intra-agency memorandum" within the meaning of Exemption 5. It then considered whether a directive "would not be available by law to a party in litigation with the agency." Rejecting the committee's claim that FOIA exempts documents whose disclosure would undermine the effectiveness of the agency's policy if released immediately, the Court concluded that directives came within "a limited form of Exemption 5 protection for 'confidential . . . commercial, information.'"[40b] The Court reasoned that since Exemption 4 gives private firms and individuals protection against

---

40a. As the Court noted, 443 U.S. at 352, "The Act makes available to any person all agency records, which it divides into three categories: some must be currently published in the Federal Register, 5 U.S.C. §552(a)(1); others must be 'promptly publish[ed]' or made publicly available and indexed, §552(a)(2); and all others must be promptly furnished on request, §552(a)(3). . . . "

40b. The Court invoked Fed. Rule Civ. Proc. 26(c)(7), which empowers federal courts to exempt from discovery "a trade secret or other confidential research, development, or commercial information," and the longstanding practice of the federal courts in giving a qualified evidentiary privilege for such information in general civil litigation. The Court asserted that there was no reason why the United States should not be able to invoke such a privilege in civil litigation, thus establishing a basis for including the privilege in Exemption 5 context.

disclosure of "trade secrets or commercial or financial information" that is "privileged and confidential," Exemption 5 should be construed to give a similar privilege to the government. The court found that directives governing purchase and sale of government securities were within the privilege because they were confidential and contained information of commercial significance. Acknowledging that the privilege was not absolute, the Court remanded the case for a determination by the district court of the committee's claims that immediate disclosure would disrupt the orderly marketing of government securities, favor large institutional investors who could quickly analyze the significance of directives, and increase the government's borrowing costs. It also directed the district court to consider whether nonprivileged portions of the directives could be separated from privileged portions and immediately disclosed.

Justice Stevens, joined by Justice Stewart, dissented. Asserting that none of the nine exemptions applied, Justice Stevens also argued that the Court had created a category of documents that need not be disclosed immediately but must be disclosed after the passage of time has deprived the information which they contain of commercial significance. This intermediate category, he argued, is inconsistent with the basic structure of the FOIA, which either requires that documents be released currently or exempts them altogether.

Page 1073. Add the following after line 26:

The Supreme Court has granted certiorari, 102 S. Ct. 565 (1981), to review Washington Post Co. v. Department of State, 647 F.2d 197 (D.C. Cir. 1981), interpreting Exemption 6 to require the State Department to disclose whether two persons residing in Iran hold U.S. passports. This information was held not "similar" to personnel or medical records. Consequently, the circuit court did not ever reach the stage of balancing privacy interests against the public interest in disclosure. The court rejected as irrelevant the department's claim that disclosure might endanger the lives of the individuals in question. Other circuits have not been so strict in requiring that the information be similar to personnel or medical files. Compare Harbolt v. Dept. of State, 616 F.2d 772 (5th Cir. 1980) (names of U.S. citizens imprisoned abroad for narcotics offenses covered by exemption 6).

Page 1078. Add the following case after line 20:

CHRYSLER CORP. v. BROWN

441 U.S. 281 (1979)

MR. JUSTICE REHNQUIST delivered the opinion of the Court.
. . . This case belongs to a class that has been popularly denominated

"reverse-FOIA" suits. The Chrysler Corp. (hereinafter Chrysler) seeks to enjoin agency disclosure on the grounds that it is inconsistent with the FOIA and 18 U.S.C. §1905, a criminal statute with origins in the 19th century that proscribes disclosure of certain classes of business and personal information. . . .

I

As a party to numerous Government contracts, Chrysler is required to comply with Executive Orders 11246 and 11375, which charge the Secretary of Labor with ensuring that corporations that benefit from Government contracts provide equal employment opportunity regardless of race or sex. The United States Department of Labor's Office of Federal Contract Compliance Programs (OFCCP) has promulgated regulations which require Government contractors to furnish reports and other information about their affirmative-action programs and the general composition of their work forces.

The Defense Logistics Agency (DLA) . . . of the Department of Defense is the designated compliance agency responsible for monitoring Chrysler's employment practices. OFCCP regulations require that Chrysler make available to this agency [written reports on its work-force composition, employment practices, and affirmative action efforts.]

Regulations promulgated by the Secretary of Labor provide for public disclosure of information from records of the OFCCP and its compliance agencies. Those regulations state that notwithstanding exemption from mandatory disclosure under the FOIA, 5 U.S.C. §552, "records obtained or generated pursuant to Executive Order 11246 (as amended) . . . shall be made available for inspection and copying . . . if it is determined that the requested inspection or copying furthers the public interest and does not impede any of the functions of the OFCC[P] or the Compliance Agencies except in the case of records disclosure of which is prohibited by law." It is the voluntary disclosure contemplated by this regulation, over and above that mandated by the FOIA, which is the gravamen of Chrysler's complaint in this case.

[The DLA informed Chrysler that third parties had made an FOIA request for disclosure of certain Chrysler reports. After objections to the DLA were unavailing, Chrysler filed suit in the federal district court for the District of Delaware to enjoin disclosure. The District Court found that agency regulation required nondisclosure of the documents. The court of appeals disagreed on this point, but found the agency record inadequate to permit review, and remanded for further proceedings. Chrysler argued that exemption 4, relating to trade secrets and commercial or financial information, precluded the DLA from disclosing the reports. The Court rejected the contention that an agency is precluded from disclosing documents that fall within an exemption.]

II

The organization of the Act is straightforward. Subsection (a), 5 U.S.C. §552(a), places a general obligation on the agency to make information available to the public and sets out specific modes of disclosure for certain classes of information. Subsection (b), 5 U.S.C. §552(b), which lists the exemptions, simply states that the specified material is not subject to the disclosure obligations set out in subsection (a). By its terms, subsection (b) demarcates the agency's obligation to disclose; it does not foreclose disclosure.

That the FOIA is exclusively a disclosure statute is, perhaps, demonstrated most convincingly by examining its provision for judicial relief. Subsection (a)(4)(B) gives federal district courts "jurisdiction to enjoin the agency from withholding agency records and to order the production of any agency records improperly withheld from the complainant." 5 U.S.C. §552(a)(4)(B). That provision does not give the authority to bar disclosure, and thus fortifies our belief that Chrysler, and courts which have shared its view, have incorrectly interpreted the exemption provisions of the FOIA. . . .

Enlarged access to governmental information undoubtedly cuts against the privacy concerns of nongovernmental entities, and as a matter of policy some balancing and accommodation may well be desirable. We simply hold here that Congress did not design the FOIA exemptions to be mandatory bars to disclosure. . . .

III

Chrysler contends, however, that even if its suit for injunctive relief cannot be based on the FOIA, such an action can be premised on the Trade Secrets Act, 18 U.S.C. §1905. The Act provides: "Whoever, being an officer or employee of the United States or of any department or agency thereof, publishes, divulges, discloses, or makes known in any manner or to any extent not authorized by law any information coming to him in the course of his employment or official duties . . . which information concerns or relates to the trade secrets, processes, operations, style of work, or apparatus, or to the identity, confidential statistical data, amount or source of any income, profits, losses, or expenditures of any person, firm, partnership, corporation, or association . . . shall be fined not more than $1,000, or imprisoned not more than one year, or both; and shall be removed from office or employment." There are necessarily two parts to Chrysler's argument: that §1905 is applicable to the type of disclosure threatened in this case, and that it affords Chrysler a private right of action to obtain injunctive relief.

A

The Court of Appeals held that § 1905 was not applicable to the agency disclosure at issue here because such disclosure was "authorized by law" within the meaning of the Act. The court found the source of that authorization to be the OFCCP regulations that DLA relied on in deciding to disclose . . . Chrysler contends here that these agency regulations are not "law" within the meaning of § 1905.

[The Court held that legislatively authorized substantive regulations that have the "force and effect of law" and have been duly adopted in accordance with applicable procedures could provide the necessary authorization to create an exception to the ban of § 1905. It found that the Labor Department's regulations fell on the substantive side of the APA distinction in §§ 553(b) and (d) between "substantive rules" and "interpretive rules, general statements of policy, or rules of agency organization, procedure or practice" because they determined "individual rights and obligations" with respect to disclosure. However, it concluded that they were not the product of a legislative grant of authority that vested them with the force and effect of law.]

Section 201 of Executive Order 11246 directs the Secretary of Labor to "adopt such rules and regulations and issue such orders as he deems necessary and appropriate to achieve the purposes thereof." But in order for such regulations to have the "force and effect of law," it is necessary to establish a nexus between the regulations and some delegation of the requisite legislative authority by Congress. The origins of the congressional authority for Executive Order 11246 are somewhat obscure and have been roundly debated by commentators and courts. The Order itself as amended establishes a program to eliminate employment discrimination by the Federal Government and by those who benefit from Government contracts. For purposes of this case, it is not necessary to decide whether Executive Order 11246 as amended is authorized by the Federal Property and Administrative Services Act of 1949, Titles VI and VII of the Civil Rights Act of 1964, the Equal Employment Opportunity Act of 1972, or some more general notion that the Executive can impose reasonable contractual requirements in the exercise of its procurement authority. The pertinent inquiry is whether under any of the arguable *statutory* grants of authority the OFCCP disclosure regulations relied on by the respondents are reasonably within the contemplation of that grant of authority. We think that it is clear that when it enacted these statutes, Congress was not concerned with public disclosure of trade secrets or confidential business information. . . .

[The Court also found that the requisite legislative authorization for the regulations was not provided by 5 U.S.C. § 301, commonly called the "housekeeping statute," providing that a head of a department may prescribe regulations for "the government of his department, the conduct of its employees, the distribution and performance of its business, and the custody, use and preservation of its records, papers, and property."]

There is also a procedural defect in the OFCCP disclosure regulations which precludes courts from affording them the force and effect of law. That defect is a lack of strict compliance with the APA. . . .

Section 4 of the APA, 5 U.S.C. §553, specifies that an agency shall afford interested persons general notice of proposed rulemaking and an opportunity to comment before a substantive rule is promulgated. "Interpretive rules, general statements of policy or rules of agency organization, procedure or practice" are exempt from these requirements. When the Secretary of Labor published the regulations pertinent in this case, he stated: "As the changes made by this document relate solely to interpretive rules, general statements of policy, and to rules of agency procedure and practice, neither notice of proposed rule making nor public participation therein is required by 5 U.S.C. 553. Since the changes made by this document either relieve restrictions or are interpretative rules, no delay in effective date is required by 5 U.S.C. 553(d). These rules shall therefore be effective immediately. . . ." We need not decide whether these regulations are properly characterized as "interpretative rules." It is enough that such regulations are not properly promulgated as substantive rules, and therefore not the product of procedures which Congress prescribed as necessary prerequisites to giving a regulation the binding effect of law. An interpretative regulation or general statement of agency policy cannot be the "authoriz[ation] by law" required by §1905.

This disposition best comports with both the purposes underlying the APA and sound administrative practice. Here important interests are in conflict: the public's access to information in the Government's files and concerns about personal privacy and business confidentiality. The OFCCP's regulations attempt to strike a balance. In enacting the APA, Congress made a judgment that notions of fairness and informed administrative decisionmaking require that agency decisions be made only after affording interested persons notice and an opportunity to comment. With the consideration that is the necessary and intended consequence of such procedures, OFCCP might have decided that a different accommodation was more appropriate.

B

We reject, however, Chrysler's contention that the Trade Secrets Act affords a private right of action to enjoin disclosure in violation of the statute. In Cort v. Ash, 422 U.S. 66 (1975), we noted that this Court has rarely implied a private right of action under a criminal statute, and where it has done so "there was at least a statutory basis for inferring that a civil cause of action of some sort lay in favor of someone." Nothing in §1905 prompts such an inference. . . .

IV

While Chrysler may not avail itself of any violations of the provisions of §1905 in a separate cause of action, any such violations may have a dispositive effect on the outcome of judicial review of agency action pursuant to §10 of the APA. Section 10(a) of the APA provides that "[a] person suffering legal wrong because of agency action, or adversely affected or aggrieved by agency action . . . , is entitled to judicial review thereof." 5 U.S.C. §702. Two exceptions to this general rule of reviewability are set out in §10. Review is not available where "statutes preclude judicial review" or where "agency action is committed to agency discretion by law." 5 U.S.C. §§701(a)(1), (2). . . .

Were we simply confronted with the authorization in 5 U.S.C. §301 to prescribe regulations regarding "the custody, use, and preservation of [agency] records, papers, and property," it would be difficult to derive any standards limiting agency conduct which might constitute "law to apply." But our discussion in Part III demonstrates that §1905 and any "authoriz[ation] by law" contemplated by that section place substantive limits on agency action. Therefore, we conclude that DLA's decision to disclose the Chrysler reports is reviewable agency action and Chrysler is a person "adversely affected or aggrieved" within the meaning of §10(a).

Both Chrysler and the respondents agree that there is APA review of DLA's decision. They disagree on the proper scope of review. Chrysler argues that there should be de novo review, while the respondents contend that such review is only available in extraordinary cases and this is not such a case.

The pertinent provisions of §10(e) of the APA, 5 U.S.C. §706, state that a reviewing court shall

> "(2) hold unlawful and set aside agency action, findings, and conclusions found to be—
> "(A) arbitrary, capricious, an abuse of discretion, or otherwise not in accordance with law. . . .
> "(F) unwarranted by the facts to the extent that the facts are subject to trial de novo by the reviewing court."

For the reasons previously stated, we believe any disclosure that violates §1905 is "not in accordance with law" within the meaning of 5 U.S.C. §706(2)(A). De novo review by the District Court is ordinarily not necessary to decide whether a contemplated disclosure runs afoul of §1905. The District Court in this case concluded that disclosure of some of Chrysler's documents was barred by §1905, but the Court of Appeals did not reach the issue. We shall therefore vacate the Court of Appeals' judgment and remand for further proceedings consistent with this opinion in order that the Court of Appeals may consider whether the contemplated disclosures would violate the prohibition of §1905. Since the decision regarding this substantive issue—the scope of §1905—will necessarily have some effect on the proper form of judicial review pursuant to §706(2), we think it unnecessary, and therefore unwise, at the present stage of this case for us to express any additional views on that issue.

Vacated and remanded.

[A concurring opinion by JUSTICE MARSHALL is omitted.]